The
AMA
Handbook of
Business
Letters

Fourth Edition

The
AMA
Handbook of
Business
Letters

Fourth Edition

Jeffrey L. Seglin and Edward Coleman

American Management Association

New York • Atlanta • Brussels • Chicago • Mexico City • San Francisco
Shanghai • Tokyo • Toronto • Washington, D.C.

This publication is designed to provide accurate and authoritative information in regard to the subject matter covered. It is sold with the understanding that the publisher is not engaged in rendering legal, accounting, or other professional service. If legal advice or other expert assistance is required, the services of a competent professional person should be sought.

Library of Congress Cataloging-in-Publication Data

Seglin, Jeffrey L., 1956-
    The AMA handbook of business letters / Jeffrey L. Seglin and Edward Coleman. — 4th ed.
      p. cm.
    Includes index.
    ISBN 978-0-8144-2012-6 (hbk.)
  1. Commercial correspondence—Handbooks, manuals, etc. 2. Letter writing—Handbooks, manuals, etc. I. Coleman, Edward, 1968- II. Amacom. III. Title. IV. Title: Handbook of business letters. V. Title: American Management Association handbook of business letters.
    HF5726.S42 2012
    651.7′5—dc23

                      2012005590

About AMA
American Management Association (www.amanet.org) is a world leader in talent development, advancing the skills of individuals to drive business success. Our mission is to support the goals of individuals and organizations through a complete range of products and services, including classroom and virtual seminars, webcasts, webinars, podcasts, conferences, corporate and government solutions, business books, and research. AMA's approach to improving performance combines experiential learning—learning through doing—with opportunities for ongoing professional growth at every step of one's career journey.

Printing number

10 9 8 7 6 5 4 3

Contents

The letters in this book are available online in easily customizable format at
www.amacombooks.org/go/AMAHbkBizLts4.

Preface to the fourth edition

It's remarkable how quickly the years have passed since the publication of the first edition of *The AMA Handbook of Business Letters*. While much has changed during that time, the basic fundamentals of letter writing have remained the same. Still, we felt it was time that we updated the book with a much wider selection of model letters as well as updates to reflect today's work setting.

People in all walks of the business world are in need of a book that can help them hone their letter-writing skills. *The AMA Handbook of Business Letters* is designed to answer that need. It will arm you with both the skills needed to be good letter writers and more than 370 model letters on which to base your own correspondence. *The AMA Handbook of Business Letters* will not just show you how to write better letters, it will show you how to write better.

Sections on grammar and usage in the first part of the book complement the sections on basic letter-writing skills. The second part of *The AMA Handbook of Business Letters* is the heart of the book. Here, more than 370 model letters have been collected. The vast majority of them are based on actual letters that were used in business. They were chosen to represent the broad spectrum of the type of letters businesspeople will most commonly have to write. We have fictionalized the names of the people, companies, and products in the letters. If a name resembles an actual name, it is purely by coincidence.

Many of the sample letters in Part II can easily be used as emails. We include them in traditional letter format, but the message of each letter can be used as the text for an email. Obviously, the sample letters can also be used as templates for letters that you can attach to emails. We give you tips on how to adapt the letters to email in Chapter 4 in the section titled "Email." You can find electronic versions of each of the letters in this book at www.amacombooks.org/go/AMAHbkBizLts4.

Part III features two appendixes that give tips on frequently misused words and punctuation.

Many people assisted us with this new edition. In particular, our spouses, Nancy Seglin and Lisa Freiman, were supportive of our efforts. And Bethany and David Whitemyer were invaluable in ensuring that this new edition came to pass.

For assistance on this and previous editions, we'd like to thank: Peggy R. Broekel, Michaela Coleman, Tess Coleman, Donna Reiss Friedman, Loren Gary, Beall D. Gary Jr., Mary Glenn, Robert Griffin, Dr. Lindsey Harlan, Adrienne Hickey, Martha Jewett, Joan Kenney, Jim Lewis, Evan Marshall, Christina Parisi, Sam Mickelberg, Howard Palay, Patti

Palay, Pat Richardson, Robert Roen, Louis J. Roffinoli, Matthew Rovner, Lester Seglin, Mike Sivilli, Mark Stoeckle, Lisa Tieszen, John Waggoner, Evan Whitemyer, Lucas Whitemyer, and Tom Williams.

We are particularly grateful to Hank Kennedy, president of AMACOM Books, for having the wisdom to believe that the time was right for a new edition of our book. Erika Spelman and Andy Ambraziejus were terrific shepherds of the book as it made its way through the production process. And Debbie Posner's substantial work as copyeditor as well as Jacqueline Laks Gorman's work as proofreader on this new edition make it a far better book than it would have been without the benefit of their extraordinary skills. We also thank our editors Ellen Kadin and William Helms at AMACOM.

We're also grateful to readers of previous editions who have sent us letters or emails with questions, suggestions, or ideas for this new edition. In an effort to continue to make future editions of the book as useful as possible, we'd like to ask your help once again. If you have ideas for new features or types of letters you'd like to see included in future editions, or if you have observations or questions, email them to us at: jseglin@post.harvard.edu.

Jeffrey L. Seglin, Boston, Massachusetts
Edward Coleman, Indianapolis, Indiana

The
AMA
Handbook of
Business
Letters

Fourth Edition

PART I

The basics

All letters methinks, should be as free
and easy as one's discourse,
not studied as an oration....
. . . .

—Dorothy Osborne (Lady Temple), letter to Sir William Temple, October 1653

Successful professionals know the importance of effective letter writing. You can't have a good business relationship with customers if they don't know what you're trying to tell them in a letter. The services or products of a company can't be marketed if a prospective customer is baffled by the service or product described. How can a salesperson expect to make a sale when, because of a muddled letter, the prospect can't even understand what it is that's being sold?

Letter writing is crucial to the success of every professional. Without letter-writing skills, the professional's effectiveness is stymied.

Approaching This Book

Our objective in *The AMA Handbook of Business Letters* is to help you write effective letters. Ineffective letters are a waste of time and money. This realization should be enough to convince every professional of the need to be a good letter writer. Letters may not seem like the crux of your business, but if you consider that effectively written letters can increase the quality of working relationships and the quantity of business you can attract, as well as decrease wasted hours and money, you can begin to see the importance of learning to write letters well.

You should be prepared to approach this book with one chief goal in mind—to learn how to write more effective letters. Remember, too, that although letter writing is not a simple skill, with practice you can become a good letter writer. Once you learn the basics and put them into practice, your letters will get better and begin to flow more easily.

Approach of This Book

Before you begin to write more effective letters, you must learn what makes up a good letter. The first part of this book takes you step-by-step through the basics of letter writing. You'll learn the importance of planning a letter and gathering all the information you need. The plan is put into practice when you decide on the approach your letter will take and the components necessary to achieve the selected approach. The components of a letter are effective only if you know the proper mechanics involved in a letter's structure and appearance. Grammar, punctuation, spelling, and language usage are important if your letter is to be understood and well accepted by its reader. You needn't fear an extensive course in grammar. What you'll receive here are the fundamental "commonsense" rules of grammar, which are easily learned and should become natural not only to your letter writing, but to all of your other writing as well.

The second part of this book consists of more than 370 sample letters, divided into categories reflecting various aspects of business. Each chapter also contains brief analyses of the strong points of many of the sample letters. Most of the sample letters are based on actual letters written and used by professionals. Names of people or corporations have been changed, but the content remains essentially unaltered. The letters chosen serve as models for ones you may have to write in your everyday business life. You can adapt them to meet your needs or use them as a touchstone to aim toward in your letter writing.

The appendixes to this book consist of helpful lists and rules to refer to in your letter writing.

As with all things, perfection can be reached only with practice. If you apply the basics learned in the first part of *The AMA Handbook of Business Letters*, and study the examples presented in the second, your letter-writing skills will improve greatly. The end result will be a letter that makes your readers think that what took much thought and planning on your part flowed as smoothly and effortlessly as discourse.

CHAPTER 1

Planning the letter

Planning is a key factor in the accomplishment of any goal. Letter writing is no exception. To successfully construct a clear, effective letter, you need a good plan.

Some letters do not require as elaborate a plan as others. A letter to a customer detailing a proposal for a product purchase will obviously need a more elaborate plan than a thank-you note for a business lunch.

Common sense can usually dictate how elaborate your plan needs to be. If the information you need to present in a letter is limited enough for you to outline it in your head, there is no real need for a detailed outline featuring Roman numeral headings and sub-points beneath sub-points. The elaborateness of your plan should suit the elaborateness of the letter to be written.

Of course, if you, as a letter writer, are more comfortable constructing a detailed outline for each of your letters, there's nothing wrong with following that procedure. With enough practice, however, the simpler letters should flow more easily, and the time you might have spent laboring over outline after outline can be directed to other areas of your business.

The following three steps are essential in the planning of any letter:

1. Researching the facts
2. Analyzing the subject and reader
3. Knowing your objectives and how to accomplish them

If you follow these steps as you are planning to write any letter, you should find that your letters will be clear and well received, and will achieve your desired goal.

Researching the Facts

Before you write a letter, it makes sense to know what you plan to talk about. If you wing it and write whatever comes into your head, chances are you'll end up with a confused, ineffective letter.

Get the facts together before you write anything resembling a first draft of a letter. For example, if you are corresponding with a customer, examine all previous correspondence with him or her. Depending upon the volume of this correspondence, and assuming the customer to be a fairly good letter writer, you can learn a good deal about the personality, interests, and values of the person to whom you are writing.

As you examine previous correspondence, jot down a note or two about some key traits you discover about this customer. For example, you have gone through your correspondence file for a potential customer named Sam Johnson. From what he has written you realize the following things about him. He:

- Is committed to existing business relationships.
- Places importance on a personal relationship between the professional and the customer.
- Often suggests ideas for improving business practices and professional/customer relationships.
- Has a strong interest in reducing costs.

After jotting down this information, try to visualize the person to whom you are writing. You know something about the customer's interests. To learn more, you might examine the file on business dealings with the customer. If you learn as much as possible about your reader, you'll find it easier to write a letter directed to him or her.

After you have collected some facts on your customer, you should direct your attention to the topic or topics to be covered in the letter. The simplest and ultimately most effective thing to do is to take a piece of paper and write down those topics you plan to cover. Under each topic you might write some examples or a few words recalling a discussion you might have had with your customer about it.

Let's stick with the example of potential customer Sam Johnson. You've already had a business meeting with Mr. Johnson and you want to write a follow-up letter. You already know something about his personality from the earlier research you did, and of course, from impressions formed during the course of your meeting. You decide you want to cover the following topics in your letter:

- Thanks for meeting
- His idea for a lockbox
  - Speeds up collections
  - Cost-effectiveness
- Appreciate his views on business
  - Loyalty to existing business relationships
  - Personal relationship
- Arrange for another meeting

The order in which you write down ideas for topics is unimportant at this point in the planning stage. The main thing is to make sure the letter covers the topics that will let customer Johnson know you are writing to him about issues that are of concern to him.

Timeliness is extremely important in any letter, including the one we are using as an example. You want to get a letter to your customer while the topics being discussed are still fresh in both of your minds. As you are doing your research, determine how long discussion has been taking place about the topics to be included in your letter and what, if any, action has already been taken. A fundamental rule to remember in all of your correspondence is that timeliness is essential for effectiveness.

Analyzing the Subject and Reader

You've completed your research. You know something about the person to whom you're writing. You have a good idea what topics will be covered in the letter. The information you've gathered must now be analyzed so you can logically organize it for the best results.

An outline is a good method of organizing topics and visualizing the order in which you wish to discuss them in the letter. You can order the letter chronologically, by importance of the topics discussed, or in whatever order is most effective. Your choice is flexible, but it must be logical and you should not mix thoughts in sentences or drop them before they are completed.

Continuing with the example of the follow-up letter to Sam Johnson, you might decide to outline your letter as follows:

Paragraph 1.   a. Thanks for meeting
                b. Appreciate views on business
                    (1) Loyalty to existing business relationships
                    (2) Importance of personal relationships

Paragraph 2.   a. Idea for lockbox
                    (1) Speed up collections
                    (2) Cost-effectiveness

Paragraph 3.   a. Arrange for another meeting

You'll notice that the only difference between this rough outline and the list of topics jotted down earlier is the order. The ordering of topics is an important function of the outline.

With a letter as simple as this follow-up to Sam Johnson, it is perfectly acceptable to outline the topics in your head and go directly to the rough draft of your letter. The important thing in writing an effective letter is not writing a good outline, but rather being able to write a letter that is ordered logically and is structured well enough for you to know where it's going. If you can do this in your head, fine. You may have to work out some kinks in the rough draft, but if you can save yourself some time and still write an effective letter, more power to you. As your letters become more elaborate, you may find that working with a written outline helps to remind you of all the facts and the best order in which to present them.

When you analyze the subject matter to be covered in your letter, you should also keep in mind the research you did on your customer. Your research can serve as a brief analysis of your customer's personality, interests, and values. This information is important to keep in mind as you organize the information to be included in your letter. What's important to you may not be as important to your reader. Your letter must be aimed toward your reader.

With outline in hand or in your head, you can now begin to write your letter. Keep in mind that, in order to be as clear as possible, you should write simple sentences, avoiding any unnecessary information. Don't try to combine ideas in sentences. In order to get your point across most clearly, write about one thing at a time. For example, when you write the first paragraph of your letter to Sam Johnson, don't try to thank him for the meeting and express your appreciation for his views in the same sentence. Take one thought at a time.

> Thank you for an interesting meeting yesterday. I appreciate the time and information you shared with me.

Avoid any excess in the sentences of your letter. If you start rambling, you are bound to get off the track and lose your reader. Remember, to be effective in letter writing you must grab your reader's attention and make that reader react positively to whatever it is you're writing about.

Another important thing to remember is that ideas placed at the beginning or end of a paragraph stand out most clearly to the reader. This placement of ideas is a good practice to use for emphasis in your letter writing.

Knowing Your Objectives and How to Accomplish Them

Set an objective for every letter you write. If you want a customer to accept credit terms you are offering, keep that goal in mind as you plan and write your letter. Stay focused on your goal as you choose the order of each paragraph and the wording of each sentence.

The research you did before beginning to write to your customer can help you decide how best to write the letter that will be most effective in getting your reader to react the way you would like. Your research can help make you familiar with your reader and what might have moved that reader to act in the past.

The objectives of your follow-up letter to Sam Johnson are to thank him and to attract his business. You know the value he places on loyalty to existing business relationships and on a personal relationship between the professional and the customer, so you might express your understanding of these values. It also might be a good idea, knowing Mr. Johnson's ability to make good suggestions, to react to a suggestion he might have made at your original meeting. Since your goal is to attract his business, closing your letter by telling him you'll call to set up another meeting is a good approach. Such a closing lets Mr. Johnson know you appreciate his ideas and are eager to meet with him again to discuss the possibility of doing business with him. Consider the following example of the complete text of a letter to Mr. Johnson:

> Thank you for an interesting meeting yesterday. I appreciate the time and information you shared with me. I understand your sense of loyalty to existing business relationships and the importance you place on knowing and being known by the people you do business with.
>
> During our conversation you suggested that a lockbox arrangement might

speed up the collection of cash available for investment. I would like to investigate this possibility and estimate the dollar benefit to your company.

I will give you a call early next week to arrange lunch together as you suggested. Thanks again for your time. I look forward to doing business together.

Judging from the final letter to customer Johnson, the research, analysis, and knowledge of objectives were handled well by the letter writer. The careful planning in the construction of a letter such as the one above should result in the increased chance of a positive response from the letter's reader.

CHAPTER 2

Components of an effective letter

Planning by itself is not enough to assure you of a positive response from your reader. There are, however, essential components of any letter that can multiply the chances of its effectiveness.

Before you begin to worry about the basic mechanics of a letter (structure, appearance, and grammar), think seriously about the attitude you wish to convey. Your attitude is conveyed through your choice of language, tone, and focus of attention. Each of these individual components is as important as anything else that goes into making up a successful letter.

The attitude conveyed in your letter can make the difference between a letter that is tossed aside and one that is read, understood, and reacted to favorably. It's basically very simple to convey a reader-oriented attitude. Remember as you write your letters that you are addressing a specific reader. Your language, tone, and focus of attention must capture the reader's interest for your letter to be successful.

Language—Clarity Versus Ambiguity

Language is a means of communication. This may seem like a foolishly simple observation to make, but remember that for communication to be completed successfully, a sender must convey his or her message so that the receiver not only receives, but also understands, the message. If language is not used clearly and accurately, the communication process cannot be successfully completed.

A simple rule to remember is that the English you use in your everyday business should be the same good English used by people in all walks of life. Granted, there may be specialized terms intrinsic to your industry, but there isn't a special type of "business English" to be learned and used when writing business letters. Good English is good English.

Be clear and straightforward in your letters. Write what you mean. Don't write in circles, making your reader guess what you mean.

Take the following example of a writer who wants to tell a customer about an important organization:

> My correspondence was initiated to inform you of the high caliber of programs and activities of an organization in which I have enjoyed being involved over the past few years. The County Business Association has served to keep me informed of, and actively involved in, the current political and economic issues affecting small businesses through its monthly breakfast meetings with interesting and impressive speakers, its newsletter on legislative activities in Washington, and several other programs outlined in the attached letter.

There are many problems with this example. Let's start by examining the clarity and directness of the statement. Since the writer of the letters wants to inform the reader about an important organization, why didn't the writer come right out and do so by writing:

> I am writing to you about the high-caliber programs and activities offered by the County Business Association, an organization in which I have been involved for the past few years.

In the writer's version of the letter, it is not until the second sentence of the paragraph that we even learn the name of the important organization. If you are writing about a particular subject, and that subject happens to be an organization, why not get its name right up front so the reader might enjoy learning about it throughout the rest of the letter instead of being left in suspense?

Instead of using many words ("My correspondence was initiated to inform you of…"), why not say simply, "I am writing to you about…"? If you come right out and say what you mean instead of beating around the bush, not only are you going to grab your reader's attention right away, but you also stand a stronger chance of convincing your reader that he or she should go on reading to find out more about what you have to say.

Be as direct as possible in your letter writing. If you can convey your message in five words instead of ten, do so.

You don't have a great deal of space in a letter to convey your thoughts. Be succinct. You're not writing a novel or a treatise on the economy. The idea is to get your message across clearly and directly.

Avoid the use of pompous or inflated language in your letters. It may sound lofty to write, "My correspondence was initiated to inform you of…," but you are not writing to see how you can turn a catchy phrase on the page (and there's nothing "catchy" about that opener). You are writing to communicate with your reader, and if you mean, "I am writing to you about…," then that's what you should write.

Be clear, direct, and unambiguous in your letter writing. Sometimes when you think you are communicating clearly in a letter, the reader receives a different message from the one you intended. If such ambiguity is present in your letters, you can't be sure that the reader will understand your message. Ambiguous language is another problem with the example paragraph above. The writer wrote:

> The County Business Association has served to keep me informed of, and actively involved in, the current political and economic issues affecting small businesses through its monthly breakfast meetings with interesting and impressive speakers, its newsletter on legislative activities in Washington, and several other programs outlined in the attached letter.

The writer did not mean to suggest that the current political and economic issues were affecting small businesses as a result of the County Business Association's monthly breakfast meetings. Because of careless wording, however, the sentence could be read to mean exactly that. The writer may be defensive and say, "Well, you knew what I meant," and in this case would certainly be correct. But if we have to read something twice to make sure of its meaning, then the chances are that it was not written clearly in the first place. The writer could have written:

> Through monthly breakfast meetings with interesting speakers, a newsletter on legislative activities in Washington, and several other programs, the County Business Association has kept me informed of and involved in the current political and economic issues affecting small businesses.

This version leaves little doubt in the reader's mind about the writer's intended meaning. It also removes the unnecessary adjective "impressive" from the text of the letter.

The meaning of an ambiguous passage often cannot be detected as easily as in the above example. A classic example is the following:

> The loan officer approved the loan for David Marshall because he was obviously of superior moral fiber.

From what is written above we cannot tell who is of superior moral fiber, the loan officer or Mr. Marshall. The pronoun "he" can refer to either the loan officer or Mr. Marshall. To avoid ambiguity, the sentence could be written:

> Because David Marshall was obviously of superior moral fiber, the loan officer approved the loan.

Or:

> Because the loan officer was of superior moral fiber, he approved the loan for David Marshall.

Tone—Personality

The tone or personality of a letter can help you get a positive reaction from a reader. The tone should be set at the very start of a letter and maintained throughout. The tone of any business letter should be courteous and friendly, and written as if you were talking with the reader. You don't want to get too technical in a letter. Write in language that the reader will understand.

The tone should help to show that someone with a personality—a human being—is writing the letter. If the reader believes that you are genuinely concerned about how the letter affects him or her, a positive response is more likely.

Consider Sample Letter 2.1. The letter sets a tone emphasizing efficiency and personal response to the reader from the beginning by addressing both the writer's past involvement with the customer and the customer's needs. Credit manager Nilges comes directly to the point by announcing that his letter contains a credit proposal for his customer's company.

In the first paragraph, the writer establishes the tone of the letter:

> We are proud to have you as a customer.

Sample Letter 2.1 is written with a positive tone directed toward its reader, which is maintained throughout the letter. If the reader is convinced that he is receiving a fair proposal from an official who is committed to helping the reader's company, then chances are the letter will be successful. A positive tone increases the likelihood of a positive response.

Sample Letter 2.1.   Business letter with effective and personal tone.

[date]

Mr. Bertrand R. Levine
Levine's Lumber Land
P.O. Box 567
Richmond, SD 57001

Dear Mr. Levine:

Welcome! Your account at Nilges Wood Supply has been approved. We are proud to have you as a customer.

As you may know, Nilges Wood Supply is a 50-year-old company, with 85 stores in nine Midwestern states. We supply a complete line of building products to our customers, including millwork, plumbing, electrical, paint, kitchen supplies, bath supplies, hardware, and tools. As a leader in this industry, we strive to provide the best service possible to our customers. Our goal is to be your most valuable supplier. Customer satisfaction is our number-one priority.

Your approved credit line is $2,000, with billing terms of net 10. Monthly statements are mailed on the first or second working day each month. A service charge is added to past-due balances that are not paid by the twenty-fifth day of the billing month.

We at Nilges Wood Supply welcome the opportunity to serve you and look forward to a long and prosperous relationship.

Your branch manager is Sheila McGulicuty. Her telephone number is 890-555-8765.

Yours very truly,

Larry E. Nilges
Vice President—Credit Sales

len/jls

Focus of Attention—The "You Attitude"

An important concept in letter writing is something called the "you attitude." The "you attitude" insists that the focus of attention in your letters be directed toward the reader, the "you" to whom you are writing.

Directing a letter toward a reader may seem very simple, but a letter writer too often incorrectly assumes that his or her interests and knowledge are the same as the reader's. Some legwork needs to be done when you are deciding how to make a letter reader-oriented. This legwork may come at the planning stage of your letter, discussed in Chapter 1.

What you need to know are answers to basic questions, such as:

- What will motivate this reader to react favorably to my letter?
- What interests this reader?
- What's this reader's viewpoint on the issues I am addressing in my letter?

Sometimes you won't know the answers to these questions. If you sit down, however, and think clearly about what will convince your reader that what you are writing is beneficial to him or her, you've attempted to direct the focus of attention of your letter to the reader, the "you" receiving the message.

The reader of your letter must be convinced that what you are trying to get him or her to do or react to is something of some personal value. If you are responding to someone about the lack of job openings at your bank, you don't want to scare off a potential employee by sending a cold form letter. Nothing overly elaborate is necessary, of course, but a cordial negative response to a potential employee now may pay off in the future when your bank does need someone with his or her expertise.

Sample Letter 2.2, acknowledging an employment application—even when no jobs are available—is courteous and considerate. Ms. Kenney has written a letter that reflects a sincere interest in Mr. Krauss. By writing, "We are complimented that you would consider the Bethany Bagel Company as a place of employment," she has flattered Mr. Krauss. This might cause him to react positively to Ms. Kenney's letter. If he does react positively now, and jobs should open up at a later date for which he is qualified, then Ms. Kenney's letter has served a good purpose by keeping a positive relationship with a prospective employee.

Ms. Kenney has not gotten caught up in the need to use only the personal pronoun "you" in her letter. That is certainly important in focusing attention on a reader, but part of the whole idea of creating a personality or tone in a letter is to let the reader know that a living person—an "I"—has indeed written the letter, as Ms. Kenney did when she wrote:

> I would appreciate it if you would notify me if you wish to cancel your application for any reason.

Sample Letter 2.2.   Form response letter reflecting use of the "you attitude."

[date]

Mr. Michael Krauss
69 Camran Terrace
Norristown, PA 19403

APPLICATION FOR EMPLOYMENT

Mr. Krauss, thank you for your recent employment application. We are complimented that you would consider the Bethany Bagel Company as a place of employment.

Your application will be retained in our open files. Currently, we do not have any openings, but should one occur you may be contacted for an interview.

I would appreciate it if you would notify me if you wish to cancel your application for any reason.

JOAN KENNEY—VICE PRESIDENT
HUMAN RESOURCES

mn

If Ms. Kenney had used a passive voice here and had written, "It would be appreciated," instead of "I would appreciate," she would have risked taking the personality out of her letter, almost as if she were reluctant to admit her involvement in the process.

A writer must focus the attention of a letter on the reader. If you choose the language and tone for your letter to convey an attitude of commitment to and interest in your reader, you will find that your letters will be more successful in grasping your reader's attention and encouraging them to respond favorably.

Length

The length of any letter or email affects its appearance. Professionals or customers who receive a lot of correspondence every day are not going to react favorably to three-page letters that could have been written in one page or emails that have the reader scrolling more than necessary.

Come right to the point in your letters and emails. They should be concise and limited to one page if possible.

Begin discussing the main topic or topics of your letter in the first paragraph. If you do, your reader will know what to expect as soon as he or she begins to read.

Planning your ideas and clarity in your writing will help to limit the length of your letter. Paragraphs should not be too long and difficult to follow. You should not, however, use a string of one-sentence paragraphs, which can result in a staccato-like reading. A concise paragraph with a few sentences that come right to the point should keep the length of your letters manageable.

CHAPTER 3

Structure: The parts of a letter

As you are reading this chapter, you'll find it helpful to refer to Chapter 4, where various letter formats are discussed. Different formats require different placement of various parts of a letter. Although placement may vary, the content and function of these parts of a letter remain constant. You'll have little difficulty in applying the principles learned here to the formats discussed in Chapter 4.

Dateline

Every letter should have a dateline. The date appears on a single line two to eight lines below the letterhead or the top margin of the page. With the exception of the simplified-letter format, three lines down from the letterhead is the usual space allotted in most letter formats. Because a letter should be well framed on a page, the placement of the dateline is flexible.

The date typed on a letter should be the date on which the letter was dictated, no matter when it is to be typed or mailed, unless, of course, the letter is a standard form letter sent out time and time again (in this case, the date the letter is sent should be used, taking care to use the same typeface as the form letter). The months of the year should always be spelled out, and the day should always be indicated by a cardinal number (e.g., 1, 2, 3), never using "nd," "th," or "st" after the number as you would with ordinal numbers.

The order of the dateline is month, day followed by a comma, and year.

May 5, 20XX

Sometimes foreign correspondence will feature a reversal in the order of day and month, omitting the comma.

5 May 20XX

The most standard order, however, for the elements in the dateline is month, day followed by a comma, and year.

The placement of the dateline varies depending upon the letter format used. In the full-block format (see Sample Letter 4.1), the dateline is typed flush with the left margin, or sometimes centered, if centering the date blends well with the letterhead. In the simplified-letter format (see Sample Letter 4.4), the dateline is typed flush with the left margin, six lines below the letterhead.

The dateline in the block (see Sample Letter 4.2), semiblock (see Sample Letter 4.3), official-style (see Sample Letter 4.5), and hanging-indented (see Sample Letter 4.6) formats is usually flush with the right margin. The last figure of the year should never overrun the right margin. However, in these formats the date can also be either centered under the letterhead, if this adds to the balanced look of the letter, or five spaces to the right of the center of the page.

Reference Line

The reference line is optional. It is a number or a series of numbers and letters referring to previous correspondence. It is usually included for the benefit of a person who must file all correspondence dealing with the same issues or topics.

The number is aligned with and typed directly below the dateline. It is usually typed one to four lines beneath the date unless your company policy stipulates that it be placed elsewhere (see Sample Letter 4.1 for an example of a reference line).

If your letter is to be more than one page long, the reference number must be carried over to all continuation sheets. On these sheets, the location of the reference line should correspond to its location on the first sheet, or as indicated by company policy.

Personal or Confidential Note

The inclusion of a personal or confidential note is optional. When you write "personal" or "confidential," however, it should always be because you want the letter to remain confidential between you and the reader. If you use such a notation as a gimmick to attract readers' attention, they will recognize that you are trying to manipulate them; it will most likely backfire.

Except with the official-style format, the personal or confidential note should be located four lines above the inside address. It doesn't need to be underlined or typed in all capital letters. If you feel it necessary to underline or capitalize, you should choose one or the other but not both.

Personal
PERSONAL
<u>Personal</u>

The personal note is rarely used in the official-style format because this format is usually reserved for personal letters. If you decide it's necessary to include a personal note in the official-style format, type it four lines above the salutation.

Inside Address

The inside address must be included in all letters. With the exception of the official-style format, the inside address is typed two to twelve lines beneath the dateline (or reference line or confidential note, should there be such notations). The placement of the inside address is flexible, depending upon the length of the letter, but four lines is the most common.

In the simplified-letter format, the inside address is typed four lines below the dateline or the last previous notation. In the official-style letter, the inside address is typed two to five lines below the last line of the signature block.

The inside address is always typed flush with the left margin of the letter. It should be no longer than five lines. No line should cross over the center margin of the page. If a line is too long, it should be broken in half and continued on the next line, indented two spaces.

The inside address of a letter addressed to an individual should include that individual's courtesy title and full name, professional title, company name, and full address. If a woman's courtesy title is unknown, use "Ms."

> Ms. Nancy Simons
> Production Supervisor
> Bethany Bagel Company
> 25 Francis Avenue
> Boston, MA 02222

If the courtesy title "Mrs." is used in a business letter, use the recipient's first name, not her husband's: "Mrs. Mary Smith," *not* "Mrs. John Smith."

If a person's name and professional title are short enough, they can be separated by a comma and placed together on the first line of the inside address.

> Mr. Robert Miles, Treasurer

If the professional title and company name are short enough, the title and the company name (separated by a comma) can be placed together on the second line of the inside address.

> Ms. Rebecca Gray
> Editor, The Tower

When a company is being addressed, the inside address should include the name of the company, the individual department desired, and the full address of the company.

> Pauly Industries, Inc.
> Distribution Department
> 79 Grand Forks Drive
> Winnipeg, VA 23444

You should always use the company's official name in the inside address, including any ampersands, abbreviations, or other items the company uses in its name when it is printed.

When the address is too long, the person's title is sometimes omitted. If you are addressing two or more people, you can either list the names alphabetically on separate lines or use the designation "Messrs." (Messieurs) for all men or "Mses." for all women. When using Messrs. or Mses., omit the addressees' first names.

> Mses. Cole, Kenney, and Long

or

> Ms. Bethany Cole
> Ms. Jane Kenney
> Ms. Marie Long

If you are unsure of the recipient's gender, it is best to try to do the research to find out. If you cannot determine the gender—for example, because the first name is gender neutral or the individual only uses initials—then you can omit the courtesy title in your letter.

> Dakota Shorter
> F. R. Dobson

Sometimes a company uses both a street address and a post office box in its letterhead. In this case, be sure to include the post office box number on the envelope. This will ensure that the post office sends your letter to the proper place.

The names of numbered streets should be spelled out for streets numbered one through twelve. Arabic numerals should be used for streets numbered 13 and above.

> 186 First Street
> 186 13th Avenue

Arabic numerals should be used for all house, building, or office numbers, with the exception of the number "one," which always should be spelled out.

> One Savin Hill Avenue
> 210 Savin Hill Avenue

When a compass direction appears before a street name, it should be spelled out. If the compass direction follows the street name, it should be abbreviated.

> 226 West 78th Street
> 3233 38th Street N.W.

A suite or apartment number following a street address should be placed on the same line as the street address, separated by a comma or two spaces.

> 25 Huntington Avenue, Suite 408
> 25 Huntington Avenue Suite 408

Attention Note

If you are addressing a letter to a company but wish to direct it to the attention of a specific person, you may include an attention note. The attention note is typed two lines below the last line of the inside address and two lines above the salutation.

In the full-block, block, or simplified formats, the attention note is typed either flush with the left margin or centered. The attention note is usually not included in the official-style format since this format is generally used for a personal letter and it would already be clear to whom the letter is addressed. The attention note can be included in a hanging-indented letter, but because the format is generally reserved for sales letters, the inclusion of an attention note would not be common.

The attention note can be written with or without a colon following the word "atten-tion." The first letter of the main elements of the attention note should be capitalized.

> Attention: David Marshall
> Attention David Marshall
> Attention: Order Department
> Attention Order Department

Salutation

The salutation appears in all letters but those using the simplified-letter format. It's usually typed two to four lines below the inside address or the attention note (if there is one). A two-line gap is most typical.

In the official-style format, the salutation is typed four to six lines below the dateline, since the inside address appears at the bottom of the letter in this format.

The word "Dear" before the person's courtesy title and name is standard. The phrase "My Dear" is no longer in style. The "D" in the word "Dear" should be capitalized. The word should be typed flush with the left margin. If the letter is informal, you address the person by his or her first name in the salutation.

Courtesy titles such as Ms. and Mr. should be used where appropriate.

> Dear Ms. Joyner
> Dear Mr. Quarrels

But, where the gender is not known:

> Dear Dakota Shorter
> Dear F. R. Dobson

If the recipient has a professional or academic title (e.g., "Dr." or "Professor"), use the title rather than "Mr.," "Mrs.," or Ms."

> Dear Professor Jones
> Dear Doctor Black

The most conventional way to address a letter when you don't know the name of the recipient is to simply use the title of the person you're addressing. For example:

> Dear Editorial Director
> Dear Sales Manager
> Dear Customer Service Representative

The simplified-letter format contains no salutation. As a result, this format can be used when you are unsure about the gender of the recipient.

Subject Line

The subject line identifies the content of a letter and is an optional addition to all but the simplified-letter formats, which always includes a subject line typed three lines below the last line of the inside address.

In the full-block, block, semiblock, or hanging-indented formats, the subject line is typed either two lines above or below the salutation. It is typed either flush with the left margin or centered, and consists of the word "subject" followed by a colon and the subject to be covered in the letter.

The subject line can be typed in all capital letters or with each important word capitalized. Sometimes when just the important words are capitalized, the whole subject line is underlined. When the subject line is typed in all capital letters, don't underline it as well.

> Subject: Proposed Distribution Arrangement
> Subject: Proposed Distribution Arrangement
> SUBJECT: PROPOSED DISTRIBUTION ARRANGEMENT

Use of a subject line is generally limited to letters in which only one subject is covered.

Paragraphs

While most word-processing programs will automatically format the various parts of a letter, it's good to know the basic formatting rules for letter writing nonetheless.

The body of a letter should begin two lines below the salutation or subject line in the full-block, block, semiblock, official-style, and hanging-indented formats. It should begin three lines below the subject line in the simplified-letter format.

The letter should be single-spaced within paragraphs and double-spaced between paragraphs. If the letter is very short, double-spacing can be used within the paragraphs, using the semiblock style of indentation to indicate new paragraphs.

Paragraphs should be indented five or ten spaces in the official or semiblock styles. Five-space indentations are usually standard. In the full-block, block, and simplified-letter formats, no indentation is used.

In the hanging-indented format, the first line of the paragraph is flush left and the rest of the paragraph is indented five spaces. Single-spacing within paragraphs and double-spacing between paragraphs are used in the hanging-indented format.

Numbered material within letters should be indented five spaces or centered. The numbers should be placed in parentheses or followed by a period. Double-spacing should be used between each item. Punctuation is used either after each item listed in the numbered material or after none of the items.

Long quotations should be blocked in the letter, setting off the quotation by indenting all of it five spaces and keeping it single-spaced.

Avoid long paragraphs. Of course, the use of brief paragraphs should not be carried to a ridiculous extreme by writing a letter full of one-sentence paragraphs. Be sensible about paragraph length. Say what you have to say and move on; avoid any padding or inconsequential information.

The first paragraph should introduce a letter's subject or refer to a previous correspondence or conversation to which you are responding. The following paragraphs should elaborate on the subject set up in the first paragraph. The closing paragraph should briefly summarize the topic and close on a positive note, encouraging a positive working relationship with the letter's reader.

Continuation Sheets

The printed letterhead is used only for the first page of a letter. The second and following pages are typed on plain sheets of paper matching the letterhead.

The heading on a continuation sheet is typed six lines below the top of the page and includes the addressee's name, the page number, and the date. The text of the letter begins again at least two lines beneath this heading. At least two lines of text, preferably more, should be carried over for a continuation sheet to be used.

In the full-block format, the information in the continuation sheet heading should be typed flush with the left margin. It should include the page number on the first line, the addressee's courtesy title and full name on the second, and the date on the third.

Page 2
Mr. David Marshall
May 5, 20X5

The block, semiblock, official-style, or hanging-indented formats can use either the flush left continuation sheet heading shown above, or a continuation typed on one line with the addressee's name typed flush left, the page number centered and set off by spaced hyphens, and the date flush with the right margin.

Mr. David Marshall   - 2 -   May 5, 20X5

Complimentary Close

The complimentary close must be included in all but the simplified-letter format. It is typed two lines below the last line of the body of the letter.

In the full-block format, the complimentary close should be flush with the left margin. In the block, semiblock, official-style, and hanging-indented formats, the complimentary close should start at the center of the page, directly under the dateline, about five spaces to the right of center, or at a point that would put the end of the longest line at the right margin. However, note that it should never cross over the right margin. The simplified letter has no complimentary close.

The first letter of the first word of the complimentary close should be capitalized. The entire complimentary close should be followed by a comma.

The choice of the proper complimentary close depends upon the degree of formality of your letter.

Among the complimentary closes to choose from are:

Yours sincerely,
Very sincerely yours,
Sincerely yours,
Sincerely,
Cordially,
Most sincerely,
Most cordially,
Cordially yours,

A friendly or informal letter to a person with whom you are on a first-name basis can end with a complimentary close such as:

As ever,
Best regards,
Kindest regards,
Best wishes,
Regards,
Best,

Signature Block

The signature block goes directly under the complimentary close. Leave four lines below the complimentary close for your actual signature, and type your name (usually the same way you will sign it) aligned with the complimentary close in the full-block, block, semi-block, official-style, and hanging-indented formats. In the simplified-letter format, type your name in all capital letters five lines below the last line of the letter, flush with the left margin.

Type your title one line below your typed name, unless it's short enough to fit on the same line as your name after a comma.

If the letterhead includes your business title and the business's name, these are not typed again in the signature block. If a letterhead is not used and your letter is a formal one requiring the business name, type the business name in all capital letters two lines below the complimentary close and aligned with it; in the case of the simplified-letter format, it should appear two lines below the last line of the letter.

The typed business name should appear two lines below the signature. Four lines below the typed business name, the letter writer's name should be typed. If the business name is long, it can be centered beneath the complimentary close in the block and semiblock format letters.

Yours truly,

BETHANY BAGEL COMPANY

Louis Leigh

Louis Leigh, President

If a woman wishes to use a courtesy title before her name, then "Ms." should be enclosed in parentheses before the typed name. This is the only title that may precede the name in the signature block. Academic degrees (e.g., Ph.D., M.B.A.) or professional designations (e.g., C.L.U., C.P.A., C.F.P.) follow the typed name and are separated by a comma.

A person signing the letter for someone else should initial just below and to the right of the signature.

Yours truly,

Louis Leigh js

Louis Leigh, President

If an assistant signs a letter in his or her name for someone else, the assistant's name and title are typed below the signature.

Yours truly,

Edward Cole

Edward Cole
Assistant to Mr. Leigh

Identification Line

The identification line is an optional addition to any letter. It consists of the initials of either the typist or the writer and the typist, and is typed flush with the left margin two lines below the signature block.

The identification line can be typed in a variety of ways. The typist's lowercase initials may be typed alone.

js

The writer's initials may be typed uppercase followed by a colon or virgule (forward slash) followed by the typist's lowercase initials.

MN:js
MN/js

The writer's initials and the typist's initials can both be uppercase, or both lowercase.

MN:JS
MN/JS
mn:js
mn/js

Any version of the identification line above can be used as long as it serves the purpose of identifying the typist of the letter.

In the unusual case that a letter should be dictated by one person, typed by another, and signed by a third, the identification line should include the signer's uppercase initials followed by a colon, followed by the dictator's uppercase initials, followed by another colon, followed by the typist's lowercase initials.

MN:JS:ms

Enclosure and Attachment Notations

If an enclosure is included with the letter, one of the following should be typed two lines below the identification line or the signature block if there is no identification line:

Enclosure
Enc.
Encl.
enc.
encl.

If there is more than one enclosure, use the plural of one of the above notations and indicate the number of enclosures before the notation, or after it in parentheses.

Enclosures (2)

> 2 Enclosures
> encs. (2)
> 2 encs.
> Encs. (2)
> 2 Encs.

The enclosures should be placed behind the letter in order of importance. If a check is one of the enclosures, it should be placed in front of the letter.

The enclosures can be numbered and listed next to the enclosure notation, one per line. If they are to be returned, indicate such in parentheses next to the item.

> encs. (2)   1. Credit analysis worksheet (please return)
> 2. International financing brochure

If you're sending a letter via email and plan to include several attached documents, you should note within the text of your email that your email contains attachments.

Distribution Notation

If you would like the recipient of the letter to know to whom you are sending copies of the letter, a distribution notation is used. Sometimes distribution notations appear only on copies of the letter. (On an email, you are automatically directed to place such names in the "cc" field of the email you are writing.)

The distribution notation consists of the words "Copy to" (or "Copies to") or the abbreviation and colon "cc:" followed by the recipient's or recipients' names.

> Copy to Louis Leigh
> cc: Louis Leigh

Multiple recipients are listed alphabetically by full name or by initials, depending upon the letter writer's preference or company policy.

> Copies to: Louis Leigh
> David Marshall

If other information about the recipient is useful (e.g., a company's name) it should be placed next to the person's name in parentheses.

> Copies to: Louis Leigh (Bethany Bagel Company)
> David Marshall (The David Marshall Agency)

> cc: LL (Bethany Bagel Company)
> DM (The David Marshall Agency)

If space is tight and a distribution notation is essential, it can be typed a single-space above either the enclosure notation or the identification line.

Postscript

A postscript is rarely used in a business letter unless it is in a sales letter to emphasize a point or to make a special offer. It is typed flush with the left margin two to four lines below the last notation in a letter. The writer should initial the postscript. The abbreviation "P.S." should *not* be used before a postscript.

CHAPTER 4

Appearance of the letter

A friend of ours is the president of a public relations company he founded in Boston. His customers include small businesses, restaurants, and financial services companies throughout New England. He is a superb spokesman for his company and is adept at convincing companies and executives that his organization can serve them better than other public relations firms can.

One reason for my friend's success is the contacts he's built over the several years he's worked as a public relations professional. Another is the good press he has gotten his clients.

But another important reason for his success is his appearance. He is well groomed and dresses well—nothing ostentatious, but when he arrives for a business meeting, the customer can tell that he or she is dealing with a public relations professional who at least appears to be very professional.

In letter writing too, appearance is very important. The message you are sending is obviously the most important aspect of your letter. However, if the reader opens an envelope and finds a note scrawled across a piece of notebook paper, the most important of messages is not going to get through.

There are certain conventions used in letter writing that are fairly well established, yet they are flexible enough to allow you to communicate exactly what you want to your reader. If you take into consideration the appearance of your letter—the stationery, format, length, and envelope—your reader will be drawn to it. Once your reader gives your letter his or her attention, your message is sure to get through.

Stationery

Letterhead design varies from business to business, but it usually consists of at least the following items:

- Business logo
- Business full, legal name
- Full street address or post office box number
- City, state, and zip code
- Telephone number
- Fax number
- Email address
- Website address

There are important considerations to make when choosing a letterhead design. The information included should be uncluttered and readable. The design should be simple enough for the reader to find the information he or she needs without being distracted from reading the rest of the letter.

Business stationery is usually white or some other conservative color. The standard size of the stationery is 8½ by 11 inches.

Margins on the typed letter should be consistent. The margins on the top and the bottom of the letter should be the same. The side margins should also be equal to one another. The size of the margins depends upon the length of the letter to be written. Long letters typically have smaller margins than short letters. Margins of one inch for long letters and two inches for short letters is a good rule of thumb to follow.

If a letter is very short, containing a few short sentences or a couple of short paragraphs, then a half-sheet of stationery can be used. The half-sheet measures 8½ by 5½ inches. It is usually imprinted with a smaller version of the letterhead, using the same logo and letterhead design as the normal-size stationery.

The full-block, block, or semiblock letter formats discussed in this chapter can be used on the half-sheet. The principles, techniques, and rules governing letter writing apply to letters written on a half-sheet as well.

Sometime a writer will choose to use an executive letterhead. In addition to the basic elements contained in a letterhead, the executive letterhead features the executive's printed name and title beneath the letterhead.

With all types of letters, the letterhead is always used only as the first sheet of a letter. If the typed letter is more than one page, a plain sheet of paper matching the letterhead should be used for subsequent pages. (See the section on continuation sheets in Chapter 3 for more information.)

One other element to keep in mind: Word-processing programs enable a writer to choose among a myriad of different type fonts and sizes. If your company does not have a standard font it uses in all correspondence, then limit yourself in how many different fonts you use with one letter. In fact, a single font should do the trick. The more readable the font, the better. Consider a font that is easy to read such as Times, Times New Roman, Courier, Arial, or Helvetica. You should choose a font size that is readable, certainly nothing smaller than 10 point, but rarely anything larger than 14-point type.

Formats

The format used for a letter is typically determined by the person writing the letter. Sometimes a company will have a house style for a format in which letters must be written.

The full-block, block, semiblock, and simplified-letter formats presented here can all be used effectively for writing any business letter. Some letter writers find that the simplified letter is not traditional enough for their taste; others find it a perfect solution to the problem of sexist language in letter salutations. Be that as it may, these four formats are the standard ones used for most business letters written today.

The hanging-indented and official-style formats discussed here are not used for everyday business letters. Their use indicates that a particular type of letter is being written. A discussion of the appropriate use of these formats is included in this chapter.

Chapter 3 discusses the placement and function of the parts of each of the letter formats discussed in this chapter. You might find it useful to look back at Chapter 3 for reference when you are studying the various letter formats in this chapter.

Full Block

The full-block format, sometimes called "complete block," is shown in Sample Letter 4.1. In this format, all the lines of the letter, from the dateline to the last notation, are flush with the left margin.

Paragraphs are not indented but rather begin flush with the left margin. Single-spacing is used within the paragraphs, and double-spacing between.

The dateline is most often typed three lines below the letterhead. Depending upon the length of the letter, however, it may be typed anywhere from two to six lines below the letterhead. If there is a reference line, it should be typed directly below the dateline.

The inside address is most often typed four lines below the dateline (or reference line if there is one) but may be typed anywhere from two to twelve lines below the dateline depending upon the length of the letter. If there is an attention line it should be typed two lines below the address and two lines above the salutation.

Sample Letter 4.1.   Example of full-block format letter.

[date]
A-354-29

Mr. Alexander Campbell
Bethany Bagel Company
14 Pendleton Road
Scots, PA 15012

Dear Mr. Campbell:

The records you requested are enclosed. Due to the technical difficulties we have in processing microfilm, I am unable to provide better quality copies.

I am sorry for any inconvenience this may cause. If I can be of any further assistance, please call me or another customer service representative on our toll-free number 1-800-555-1212.

Sincerely,

Ambrose Kemper
Customer Service Representative

jls

Enclosure

As you see in Sample Letter 4.1, the salutation has been typed two lines below the inside address; had there been an attention line, the salutation would have been two lines below that. If there had been a subject line, it would have been typed two lines above or below the salutation. The body of the letter begins two lines below the salutation or subject line if there is one.

The complimentary close was typed two lines below the last line of the letter and the signature block was typed four lines below the complimentary close.

An identification line was typed two lines below the signature block. All other notations (e.g., enclosure, distribution) are typed two lines below the identification line.

All letters in the full-block format will look like this one.

Block

The block format, sometimes called "modified block" to distinguish it from the full-block format, is shown in Sample Letter 4.2. This format differs from the full-block in the position of the dateline (and reference line if there is one) and of the complimentary close and signature block.

The dateline is usually aligned with the right margin, although sometimes it is centered in relation to the printed letterhead if this presents a more balanced look. In the samples in this book, the dateline is flush with the right margin.

The complimentary close and signature block can correctly be placed in any of several locations (see Chapter 3). Whatever position you choose for the complimentary close must be used for the signature block.

Paragraphs are not indented. The spacing of various parts of the block-format letter is the same as for the full-block format.

Sample Letter 4.2. Example of block ("modified block") format.

[date]

Mr. Jacob L. Martin
Investigative Management Magazine
25 Huntington Avenue, Suite 408
Boonton, NJ 07005

Subject: Membership of Bill Senyl

Dear Mr. Martin:

As we feared, Mr. Senyl is no longer a member of the Investment Managers Society of America. He was a member for just one year from May 20X6 through May 20X7, at which point he allowed his membership to lapse.

In his application, he indicated licenses and registrations in accounting, life insurance, law, real estate, and securities. He also indicated he was a registered investment advisor with the Securities and Exchange Commission. He indicated his highest level of education was a Ph.D., not a Masters degree, as you mention he suggested to you. He also stated that he had memberships in the American Bar Association, American Society of Certified Life Underwriters, and the Million Dollar Round Table.

We certainly appreciate your interest and assistance. Your information will be lodged with the membership department of the Investment Managers Society of America.

Sincerely,

Lisa Antolini
General Counsel

la/js

The block format is sometimes used because of the balanced look it gives to a letter. Since everything is flush with the left margin in the full-block format, it almost appears as if the letter might tip over to the left. In the block format, since the date is flush right and the complimentary close and signature block are *toward* the right, the letter is balanced in place and not tipped to either side.

Semiblock

The semiblock format is shown in Sample Letter 4.3. The only difference between this and the modified block format is that the paragraphs in the semiblock format are indented.

Sample Letter 4.3. Example of semiblock format letter.

[date]

Mr. Roger Perkins
95 Belltoll Road
Ketchum, ID 83340

Dear Mr. Perkins:

Thank you for sending your work samples and discussing your views about the editor's position we have open. I've reviewed your work and reflected at length on our last conversation, particularly your hesitancy to take on an assignment to demonstrate your editorial approach to analytical topics. Since we talked I've interviewed several other candidates with substantial editorial credentials and have become convinced that proven analytical skills or technical knowledge of the investments area are important prerequisites for the job.

My conclusion is that your background is not appropriate for the position and, frankly, that you would not enjoy the job during a necessary period of training. If, however, you are interested in establishing a freelance relationship with our publication, I'd be happy to consider using you.

Thanks again, Roger, for your interest in the job.

Cordially,

Gloria Hoagland
Publisher

GH/ec

Simplified Letter

The format of the simplified letter departs significantly from the formats described thus far; an example appears in Sample Letter 4.4.

Sample Letter 4.4.   Example of simplified-letter format.

[date]

Professor Alan Campbell
Lazarus College
43 Lorraine Terrace
Plattsburgh, NY 12901

OPINION LETTERS ON MARKETING TEXTBOOK

Enclosed is a group of opinion letters for your text, *Marketing: A New Approach*. We hope these letters will be of considerable interest to you and help you in making revisions to the second edition of the book.

As more of these letters come in, I will send groups of them along to you so that you may read the comments your colleagues have made about your book.

OTTO SCOTT—EDITOR

OS/js
Enclosures

The most obvious variation in the simplified-letter format is its lack of salutation and complimentary close. In addition to addressing a known recipient, the simplified-letter format is a good way to address an unknown audience that may consist of both men and women or only one of these two groups.

In a simplified letter, all lines are flush with the left margin, including the dateline, reference line (if there is one), and the signature block. The dateline is typed six lines below the letterhead. The inside address is typed four lines below the dateline or reference line.

A subject line always is included in the simplified-letter format. Type it in all capital letters, three lines below the inside address and three lines above the body of the letter.

Paragraphs are not indented in the simplified-letter format. Five lines below the body of the letter, the signature block is typed in all capital letters. Your signature goes above the signature block. If there is an enclosure notation it is typed a single space below the identification line. Any other notations are typed two lines below the enclosure notation.

If a continuation page is needed, the heading should be the same as used with the full-block format. The addressee's name should appear six lines from the top of the plain sheet, flush with the left margin. The page number should be typed directly below the name, and the date directly below the page number.

Official Style

The official-style format is used mostly for personal correspondence and is often written by executives on their personalized business stationery. This format is the same as the semi-block format with the exception of the placement of the inside address, which is typed two to five lines below the signature block. See Sample Letter 4.5 for an example of an official-style letter.

If there is an identification line in the official-style format, it is typed two lines below the inside address. Any enclosure notations are typed two lines below the identification line.

Sample Letter 4.5. Example of an official-style format letter.

[date]

Dear Ambrose:

Your article that appears in December's *Guam City Magazine* made good reading. It was informative and well written for the layman like me.

On behalf of Alan, Mike, and Gus, whom you cited in the article, as well as the whole crew here at Natick Nautical, I want to thank you for including us in the article. The exposure is great, especially in such a well-written and widely read piece.

Thank you again.

Regards,

Paul Pendelton

Mr. Ambrose Kemper
Guam City Magazine
One Symphony Place
Guam City, AZ 85001

PP:js

Hanging Indented

The hanging-indented letter format is reserved for sales or advertising letters. This unorthodox format, shown in Sample Letter 4.6, is believed to attract the attention of the reader.

The first line of each paragraph of the hanging-indented letter is flush with the left margin. The remaining lines of that paragraph are indented five spaces. Single-spacing is used within paragraphs and double-spacing between.

The dateline is flush with the right margin and typed three lines below the letterhead. The inside address and salutation are flush with the left margin and blocked exactly as in the block format ("modified block") discussed earlier in this chapter. The complimentary close, signature block, and all subsequent notations are also positioned similarly to the way they are placed in the modified-block and semiblock letter formats.

The main difference between the hanging-indented format and the semiblock format is the difference in the indentation of paragraphs. If there is a postscript, it is also typed with the first line flush left and the remaining lines indented five spaces.

Sample Letter 4.6.   Example of a hanging-indented format letter.

[date]

Ms. Jane Kenney
1978 Malden Place
Summit, NJ 07901

Dear Ms. Kenney:

For a very limited time—and only to a select, qualified group—I'm authorized to send
    the next issue of *The Armchair Reader's Review* absolutely free.

Reply by March 1, 20X5, and you'll receive—without risk or obligation—the one publi-
    cation dedicated to giving the inside knowledge on the latest in economic devel-
    opments.

Mail the enclosed postage-paid reservation card by March 1, 20X5, and the next issue of *The Armchair Reader's Review* is yours free. At the same time, we'll reserve in your name a full year's subscription at a special introductory rate.

When you receive your free issue, read it and then decide. If you can do without *The Armchair Reader's Review*, write "cancel" on the bill when it comes. You'll owe nothing. Your first issue will be your last. Or you can pay just $11.95 for 11 more issues—saving $24.05 off the newsstand price—and enjoy the insight that each monthly issue of *The Armchair Reader's Review* delivers.

Remember that this is a special offer good for a limited time only. Please reply today.

Cordially,

Alan Sitton
Publisher

AS:JS

Enclosure

Well, that's an awful lot of information, isn't it? Don't despair! You don't have to try to memorize each of these styles. Choose one that you feel comfortable with, and get that down pat. Be aware that there may be occasions when a personal note in the official-style format would be appropriate, or the more impersonal simplified-letter format. And when that time comes, you'll turn to the chapter and refresh your memory.

We, too, have a favorite style. You will find that 99% of the sample letters in Part II are presented in the full-block format, because that's the one *we* happen to like best.

Envelopes

The appearance of the envelope adds to the overall professional appearance of your letter. The address should be typed in the approximate horizontal and vertical center of the business envelope. The address on the envelope should appear exactly as in the inside address of the letter (see Chapter 3), although it must also include the P.O. box number if there is one.

The addressee's name should be typed on the first line. If there is space, the addressee's title can be typed next to the name on the first line, separated by a comma. On the second line, a single-space down, the person's title is typed if it did not fit on the first line. If the company's name will also fit on the second line, type it next to the title, separated by a comma. The complete street address or post office box number is typed on the next line. The city followed by a comma, the two-letter state abbreviation, followed by two spaces, and the zip code are typed as the last line of the address.

If you are addressing a company rather than an individual, type the company's name on the first line and the department name or attention line on the second line.

Your full name and address should appear in the upper-left corner of the letter. Usually the business name is imprinted on the envelope. If it isn't, add it in that same corner, just below your name and above your address.

The stamp is placed in the upper-right corner of the envelope. Any special mailing notations ("SPECIAL DELIVERY," "CERTIFIED MAIL," or "AIRMAIL") should be typed in all capital letters directly below where the stamp is to go. On-arrival notations ("PRIVATE" or "CONFIDENTIAL") should be typed in all capital letters about nine lines below the top left of the envelope, aligned with the end of the return address. Italics and script writing should not be used because they might confuse the postal service.

Memorandums

More often than not, memorandums are written as interoffice correspondence. Different businesses use different formats for their memos. Businesses often have preprinted memo forms that resemble the company's stationery. Usually these forms will feature the following information at the top:

> TO:
> FROM:
> DATE:
> SUBJECT:

In many word-processing software packages, a memo feature allows you to call up one of many templates, all of which include the above headings.

When a business does not have preprinted memo forms available, you can use the above format on a blank piece of stationery. You should begin the memo's message two to four lines below the subject line.

When you consider writing a memo, remember:

1. Write a memo only when it is necessary. Professionals are already drowning in a sea of paper. Don't compound the problem by adding unnecessary missives to the flood. If you don't really need to write the memo, don't.

2. Keep your memos as brief as possible. The memo is the ideal place for you to show how competent a writer you are. Be sure the memo is clear, concise, and to the point. The reader must be able to grasp the message quickly and clearly. Memos can run on to more than one page, but only when absolutely necessary.

Memorandum 4.1 shows these considerations in action.

Memorandum 4.1. Memo to employees about new benefits.

TO: Employees Participating in Disability Insurance Plan
FROM: Etsuko S. Yukki, Benefits Administrator
DATE: August 13, 20X4
SUBJECT: Long-Term Disability Plan

Your long-term disability insurance carrier until now has been Security of America. The cost to you for this coverage has been $.30 per $100.

As of August 1, we are pleased to announce that we have changed long-term disability carriers. As a result, your costs have been reduced by 25%. The new carrier on the long-term disability plan is Sambuki General Life Insurance Ltd.

Plan benefits through Sambuki General will remain the same, but rates have been reduced retroactive to August 1. As a result, you will see a rate reduction in your August paycheck. Your cost will be reduced to $.22 per $100 in monthly earnings. The company will continue to pay 50% of the cost of your plan.

Please call me in the New York office if you have any questions.

Email

Email—in part because it is simpler, faster, and less expensive—has taken the place of memos, faxing, and even casual hallway conversation in many businesses. It has also replaced traditional letter writing in many cases.

The immediacy of email makes it very tempting. It's all too common for someone to bang out an email on the computer or a smartphone, and then fire it off. Try to treat email with the same thoughtful consideration that you do letters or memos you send out. While it's tempting to send off an email in response to something that has angered or disappointed you, resist the urge. Sure, type out the email if you want to, but then use the "save draft" function. When you're calmer, go back and read the email to see if you really want to send it. When using email in any business or professional setting, you should follow the same rules about grammar, usage, and the construction of your thoughts as you would if you were writing a well-crafted business letter. While it may be faster to type everything lowercase and not bother with periods or other punctuation, it's best to take the time to reread your email and to make sure it is correct, clear, and concise. While it's a good practice to do this with interoffice email, it's even more important with email sent to outside parties. Just as a letter will give an impression of your company, so too will the emails you send. Remember: what may be your practice in a text message to a friend may not be appropriate for the business world.

Many of the sample letters provided in Part II of *The AMA Handbook of Business Letters* can easily be sent as an email. Sample Letter 6.41, for example, is a letter accompanying enclosed materials requested in a phone call and confirming the appointment made in that call. It was easily adapted to email format, as shown below, by simply copying the text of the letter in the message field of an email and modifying it slightly—the author only needed to change "enclosed" to "attached" in the opening sentence.

From: Mack Nilton <MNilton@nespr.com >
To: Walter Jingle <Walter_Jingle@clp.com>
Sent: Thu Sept 14 07:18:12 20X1
Subject: Follow-up to our conversation

Dear Mr. Jingle:

I've attached a copy of our press kit, which you requested when we spoke on the telephone yesterday. Among other things, the press kit contains articles I've written, stories in which I've been quoted, biographies of me and our senior staff, and a client list.

I look forward to meeting you the week of October 5. Thank you very much for your interest in NES Public Relations. I'll speak with you soon.

Yours truly,

Mack Nilton

With more formal or longer letters, you're likely to decide to write the letter in traditional format and either mail it or include it as an attachment to an email. But for shorter, less formal letters, you may decide that using email provides a more immediate way of getting your message to your recipient.

From a legal perspective, there's been little argument over the fact that companies have the legal right to monitor email sent over the company's computer network on company time. Employees may argue that monitoring their email is an invasion of privacy, but companies can also make a compelling case that if they don't monitor the email going out over their systems, they could be exposing themselves to internal problems related to employee misconduct as well as to outside legal liabilities.

It's important then to remember when using email within a company that what you write becomes a written record that can be subpoenaed should the company be sued. In some cases, for example, claims of sexual harassment because of off-color jokes being sent around the office have led to the dismissal of not only the employee who originated the email but also those who forwarded it on throughout the company. One such case at the St. Louis brokerage firm of Edward Jones & Company resulted in the dismissal of 19 employees, 1 resignation, and 41 warnings.

Because of its immediacy and ease of use, people sometimes forget that unlike a telephone conversation or chat at the water cooler, emails composed on company networks become written records that get stored. That alone offers a compelling reason why you should be thoughtful about the emails you write.

Some basic rules of thumb for email usage in business:

- Make sure the subject line of your email is descriptive and short—no more than four or five words. Because readers receive many emails every day, using a short, descriptive subject line helps ensure that your recipient will know right away what to expect from your email. It can also help a reader determine the importance of your email and when he should respond.

- Keep the email itself short and focused as well. Many people scan through their emails not just on their desktop or laptops, but also on their cell phones and other devices. The more focused you can make your emails, the more likely they'll get fuller attention from their readers.

- Use the same good grammar and spelling that you would use in a letter.

- Avoid cute abbreviations (e.g., imho for "in my humble opinion") and emoticons in your business email; it's just not professional, and says you aren't either.

- Never write in all capital letters. It gives the impression you're shouting at the recipient. If you need to stress a word, underline it or make it italic.

- Don't be too informal. Remember that your message still reflects your professionalism.

- Avoid spamming recipients by sending out mass emails about your business.

- Consider setting up a consistent signature that goes out with each email that gives your contact information. (Email programs and Web-based services allow for an easy set-up of a signature.)

- Don't forward chain emails or the latest jokes that you receive from friends.

- When you reply to an email, if your program permits, don't return the entire e-mail that you were sent. If you need to refer to select parts of it, then just include those. Otherwise, the email can become long, confused, and difficult to follow.

- Only send attachments that are necessary and make sure those you do send are free of any viruses by regularly running a virus check on your computer files.

CHAPTER 5

Grammar

People who are frightened about making mistakes often have tremendous difficulty writing. Grammar can appear to be a minefield of potential error and thus, for many, it is the most frightening element of writing.

You can combat this fear. Relax and try to write as naturally as possible. You'll usually find any grammatical errors when you do a careful proofreading. When I asked one professional how she managed to write such good letters, she replied: "Simple. I have a good secretary." Her secretary filled the role of proofreader. Most people don't need a secretary, however, to find and fix their errors. But first, they have to get something down on paper.

Relax and just start writing—after you've done the planning we talked about in Chapter 1. That's the key: get something down on paper. If you find you have a real problem with grammar, there are many easy to-understand grammar and usage books that should help you avoid any mistakes you might be making. Two books that are particularly useful are *The Chicago Manual of Style, 16th Edition* (University of Chicago Press, 2010) and William Strunk, Jr. and E. B. White's *The Elements of Style, Fourth Edition* (Longman, 1999). There are also many good online sources of grammar and usage information. Among the best is Purdue University's Online Writing Lab (OWL) at http://owl.english.purdue.edu/. Strunk and White's *The Elements of Style* is available online for free at http://www.bartleby.com/141/.

Word-processing programs also feature a grammar-check function. While these can be useful, it's still best to know the basic rules of grammar when writing. Knowing these basic rules will help you be able to fix mistakes identified by your grammar check, or, even better, will keep you from making them in the first place. This chapter gives you the grammar basics you need to create a well-written letter.

Grammar

The rules of grammar define how to speak and write clearly. Most of these rules are logical. Some may not seem as logical as others, but, on the whole, following the rules of grammar helps your writing to be consistent and understandable. If you get the basics correct and write with clarity and precision foremost in your mind, you will most likely produce correctly written English.

All types of grammatical errors are possible. In the next few pages, we discuss some of the most common problems, which—luckily—happen to also be the easiest to find and correct. Remember, most errors can be detected in a careful proofreading after you've finished the first draft of your letter.

Wrong Pronouns

Some writers have a tendency to want to write "I" instead of "me," even when the latter is correct. For instance, the sentence:

> He gave the book to Eddie and I.

is incorrect. The sentence properly should be written:

> He gave the book to Eddie and me.

The above error is common when two or more people are the recipient of the action. If you find yourself having difficulty in such a case, simply say the sentence to yourself as if you were the *only* receiver of the action.

> He gave the book to me.

It is easy to add other receivers of the action after you have determined the proper pronoun to use. This is a simple way to avoid using the wrong pronoun.

Another way to avoid using the wrong pronoun is to remember that there are three "cases" of pronouns. The *nominative case* pronouns are the subject of the verb. The nominative case pronouns are:

Singular	**Plural**
I	we
you	you
he, she, it	they

You would never write:

> Her and me are going to the movies.

but rather:

> She and I are going to the movies.

In the above sentence, because the phrase "She and I" is the subject of the verb, the nominative case pronouns are used.

The *objective case* pronouns are used as the direct or indirect object of a verb's action or as the object of a preposition. The objective case pronouns are:

Singular	**Plural**
me	us
you	you
him, her, it	them

The object of the verb can usually be determined by asking "what" or "who" is the receiver of the verb's action. In the sentence

> I gave it to her.

"her" is the indirect object of the verb because it answers the question: "To whom did you give it?"

One of the most problematic pronouns is "who." Some situations are no-brainers:

> *Who* goes there? [nominative case]
> With *whom* are you going? [objective case]
> *Whose* is this? [possessive case]

But when "who" is the subject of a clause ("The voters *who elected her* have been sorely disappointed."), you must use the nominative case.

Remember that an objective case pronoun is always used as the object of a preposition as well, so when you see a sentence that includes a prepositional phrase such as "at him," "with her," or "about me," it should immediately trigger your memory to use one of the objective case pronouns.

Possessive case pronouns indicate possession and are usually used correctly by native speakers of English. The possessive case pronouns are:

Singular	**Plural**
my, mine	our, ours
your, yours	your, yours
his, her, hers, its	their, theirs

Another common error involving the use of pronouns occurs when the words "than" or "as" precede an incomplete sentence construction. For example, let's look at the following sentence:

> Mr. Bradford is richer than I.

To determine the proper pronoun to use, complete the sentence:

> Mr. Bradford is richer *than I am.*

As we see in the completed structure ("richer than I am"), you would use "I," so indeed, that first example ("richer than I") is correct.

There are many more rules governing the proper use of pronouns. The ones we've discussed here are particularly useful to remedy some common problems. If you are unsure of the pronoun to use, you can usually determine whether or not your sentence is correct by listening to how the sentence sounds once you have written it. If you remain unsure, check the examples above or consult a grammar reference.

Pronouns and Antecedents

The most common mistake concerning pronouns and their antecedents occurs when it is unclear to what or whom a pronoun refers. To avoid any confusion in your letters, make sure that when you begin a sentence or a clause in a sentence with "he," "she," "it," or other pronouns, it is absolutely clear to whom or what these pronouns refer.

A couple of simple examples of unclear references involving pronouns and antecedents follow:

> Loren Gary and Guy Martin prepared the advertising presentation and visited the customer's new office building. It was a handsome piece of work. [<u>What</u> *was a handsome piece of work? The advertising presentation? The office building?*]

> Brian Palay spoke with Robert Long about the possibility of working together. He thought it was a good idea. [<u>Who</u> *thought it was a good idea? Brian? Robert?*]

Subject and Verb Agreement

Sentences consisting of a disagreement in number (plural versus singular) between subject and verb often result from quick, careless writing.

A word that is said to be singular refers to only one person or thing, whereas a word that is plural refers to more than one person or thing.

Singular	Plural
check	checks
this	these
loan	loans
client	clients

Remember these two basic rules:

1. Singular subjects take singular verbs.

   The check *is* here.
   This *is* unsatisfactory.
   The loan *is* adequate.
   The client *coughs* a great deal.

2. Plural subjects take plural verbs.

   The checks *are* here.
   These *are* unsatisfactory.
   The loans *are* adequate.
   The clients *cough* a great deal.

In a simple sentence, making subjects and verbs agree is not too difficult. But when a phrase appears between the subject and the verb or a word whose number you are unsure of is in a sentence, it becomes more difficult.

Remember that the verb must always agree with the subject. No matter how many words separate the subject and the verb, check to make sure they agree.

> The cancellation was final.
>
> The cancellation of the contracts was final.

Even though "contracts" would take a plural verb if it were the subject of the sentence, "cancellation" is still the subject, so you still use a singular verb.

When you use an indefinite pronoun as the subject of a sentence, it is sometimes difficult to tell whether the pronoun is singular or plural. Some take a singular verb while others take a plural.

These indefinite pronouns take a singular verb:

anybody	everybody	one
anyone	everyone	somebody
each	neither	someone
either	no one	

These indefinite pronouns take a plural verb:

both
few
many
several

With the following indefinite pronouns you must judge from the context of the sentence whether to use a singular or plural verb:

all
any
most
none
some

For example:

1. All of the secretaries *are* talented.

   All of the money *is* green.

2. Any desk *is* fine.

   Are any of the proceedings to be taped?

3. Most of my days *are* busy.

   Most of my dinner *is* cold.

4. None of the stores *were* open.

    None of the ledger *was* saved.

5. Some of our orders *are* processed incorrectly.

    Some of the order book *is* missing.

Another simple rule to remember is that *compound subjects always take a plural verb.*

> Mr. Hemingway *has* arrived.
> Mr. Hemingway and Mr. Grimes *have* arrived.

When "or" or "nor" connects the two subjects, however, a singular verb is used.

> Neither Mr. Hemingway nor Mr. Grimes *has* arrived.

If you carefully check to make sure that the subjects and verbs of your sentences agree in number, you will most likely not make any errors. Sometimes, however, when it is difficult to determine whether a singular or plural verb should be used, a quick reference to my pointers above or a grammar book will set you straight.

Dangling Modifiers

When a phrase doesn't clearly refer to the word it is modifying, it is said to be "dangling." The sentence

> Preoccupied with the business negotiation, her assistant surprised her.

is unclear. What does the phrase "preoccupied with the business negotiation" modify? It is a dangling modifier. It appears to modify "assistant" because that's the noun it's closest too, but it's more likely that it's meant to modify the "her" of the sentence. A word that the modifier can refer to sensibly in the sentence is needed:

> Because she was preoccupied with the business negotiation, she was surprised by her assistant.

When you write a sentence that contains a modifying phrase, always make sure that it clearly modifies what it's supposed to. Most dangling modifiers result from carelessness. You can usually tell after a careful proofreading of your letter whether or not the sentences you have written make sense.

Split Infinitives

You may remember your English teacher telling you: "Now remember, don't split an infinitive," probably sometime back in junior high. But splitting infinitives is not always wrong. Some people will go to such great lengths to make sure infinitives are not split that the sentences they write are awkwardly constructed.

As a rule of thumb, you should not split an infinitive when the splitting results in an awkwardly constructed sentence. For example, the infinitive "to pass" is awkwardly split in the following sentence:

The legislation is the proper one to, whether or not you approve of deficit spending, pass in the upcoming session.

A better way to write the above sentence is:

Whether or not you approve of deficit spending, the legislation is the proper one to pass in the upcoming session.

If splitting an infinitive is less awkward than leaving it intact, however, it is acceptable to split it. For example:

For the client to never lose is unusual.

If the scriptwriters had blindly followed the rule, the *U.S.S. Enterprise* would never have boldly gone where no man had gone before!

Parallel Structure

Perhaps the most common error involving parallel structure occurs with elements in a series. When you write a sentence that lists a series of items, make sure all of the elements are written in the same grammatical form. The use of parallel structure makes your writing more consistent and clearer to your reader.

Faulty parallel structure: To sell her proposal, the marketing director presented her marketing plan, asked for reactions to her presentation, and many other things to involve her audience.

Better: To sell her proposal, the marketing director presented her marketing plan, asked for reactions to her presentation, and did many things to involve her audience.

Faulty parallel structure: The personnel director was requested to handle terminations of employees as well as writing commendations.

Better: The personnel director was requested to handle terminations of employees as well as to write commendations.

Faulty parallel structure can be corrected no matter what part of speech the items in a series are. The important thing to remember is to be consistent with the grammatical form you use for writing items in a series.

Punctuation

Punctuation is used in writing to distinguish or separate one group of words from another to convey some meaning to a reader. The use of punctuation creates pauses and stresses where the writer feels they are necessary.

Appendix II goes over various aspects of punctuation that will help you use it correctly and effectively in your letter writing.

The most important thing about punctuation is using it consistently. Ralph Waldo Emerson might have thought that "foolish consistency is the hobgoblin of little minds," but you can rest assured that consistency in the use of punctuation is not foolish. It helps to clarify your message to your reader. By the same token, avoid overpunctuation; it impedes understanding.

Capitalization

Capitalization is another area that calls for consistency. Obviously you should capitalize the first word of every sentence as well as proper nouns and proper adjectives. There are, however, many quirks to the proper use of capitalization. When in doubt, it is usually best to lowercase or to check a reference such as a dictionary. For a discussion of proper capitalization within the various letter formats, see Chapter 4.

Spelling

Many books have been written to help writers with spelling problems. Most often, however, the best help is a dictionary. To avoid careless spelling mistakes, you should look up those words about which you have even the slightest doubt. The two best tools to guard against spelling errors in your letters are care in writing and a dictionary at your side.

Word-processing software packages feature spell-check. If you have any doubts about your spelling ability, a spell-check can be a saving grace. It will highlight any misspelled words and help you choose a correctly spelled alternative. Spell-check will not, however, catch misused words (e.g., "cat" for "can" or "lamb" for "lamp"), and your spell-check program may drive you crazy with its "false negatives" (it will accuse you of misspelling any word not in *its* meager list; this will include Mr. Jones's last name—who could misspell "Jones"?—and "smartphone," along with other words too recent to have been included). A careful proofreading is still the best guard against misuse.

Jargon

Jargon is a curse to any writer who wants to get a clear, precise message across to a reader. The word "jargon" has two meanings. The first is "incoherent language." The second is "the technical language of a profession." Usually both of these types of jargon should be avoided in letter writing. Of course the first, incoherent language, must be avoided at all costs. Technical language should be kept to a minimum in your letters to avoid confusing your reader.

A person who writes jargon is usually more impressed with the way the words sound than with getting a message across. You are writing to convey a message, not to impress your reader with how many big words you know. People who write in lofty language or jargon will often string together complex words that sound great but mean nothing.

Avoid pretension and strive for clarity in your letter writing. Forget about jargon!

Use simple language. Your reader will appreciate it.

Clichés

Clichés are words or expressions that become stale from overuse. Clichés often take the form of metaphors or comparisons, such as "big as an ox" or "slept like a log." They are trite and show a lack of originality in writing.

In business, expressions such as "put on the back burner," "caught between a rock and a hard place," and "thinking out of the box" have been used so often that they can be considered clichés. Nothing is grammatically wrong with these trite expressions. They are just so stale that they have lost the power to convey much meaning to the reader.

Avoid clichés by writing exactly what you want to convey. Make every word in your letters mean something. After you've written your first draft, clarify your message by deleting any clichés or trite expressions.

Be original in your letter writing. If you need to make a comparison, try to make an original one. Avoid drawing from the stock of clichés that have been used for years.

Wordiness

In Chapter 2, I warned that if you don't write what you mean, your writing will be full of ambiguity. I can't emphasize this point too much. Write what you mean, not what you think sounds good.

The following pointers may be helpful in guiding you away from the curse of wordiness. Remember the following "five avoids" and you will be on your way to writing in a clear, direct style:

1. *Avoid pretentiousness.* Don't overcomplicate your writing by trying to impress the reader with your vocabulary or your great literary style. Write simply, clearly, and directly.
2. *Avoid redundancy.* Don't use superfluous or repetitious words. Write what your reader needs to know and he or she will most likely get the message. There is no need to repeat your message over and over.
3. *Avoid padding.* Be direct in your letter writing. Strike out all unnecessary words or sentences. If you write more than you have to, your reader might become impatient. Strive for clarity and precision.
4. *Avoid weak intensifiers.* Words like "very," "quite," and "completely" usually add little or nothing to the meaning of your sentences.
5. *Avoid unnecessary definitions or explanations.* Explain only what absolutely needs to be explained. Don't insult your reader by explaining something that is obvious or that he or she would already know.

Revisions can help you eliminate any problem with wordiness you may be having. In the revision process you should:

1. Reread the letter to make sure you've said what you wanted to say.
2. Edit out all unnecessary words and phrases.
3. Clarify until your letter is precise enough to get the proper message across.

PART II

The letters

You have learned the basics. From planning and structure to appearance and grammar, you have learned what it takes to write a good letter.

Part II of *The AMA Handbook of Business Letters* takes you a step further. In the chapters that follow you will see the basics of letter writing at work in more than 370 sample business letters, also available to customize at www.amacombooks.org/go/AMAHbkBizLts4.

These letters, which show you the application of the basics discussed in Part I, were chosen for two major reasons. First, this sampling of letters gives you access to many of the more common letters written in everyday business. Second, the letters are particularly well-written examples upon which you can model effective business letters.

You can use many of the letters in Part II as form letters or as prototypes for your own letters. Change the names and addresses in these letters, tweak them a little, and use them with your own customers.

The caption at each of the sample letters gives you a concise description of its purpose. The narrative interspersed among the letters gives you a brief analysis of each letter's strong points.

We don't expect you to diligently read through every sample letter in every chapter of Part II. Read those sample letters that can best help you improve or increase the scope of your letter writing. Study them and, if you apply the basics learned in Part I, you'll be well on your way to writing better, more effective letters.

CHAPTER 6

Sales, marketing, and public relations letters

The object of a sales, marketing, or public relations letter is to elicit a positive response from your reader toward the product or service you are trying to market. Successful sales, marketing, and public relations letters must therefore grab readers' attention and convince them that your product or service will satisfy their needs or desires.

Use a friendly, personal tone. Customers, whether they are consumers or business users, crave personal attention, and a very formal letter suggests just the opposite.

While all the letters in Part II could be considered sales and marketing letters in the broad sense that they are trying to convince a reader to take some sort of action, the letters in this chapter are sales and marketing letters in a more literal sense. They were written specifically to market a product or service.

Many of the letters in this chapter can be sent as emails or as attachments to emails. For those letters that can be adapted to emails in this section, it's simple enough to copy the text of the sample letter into the text of your email.

Letters of Introduction

Sample Letters 6.1 through 6.6 are all letters introducing salespeople or companies.

Sample Letter 6.1 was written by a salesperson to an existing customer informing him that she is being promoted and will be replaced by someone new. The current salesperson comes right to the point in announcing her promotion and replacement. She then seeks to set up an appointment with the customer so the customer can meet the new salesperson. Finally, she expresses confidence in her replacement, and stresses the continuity of service.

Sample Letter 6.1.   Letter introducing new salesperson.

[date]

Mr. Lawrence Volpe, Treasurer
Boonton Medical Center
100 Harlan Drive
Milwaukee, WI 53201

Dear Mr. Volpe:

Last week I mentioned to you that I am being promoted to vice president at Gleechie Medical Equipment Supply Company. Taking over my territory as your sales representative will be Felicia Mamet. Felicia has been with Gleechie for four years in our Indiana office.

Felicia and I will be in your area on May 25 and 26. We would like to take some time on one of those two evenings to take you and Mark McIntyre to dinner and a baseball game. I'm hoping that this will give both of you the chance to get to know Felicia.

Felicia is my handpicked replacement. I know she will give Boonton Medical Center the attention it deserves. I have little doubt that you will be pleased with my choice.

I look forward to hearing from you to confirm our meeting.

Best regards,

Alice Krauss
Sales Representative

AK:js

cc: Mark McIntyre
     Felicia Mamet

Sample Letter 6.2 was written by a new sales representative to an existing customer. Like Sample Letter 6.1, the writer immediately gets to the point by introducing herself and explaining whom she will be replacing. The writer goes on to instruct the customer how to get in touch with her and expresses a desire to set up a meeting so they can get to know each other.

Sample Letter 6.2. Letter from new salesperson.

[date]

Ms. Patsy Palay
Palay Sporting Goods
139 Howard Place
Carfer, WV 26000

Dear Ms. Palay:

I am your new Glorious Racquets sales representative. I arrived in the territory about a month ago and have been working with Bob Sheffield, your former rep, to familiarize myself with both the territory and all of the dealers in it.

If you should ever need to reach me when I am on the road, feel free to call my cell phone or text message me. My cell phone number 617-555-3232.

You can also call my personal extension at Glorious Racquets, which is 617-555-2345, and leave a message for me.

I look forward to meeting you and all of the people at Palay Sporting Goods. I'll call soon to set up a mutually convenient meeting time. Thanks for your patience during this transition.

Cordially,

Bethany J. Cole
Sales Representative

bjc:nlc

Sample Letters 6.3 through 6.6 introduce companies to customers. Sample Letter 6.3 introduces a new company to a current customer. The writer announces the formation of the new company in the opening paragraph and spends the rest of the letter detailing the company's chief employees, the desire to provide services to the reader, and the desire to set up a meeting with the reader.

Sample Letter 6.4 was written to a prospective customer by an official of an existing company. In the letter she explains what the company does and how it might benefit the reader. The letter elaborates on specific services provided as well as services that may be of particular interest to the party addressed.

Sample Letter 6.5 also introduces an existing company, but this letter is sent as a follow-up to a brief meeting. Like the earlier letters, this one gets right to the point by clearly indicating why it is written—to inquire about the recipient's public relations needs. The letter continues with a brief description of the writer's company, indicates that a press kit is enclosed with the letter, and closes by stating that she will get in touch with the reader.

Sample Letter 6.3.   Letter introducing new company.

[date]

Ms. Adrienne Leigh
186 Alpine Rock Road
Boston, MA 02125

Dear Adrienne:

I've enclosed a copy of our new corporate image brochure for the financial planning company our bank has recently purchased. New Bedford Financial Planning Services Inc. provides complete financial planning consulting services through our staff of 50 financial services professionals.

The individuals who run this company have extensive experience in all forms of financial planning. They and other senior staff members have done financial planning for some of the country's largest corporations, including: Mom's Bagel Company, General Hospital, Broughton & Brady Corporation, STL Hotels, and a host of others. They have also completed financial planning services for many fast-growing small to midsize companies.

Adrienne, we would be pleased to provide whatever financial planning services you may need or, if you use other financial planning services, we will be pleased to offer you competitive quotations for your entire financial planning program or any portion of it. We are certain that we can earn the privilege of being your financial planning provider if you give us the chance to compete.

At your convenience I would like to introduce you to some of the key members of our staff. Please let me hear from you if you'd like to find out more about New Bedford Financial Planning Services and what we can offer you.

Regards,

Quentin Compson
President

QC/js

Enclosure

Sample Letter 6.4.   Letter introducing existing company and its services.

[date]

Ms. Eliza Gruber
Long & Berrigan
200 Andover Street
Bar Harbor, MI 48001

Dear Ms. Gruber:

I am pleased to enclose a copy of a recently published "tombstone" advertisement covering selected corporate finance transactions completed during the past year by our corporate finance department. As indicated in the advertisement, we provided a variety of services to our Michigan public and private clients, including:

1.   Underwriting common stock and debt offerings
2.   Handling private placement of debt securities
3.   Managing corporate sales and acquisitions

Our company is one of the securities industry's largest and most preeminent international firms. The objective of our Detroit corporate finance department is to combine the capital resources and specialized skills within the firm with the financial expertise of the Detroit department to provide an exceptional level of corporate finance service to Michigan public and private companies.

We would welcome the opportunity to become acquainted with you and your company and to be of service in achieving your corporate and financing objectives. The objectives for the management of a company such as yours, which has gone public during the past several years, may include:

1. Raising additional equity or long-term debt capital to support continued corporate growth
2. Pursuing growth through selected acquisitions
3. Increasing corporate exposure to the institutional and retail investment community

Please don't hesitate to call me if we can be helpful to you in any way. I look forward to discussing any aspects of our activities of particular interest to you, as well as any other issue in which we may be of assistance.

Kindest regards,

Susan Crooms
Vice President

SC/mn

Enclosure

Sample Letter 6.5. Short letter introducing existing company as follow-up to brief meeting.

[date]

Peter Velasquez
President
Commonwealth Pro Systems
54 Garland Drive
Hamilton, CA 90001

PUBLIC RELATIONS NEEDS OF COMMONWEALTH PRO SYSTEMS

Not too long ago I had a brief discussion with Jennifer Silex about your company's public relations needs. Commonwealth Pro is certainly an exciting company with an interesting history. It's a public relations professional's dream.

I thought it might be appropriate to introduce my company for your consideration, should you decide to enhance your current marketing program with public relations. Berenson Public Relations specializes in marketing for clients in the sporting goods industry.

I've enclosed our press kit. It will help familiarize you with us. After you've had time to look through the enclosed material, I would like to make an appointment to meet with you and Rhonda Berringer, your marketing director.

Thank you, in advance, for your time. I'll call next week to arrange an appointment at your earliest possible convenience.

MARY NESINE
PRESIDENT

Enclosure

mn/ph

Sample Letter 6.6 was written by someone who wanted to introduce himself to a new contact person who had just been promoted at a client company. Recognizing that this person is in a decision-making position, the letter writer does his best to shore up the relationship he has built over the years with the recipient's company.

Sample Letter 6.6. Letter to new contact at client company.

[date]

Ms. Catherine Serven
Vice President
Boonton Labor Services
312 West Main Street
Boonton, VT 05001

Dear Ms. Serven:

Congratulations on being named chief operating officer for Boonton Labor Services. I'm looking forward to working with you to help ensure that the employee leasing services we provide are tailored to meet your needs as you lead your company into the future.

I realize that you must have your hands full these days, but I'd really like to meet with you soon so we can assess your future plans and develop a partnership that will ensure the success of both of our companies as well as meet the needs of the employee leasing community. At a time when the industry is rife with consolidation and uncertainty, I am glad we can look to you to take a leadership position.

Georgia Sweet, our director of trade relations, and I would like to meet with you at your earliest convenience. I'll give your office a call early next week to set up a meeting time that works for all of us.

Again, congratulations on your new position. I look forward to a long, fruitful partnership in the years to come.

Sincerely,

Guy Lewis
Senior Vice President

Sales Letters

Sample Letters 6.7 through 6.21 are all directly selling something.

Sample Letter 6.7 was written to sell a consumer product. The writer makes a special offer to a previous customer. The offer is established in the first paragraph of the letter, followed by suggestions about how to take advantage of it. The writer winds up the letter cross-selling other products the company offers, backs up her offer with the company's money-back guarantee, and closes with the date by which the offer must be taken. By being direct, enthusiastic, and personable in the letter, the writer clearly gets her sales point across to the prospective consumer.

Sample Letter 6.8 was written to sell a business product. The author of the letter makes clear what he is selling in the first two paragraphs of the letter. The next paragraphs detail the features of the product and spell out its convenience and results-oriented nature. The writer then offers the reader a no-risk trial period, and closes with a reminder to order the product today.

Sample Letter 6.9 was written to sell a consumer service. As in the earlier product sales letters, the author here clearly establishes what is being sold in the first paragraph. The next paragraph emphasizes the competitive qualities of the service and the convenient method of signing up. The letter closes by referring to an enclosed brochure and encouraging the reader to call and sign up now.

Sample Letter 6.7. Letter selling consumer product.

[date]

Warren Laylor
78 Andover Street
Alabaster, KS 66012

Dear Mr. Laylor:

Because you're a valued customer, I've been authorized to make you this very special offer: For a limited time only, you can save 50% when you buy 4 pairs of Slacks Favorites slightly imperfect men's slacks!

That's right. Usually you save 40% when you buy 4 pairs of slightly imperfects. But we've slashed our prices, so now you pay only half the normal first-quality price.

Take advantage of these low prices to try some spring and summer favorites like Slacks Favorites Cotton Twills at only $22.99 per pair, or Summer Slacks at just $19.99 per pair. With prices this low, you can try several different colors to go with every conceivable outfit.

And it's the perfect time for you to stock up on your favorite slacks styles, like:

Slacks Favorites all cotton work pants—only $15.99 per pair.
Slacks Favorites cotton/polyester blend dress slacks—only $17.99 per pair.
Slacks Favorites bestselling durable casuals—only $18.99 per pair.

Remember Slacks Favorites, Inc. guarantees your satisfaction—no matter what. If you are not completely satisfied, just return the item for a full refund or replacement, whichever you prefer.

I only have authority to extend these special half-off prices through July 31, so I urge you not to delay. Order now and stock up on your favorite Slacks Favorites styles at these super-saver prices.

Sincerely,

Lorraine Gabor
Vice President, Marketing

ls

enc.

Sample Letter 6.8. Letter selling business product.

[date]

Mr. John Hill
327 Richmond Avenue
San Diego, CA 90006

Dear Mr. Hill:

The new edition of *The AMA Handbook of Business Letters* shows you how to write effective letters and memos that get the results you want. By taking advantage of our 15-day free trial offer, you can see those results immediately.

You'll get dozens of new sales, marketing, and customer service letters that are ready to use. *The AMA Handbook of Business Letters* covers the broad range of correspondence handled in almost every business setting. There are tools for salespeople, personnel directors, assistants, and managers. This convenient and comprehensive guide will help you, your staff, and your colleagues write results-oriented letters quickly and correctly.

These are actual letters used by businesses that are proven effective. Each sample was selected for its ability to generate positive results. In addition to the many sample letters, *The AMA Handbook of Business Letters* provides information on the fundamentals of good letter writing—from planning and formatting to phrasing and closing. You'll learn techniques that enhance and improve communication and make all of your correspondence more effective.

Send for your 15-day free examination copy today. Just mail in the enclosed order card to receive your copy. Use it for 15 days and see for yourself how much time you save and how easy it is to write letters that produce positive results.

You are under no obligation to purchase the book during the examination period. If you are not convinced that it will improve the quality of your writing and save you time, simply return the book to us and owe nothing. Should you decide to keep the book, approve the invoice for $69.95 plus shipping and handling.

Start getting the response you want from your letters and improve your communication skills by ordering your copy of *The AMA Handbook of Business Letters* today.

Sincerely,

Maury Notches
Publisher

jls

Enclosure

Sample Letter 6.9.   Letter selling consumer service.

[date]

Ms. Joanne Wagner
456 Allegheny Road
Southside, NJ 07005

Dear Ms. Wagner:

There is not a single reason why you should continue using Blotto Laundry Service. Because anything Blotto can do, Spotless Laundry's professionals can do better—for less. And if you switch to Spotless before April 30, 20XX, you'll receive a free week of laundry service.

Why would you want to pay the high cost of Blotto's weekly pickup and delivery service? Come over to Spotless. You'll get the best laundry service at the best price and you won't give up a thing.

Our complete fleet of trucks operated by professional drivers will give you the service you deserve. Our brand new state-of-the-art industrial laundry facilities increase the efficiency of our operations, allowing us to give you the highest quality service at the lowest prices available.

Spotless Laundry is fully equipped to provide all the services you'd expect—even morning pickup and same afternoon delivery. And our quarterly billing plan is the ultimate in making it easy for you to pay for the service without receiving a bill every week.

Rest assured that once you sign on with Spotless, there'll be no interruption of your laundry service and no inconvenience to you whatsoever.

Read the brochure enclosed with this letter. It includes our menu of services and prices. Then return the authorization form without delay so you don't miss out on our special offer of a free week of laundry service.

Better yet, get Spotless quality, savings, and service right now by calling us toll-free at 1-800-555-8537 or sign up on our website at www.spotlesslaundry.com now. We're waiting for your business!

Sincerely,

Beverly G. Krauss
Vice President
Sales and Marketing

bgk/lls

Enclosure

Sample Letter 6.10 was written to sell a business service. Unlike the previous product and service sales letters, here the author has decided to create the perceived need in the reader's mind before even mentioning the company's name. While it's clear from the opening paragraph the type of service being sold, the first two paragraphs are used to raise questions in the reader's mind. In the third paragraph, the writer presents his service as the solution to the customer's problems. The letter continues to elaborate on the company's no-risk guarantee and its specialization with the reader's type of business, and closes with a special offer.

Sample Letter 6.11 was written to sell a subscription to a publication. The writer here pulls no punches, but gets right to the subscription offer in the first paragraph. In the first four paragraphs, the writer clearly explains the offer to the reader. In the closing paragraph he reminds the reader that the offer is for a limited time so she should reply today. Like the earlier sales letters, Sample Letter 6.11 does not try to sell by bamboozling the reader with an array of sales offers. Sales letters work best when the reader knows what is being offered, how it can help him or her, and how to take advantage of the offer.

Sample Letter 6.12 is a brief letter selling a subscription renewal to a subscriber. Paragraph 1 explains the letter's purpose. Paragraph 2 highlights some benefits of renewing soon. And paragraph 3 explains how to renew.

Sample Letter 6.10.   Letter selling business service.

[date]

Ms. Beatrice Alexandria
Office Manager
Pixadiddle & McCormick, Inc.
34 Runter Road
Luckier, NM 87001

Dear Ms. Alexandria:

Have you ever wondered why every time your copy machine goes on the blink your copier service company's phone is busy?

If your company is like most, every lost day of your copying capabilities can spell headaches, delays, and the expense of having to send materials out to be copied.

Rest easy. Anderson Copy Repair guarantees that as your copier service company, we'll be there when you need us with the solutions to your copier problems. Our trained staff has years of experience, experience that gets your machine off the blink and back into A-1 condition.

What's more, there's no risk that you will be without a machine for long. While we are servicing your machine, we'll provide you with a temporary machine until yours is up and going. Most repairs will take less than an hour. But just in case, there will be a top-of-the-line machine at your disposal.

Anderson Copy Repair specializes in servicing small businesses like yours. I've enclosed a partial list of our current clients. Feel free to check our reputation with any of them. I think you'll find the response is unanimous praise.

As a special offer to new customers, we are offering a 6-month contract for copier repair service at our 3-month rates. But the offer's only good if you sign up by May 31. Simply fill out the enclosed postage-paid card, mail it back to us, and we'll get you started on worry-free copier service. Or, go to our website at www.andersoncopyrepair.com and sign up there.

Act now to get the special introductory offer.

Sincerely,

Ralph L. Anderson

rla/jls

enc.

Sample Letter 6.11.   Letter selling a subscription.

[date]

Ms. Jane Kinneally
1978 Malden Place
Summit, NJ 07902

Dear Ms. Kinneally:

For a very limited time—and only to a select, qualified group—I'm authorized to send the next issue of *The Armchair Reader's Review* absolutely free.

Reply by March 1, 20X2, and you'll receive—without risk or obligation—the one publication dedicated to giving the inside knowledge on the latest in economic developments.

Mail the enclosed postage-paid reservation card by March 1, 20X2, and the next issue of *The Armchair Reader's Review* is yours. At the same time, we'll reserve in your name a full-year's subscription at a special introductory rate.

When you receive your free issue, read it and then decide. If you can do without *The Armchair Reader's Review*, write "cancel" on the bill when it comes. You'll owe nothing. Your first issue will be your last. Or you can pay just $11.95 for 11 more issues—saving $24.05 off the newsstand price—and enjoy the insight that each monthly issue of *The Armchair Reader's Review* delivers.

Remember that this is a special offer good for a limited time only. Please reply today.

Cordially,

Mark Naddes
Publisher

MN:JS

Enclosure

Sample Letter 6.12.   Letter selling subscription renewal.

[date]

Mr. Erik Hane
1045 Harcross Plaza
Roswell, GA 30075

Dear Mr. Hane:

Our message to you is brief, but important: Your subscription to *The Armchair Reader's Review* will expire soon and we haven't heard from you about renewing.

We're sure you don't want to miss even one issue. Renew now to ensure that your subscription will continue uninterrupted. You'll guarantee yourself continued delivery of the excellent features, fiction, and insight that make *The Armchair Reader's Review* the fastest growing journal in America.

To make it as easy as possible for you to act now, we've enclosed a pencil for you to complete the postage-paid reply card enclosed. Simply send back the card today and you'll continue to receive your monthly issue of *The Armchair Reader's Review* without any interruptions.

Best regards,

Thomas Strout
Circulation Director

TS/ny

Enclosure

Sample Letter 6.13 was written to welcome a new subscriber to a publication. It could be written as a follow-up to a successful subscription sales letter. The letter briefly welcomes the new subscriber, asks her to check her invoice for accuracy, and instructs her on the procedure for forwarding or holding her publication should she be out of town for any period of time. By showing a concern for the subscriber and letting her know how the system works, the publisher builds goodwill, increasing the likelihood of further subscription renewals.

Sample Letter 6.14 was written to sell an educational seminar. Since seminars are intangible, the writer sells the benefits of attending the seminar. The first paragraph briefly tells the reader that the topic of this particular seminar, compliance, is more important than ever. The second paragraph recounts the benefits of attending, and the close allows the prospective attendee to have a say in some of the issues covered.

Sample Letter 6.13. Letter welcoming new subscriber.

[date]

Ms. Jane Thomson
Brian, David & Lauren, Inc.
55 Congregation Drive
Boonton, MA 02125

Dear Ms. Thomson:

We're delighted to welcome you as a subscriber to *The Armchair Reader's Review*.

Please take a moment to review the enclosed invoice to make sure we have recorded your name and address properly. If any corrections are necessary, please make the changes on the portion of the invoice you return with your payment.

If you plan to be away for a month or longer, we will be glad to change your address label so you'll receive *The Armchair Reader's Review* at your temporary address. Delivery can always be suspended for a week or so while you are away and started again when you return. We'll credit your subscription so you receive every issue you've paid for. Let us know about three weeks before you leave and we'll make the necessary arrangements to ensure that you receive the *Review* when you want it where you want it.

Thank you for your subscription. We are glad to be able to serve you.

Sincerely,

Yvonne Surrene
Associate Publisher

ys/nw

Enclosure

Sample Letter 6.14.   Letter selling an educational seminar.

[date]

Mr. Samuel Johnson
Auditor
Missoula Accounting Services
P.O. Box 3452
Missoula, MT 59011

Dear Mr. Johnson:

Never before have accountants faced so many compliance issues. Countless questions have arisen and often accountants have difficulty knowing where to turn for correct answers to these questions.

To meet that challenge of compliance, you should plan to attend the Tenth Annual Southwest Accountants Group Compliance Seminar, described in the enclosed brochure. Our compliance committee has developed a program that will answer many of your questions and help you establish personal contacts for future assistance.

We have also enclosed a survey form to determine the issues you would like covered in the afternoon session. Your responses will determine the make-up of that session. Complete the form and send it back with your registration.

We look forward to your participation.

Sincerely,

Jim Boswell, Chairman
SAG Seminar Committee

jb/js

Encs.

Sample Letter 6.15 was written to sell an existing customer additional services after an expansion in the company's production capabilities. The writer thanks the customer for his business and clearly lays out the specifics of a special offer to existing customers.

Sample Letter 6.15.   Letter selling customer additional services.

[date]

Mr. Brian Palay, Purchasing Manager
P.O. Box 3452
Grand Forks Opera House
Grand Forks, NE 68015

Dear Mr. Palay:

It's been a real pleasure working with you over the past several years at the Grand Forks Opera House to provide you with high-quality performance programs for each of the operas you have staged. We think you'll agree that we've delivered high-quality goods at prices that fit your budget.

Now we are expanding our services to offer you assistance in designing and printing souvenir programs for your productions as well. These four-color books can be tailored to the production you're presenting and can give your patrons a lasting remembrance of a wonderful experience at your opera house.

We are making a special offer on these souvenir programs to our regular customers. For orders of 2,000 or more, we are offering a 20% discount on our published prices. We'll work with you to design the programs, and once we have the design complete we guarantee that we'll have the programs printed and in your hands within seven working days.

If you're intrigued, please give me a call at 999-555-8458 to set up a meeting. We look forward to continuing to give you the same top-notch customer service you've come to expect from us over the years. I think you'll agree that our expanded offerings will add to your satisfaction.

Sincerely,

Rachel Digs
Regional Sales Manager

Sample Letters 6.16 through 6.21 are all sales letters that were written to market membership in one form of club or another.

Sample Letter 6.16 extends an offer of membership in a professional organization. It is written as a follow-up to an inquiry from a member of the profession. The letter acknowledges the inquiry, lists the services the professional will receive, details the costs of membership, and expresses a desire for the prospect to join the association.

Sample Letter 6.17 is written to a prospective member of a local professionals' organization. The letter is a follow-up to someone who attended one meeting as a guest. It's brief but to the point, expressing pleasure that the prospective member attended the meeting and offering him membership in the organization. Because the prospect has already attended a meeting, he has a fair idea of the type of issues that will be covered at these events, so a detailed analysis would be unnecessary.

In Sample Letter 6.18 the purpose is to sell membership in a local health club. First, the writer welcomes the reader to the community. In the first paragraph, he associates his health club with the community by expressing his fondness for the city. The next paragraph describes the benefits of the club. It is followed by an offer of special membership rates. The organization of the letter builds goodwill and leaves the reader with an impression that this organization really wants to serve her and her new community.

Sample Letter 6.16. Letter extending membership.

[date]

Mr. Joseph Y. Smith
Ventilating Experts
45 Archie Way
Elizabeth, PA 15010

Dear Mr. Smith:

Thanks for your inquiry about membership in the Associated Ventilators of America. In the interests of providing more adequate services to AVA members, the National Plumbers Club has assimilated the AVA membership as a special division of NPC.

As a ventilation professional you will receive not only all of the NPC services, but also special market information and other news relating specifically to ventilation. You will also have an opportunity to be listed in the Plumbing Professionals Directory for a small fee.

If you wish to join the AVA division of the NPC, your dues will be $50, plus a one-time initiation fee of $15. A brochure describing the activities and services of the National Plumbers Club and an application form are enclosed. To qualify for the AVA division of NPC you must apply for professional membership.

If you have any further questions, please call on me. We look forward to having you as a member.

Best regards,

Bud Gener
Executive Director

bg/mn

Enclosures

Sample Letter 6.17. Follow-up membership offer.

[date]

Mr. Rodney McDonnell
McDonnell Associates
11 Tepler Drive
South Zane, IL 60004

Dear Rodney:

It was a pleasure to see you at the South Zane Chamber of Commerce's Business After Hours Club (BAHC) co-hosted by South Zane Inn and the East Zane Medical Group. The BAHC is one of our most successful programs. It was created to provide a relaxed social atmosphere in which our members can network with other professionals.

We have many more exciting new programs planned for our membership during 20X5. We would love to have you as a member. I've enclosed an application. If you have any questions, I'd be happy to talk with you.

I look forward to hearing from you.

Sincerely,

Zoe Nelson
Program Manager

zn/mn

enc.

Sample Letter 6.18. Letter selling membership in health center.

[date]

Ms. Ellen P. Thrall
908 Visitation Drive
Hawthorne, MA 02127

Dear Ms. Thrall:

Welcome to Hawthorne. I sincerely hope that you will enjoy your new community. We at The Hawthorne Fitness Club feel that Hawthorne is a great place to live and work.

The Hawthorne Fitness Club has been part of this community for more than 25 years. Our facilities include two gyms, an Olympic-size swimming pool, two weight rooms (one especially designed for women), a Nautilus Center, locker rooms for men and women, a jogging track, six racquetball and handball courts, four squash courts, an exercise studio, and a drop-in nursery and preschool center. We have more than 100 program offerings from which to choose.

To help you meet new friends and get started in a program of health, fun, and fitness, we are offering you a free 30-day family or individual membership. Just fill out the enclosed application, bring it to the Club, and receive your complimentary membership card and schedule of activities. Then you can begin to enjoy your new membership.

Again, welcome to the Hawthorne area. If you need additional information, please phone me at 999-555-6666.

Sincerely,

Simon Thorn
Executive Director

st/mn

Enc.

Sample Letter 6.19 was written as a follow-up to Sample Letter 6.18, offering congratulations to a new member for joining up. The letter opens with a repeat of the club's benefits and its commitment to helping its members.

Sample Letter 6.20 is a health club membership renewal letter. The letter's purpose is clearly stated in the opening paragraph. A reminder of the club's benefits follows. The methods of payment available are highlighted in the next paragraph. The final paragraph urges the member to continue to take advantage of the club's offerings.

Sample Letter 6.21 is a second membership renewal notice written as a follow-up to Sample Letter 6.20. The letter writer clearly states that he is reminding the member to renew, highlights in greater detail the methods of payment available, and reminds the member not to let her membership lapse so she can avoid paying the application fee again. Rather than giving a hard sell pressuring the member to renew, the writer makes it clear he wants the member to continue reaping the club's benefits and reminds her not only of the ease of paying but also of the consequences of letting her membership lapse.

Sample Letter 6.19.   Follow-up to Sample Letter 6.18 congratulating person on new membership.

[date]

Ms. Ellen P. Thrall
908 Visitation Drive
Hawthorne, MA 02127

Dear Ms. Thrall:

Congratulations and welcome to a year of health, fun, and fitness as a new member of The Hawthorne Fitness Club. You're now one of the many individuals who have chosen The Hawthorne Fitness Club as the best way of feeling good through getting and staying fit, learning new skills, and simply having fun.

This year at the Club you can do it all. We look forward to helping you make good use of our facilities, try new programs, and meet new people. To help you make your program choices, please review the enclosed program schedule.

If at any time you have any questions, please feel free to call on me or any of our staff. The Club has earned its reputation as a "people place" because we're always listening to our members and making every effort to fulfill their needs and desires.

Sincerely,

Simon Thorn
Executive Director

st/mn

Enc.

Sample Letter 6.20. Membership renewal letter.

[date]

Ms. Ellen P. Thrall
908 Visitation Drive
Hawthorne, MA 02127

Dear Ms. Thrall:

It's time to renew your membership at The Hawthorne Fitness Club. To keep yourself in top condition—physically, mentally, emotionally—and to look good and feel good, you know there's no better way than the Club.

We offer you modern, clean, and well-equipped facilities, a friendly staff all dedicated to offering the widest range of sports, fitness, and relaxation facilities, and an interesting variety of instructional and recreational programs. The beauty of it is that you can find it all in one convenient location for one low fee.

Renewing your membership is easy with a number of convenient payment methods from which to choose. We suggest the monthly automatic withdrawal. But you may also choose to charge the membership fee on your Visa or MasterCard or to send a check in the enclosed envelope.

Don't put off renewing your membership. We look forward to helping you enjoy another year of health, fun, and fitness at The Hawthorne Fitness Club.

Sincerely,

Simon Thorn
Executive Director

st/mn

Enc.

Sample Letter 6.21.   Second-notice membership renewal letter.

[date]

Ms. Ellen P. Thrall
908 Visitation Drive
Hawthorne, MA 02127

Dear Ms. Thrall:

I just wanted to make sure that you have not overlooked your first membership renewal notice. We look forward to you continuing your membership at The Hawthorne Fitness Club for another year. There are several payment options:

- Monthly automatic withdrawal. We will continue your membership indefinitely. Should you wish to cancel at a later date let us know prior to the first of the month.
- A discount for cash. Paying up-front, you will receive the lowest rate possible.
- MasterCard and Visa are both accepted.

Remember, if you renew now you will avoid having to again pay the $30 application fee should you cancel and pay at a later date.

We look forward to having you continue your activities at The Hawthorne Fitness Club.

Sincerely,

Simon Thorn
Executive Director

st/mn

Enc.

Letter Accompanying Renewal Notice

Sample Letter 6.22 was written as a renewal notice to someone whose annual insurance payment was due. While the letter writer is blessed with a seemingly automatic sale since most drivers are obligated to renew their insurance, she is concerned that the reader check over the facts in his previous year's application for accuracy. She clearly states the letter's purpose in the first paragraph, explains the consequences of not checking the application, and closes with an offer of assistance to the insured.

Sample Letter 6.22.   Letter accompanying a renewal notice.

[date]

Mr. Harold Lester
100 Newton Street
Binghamton, ME 04003

Dear Mr. Lester:

Your automobile insurance renewal application is enclosed. While your insurance will be automatically renewed, it is important that you review the application to make sure that all drivers are listed and the coverage is adequate.

In the event of a serious accident, you may be held personally liable for damages that exceed the bodily injury and property damage limits on your policy. To avoid financial risk, we recommend that you review your coverage and call or write us to make whatever changes are necessary.

Please call or come into our office if you have any questions or wish to make any changes. If you have no questions, simply complete, sign, and return the renewal application in the enclosed return envelope.

Sincerely,

Theresa J. Cove
Vice President

mn

Encs.

Letter Announcing a Special Presentation

Sample Letter 6.23 was written as a letter to prospective customers announcing a special presentation of product offerings. The letter writer announces the success of this event in the past and invites the recipient and any friends to attend an upcoming presentation. The letter clearly explains how to register for the special presentation and makes it clear to the reader that this will be a wonderful opportunity to preview the products of this company.

Sample Letter 6.23.   Letter announcing a special presentation.

[date]

Mr. Alan D. Simpson
1980 Svenson Avenue
Biloxi, NJ 07006

SPECIAL SLIDE PRESENTATION OF VIOLIN PRODUCTS

Mr. Simpson, our Stradivarius Violin Slide Show Tour of the Factory was extremely well received this past February. In fact, we've had so many requests for a repeat performance that we're having another presentation so that other family members and friends can attend.

Please register for the presentation on April 14 by filling out the enclosed form indicating what time of day you would like to attend. Also include the names and addresses of friends you would like us to invite to this or future presentations.

Feel free to call me any time I can be of further help to you.

JOHN SAVITHSON
VICE PRESIDENT

js/mn

Enc.

Letter Expressing Appreciation to Customers

Sample Letter 6.24 is written to let valued customers know they are appreciated and that the letter writer plans to make an extra effort to service their needs.

Sample Letter 6.24. Letter announcing client appreciation program for valued customers.

[date]

Mr. and Mrs. Barry White
1876 Grampite Road
Dottie, RI 02804

Dear Mr. and Mrs. White:

I am writing to let you know about the client appreciation program I have instituted for people like you who are my most valued clients.

Each month, I send out valuable tips and information about the real estate industry to this select group of people. You will receive articles on topics ranging from home budgeting and home remodeling to refinancing and home equity lines of credit.

I am constantly trying to improve the level of service I provide because in my business your trust and respect are essential to my success.

I will contact you soon to see how I might be able to help you meet any new real estate needs you might have.

Yours sincerely,

Lorraine Benjamin, Broker
Altobelli Real Estate

Catalog Letters

Sample Letters 6.25 through 6.27 were all written to accompany catalogs.

Sample Letter 6.25 was written to accompany a professional catalog. The writer first introduces the company, then highlights the enclosed catalog, and closes with an offer to help the prospective customer with any business products she might need.

Sample Letter 6.26 was written as a response to a request for a professional catalog. The letter writer first acknowledges the request, then mentions a specific product the prospective customer asked about, and offers special help to the prospect. The letter is short and to the point, and addresses the needs of the prospect.

Sample Letter 6.27 was written to accompany a consumer catalog. This letter is longer than the previous two, and it is written with a more folksy style to attract its target market. While the style is different, the clarity is comparable. The writer mentions the catalog's highlights, describes a special offer as an incentive to get the customer to order early, and closes with information on how to order.

Sample Letter 6.25. Letter accompanying a professional catalog.

[date]

Mrs. Bess Cooperburg
Cooperburg Department Stores
One Park Place
Sibling, OH 43044

Dear Mrs. Cooperburg:

Bertram and Bertram Store Displays is a full-service company offering store layout and designs as well as fixtures and supplies.

Enclosed are our current catalog and price list. You will find that our prices are competitive. We also offer quantity discounts.

If there is something you are looking for and you don't find it in our catalog, please call me. We'd be glad to fill your needs. Our phone number is 1-800-555-5467.

Yours truly,

William Berran
Vice President

wb:gm

Encs.

Sample Letter 6.26.   Letter responding to request for a professional catalog.

[date]

Mr. Justin Longen
Hartford Longs Department Store
186 Grampian Way
Dorchester, NC 27009

Dear Justin:

I've enclosed a copy of our catalog and the flyer on wire grid cubes that you requested. As I mentioned on the telephone, the wire grid cubes are an excellent way to display blouses and sweaters and will add a high-tech look to your stores at a low cost.

Please get back to me, Justin, and I'll work out special prices on our whole line of display fixtures for Hartford Longs stores.

Kindest regards,

Alison Kraw
Sales Representative

ak/mn

Encs.

Sample Letter 6.27. Letter accompanying a consumer catalog.

[date]

Mr. Greg Dendrinos
1966 Myron Boulevard
Goddard, NJ 07007

Dear Mr. Dendrinos:

In the enclosed catalog for Mead's Seeds, we have a greater variety of vegetable and flower seeds than ever before.

We have spent the entire season poring over a variety of seed offerings. You will find a grand selection of new products as well as your old favorites.

This year we feature more than 100 varieties of the world's most beautiful flowers and tasty vegetables. You get the same quality products, good value, and super service that Mead's Seeds has offered for more than 100 years. You also get our money-back satisfaction guarantee.

If you order before March 30, 20X3, you get something more: a $5 savings on your total order. Just enclose the coupon from the catalog with your order and deduct $5 from the total where indicated on your order form.

You can use the coupon to load up on the seeds that will blazon your garden with color this summer: blue ribbon asters, ultra crimson petunias, bronze giant mums. Choose your family's favorite vegetables from among the hundreds in our catalog.

Since this is a preseason catalog, nearly all the seeds are priced 20 to 25 percent lower than the prices in our spring and summer catalogs. So send in your order today for even greater savings.

If you wish to order by telephone, call our toll-free number, 1-800-555-3733, Monday through Friday, 9 A.M. to 9 P.M., E.S.T. Or visit our website any time, 24/7, at www.meadsseeds.com. You can charge your order to any major credit card. You won't be billed until April, when your seeds are shipped.

Best wishes for a glorious spring and summer of planting.

Sincerely,

Cyndee G. Mead
President

cgm/bjc

Enc.

Sales Inquiry Response

Sample Letter 6.28 was written as a response to an inquiry about a particular product. The author clearly addresses the prospective customer's question and follows by stressing his company's reputation. He closes by offering to help the prospect make purchase decisions.

Sample Letter 6.28.   Letter responding to an inquiry.

[date]

Mr. Ned J. Waggoner
Keith, Simons, and Underthal
343 Twilite Drive
Encino, OR 97004

Dear Mr. Waggoner:

Thank you for your interest in FLOORBOARD™ products and systems. We have enclosed the information you requested for your review.

Since 1886, the M. L. Nilgest Company has provided quality construction products to the industry. We would like to provide any assistance you might require in your project.

If you have any questions, please feel free to call our office at 617-555-6666.

Best regards,

Martin Nilgest
Sales and Marketing Manager
Architectural Products

mn/js

enclosure

Appointment Requests

Depending on the nature of your business and the level of formality you are trying to maintain, appointment requests can often be done through email. Each of the letters below can be easily adapted to an email by using the message of the letter itself as the content of your email.

Sample Letters 6.29 through 6.32 were all written to request sales appointments with prospective customers.

Sample Letter 6.29 is a very short letter telling the prospect that the letter writer will be in his area and would like to set up an appointment when she is in town. The writer makes it clear what procedure she will take to set up the appointment and leaves little doubt whose court the ball is in.

Sample Letter 6.30 was written as a follow-up to a brief discussion. The writer thanks the reader for his time, refers to the reader's colleagues who recommended him, and closes by saying he will call at the end of the next week to set up a meeting at a mutually convenient time.

After being referred to yet another person, the writer of Sample Letter 6.30 wrote Sample Letter 6.31. He recounts his history with the company, mentions the referral, and closes by requesting a meeting. Again, the writer makes it clear when he will call to set up a convenient meeting.

Sample Letter 6.32 was written to inform the reader of a rescheduled trip and requests a specific meeting time with the reader. The writer and reader had been in contact before the letter was written and this letter confirms the actual date the writer will be in town for a possible meeting.

Sample Letter 6.29.   Short letter requesting an appointment.

[date]

Mr. Simon Rone
Acme Film Labs, P.O. Box 3452
Cosgrove, ID 83201

Dear Mr. Rone:

I plan to be in Cosgrove on September 1, and would like to discuss the possibility of working with you on the Bimini project.

I'll give you a call next week to see if we can set up a convenient time to meet.

Sincerely,

Alice Berg
President

ab/rb

Sample Letter 6.30. Letter requesting an appointment after initial discussion.

[date]

Mr. Ralph Hamill
Thomson Enterprises
111 Prospect Street
Hamilton, CA 90001

Dear Mr. Hamill:

Thank you for taking the time to talk to me last Friday.

Alice Crafton suggested that I meet with you and Sondra Narsak to discuss the public re-lations needs of Thomson Enterprises. I have enclosed copies of the publicity we've been able to secure for one of our high-tech clients—Wheaton Softprodisk. Building an image through publicity is one part of the marketing services we can offer Thomson Enterprises.

At your earliest convenience, I would like to meet with you and Ms. Narsak to learn about your company and its public relations goals. I will call at the end of next week to see when a meeting might be possible.

Congratulations and best of luck. I know your company will be well received in the Hamilton community.

Yours sincerely,

Gene O'Connor

go/mn

encs.

Sample Letter 6.31. Follow-up to Sample Letter 6.30, requesting meeting with appropriate person at company.

[date]

Mr. Loren Gray, President
Thomson Enterprises
111 Prospect Street
Hamilton, CA 90001

Dear Mr. Gray:

Alice Crafton recommended I meet with Ralph Hamill and Sondra Narsak to discuss the public relations needs of Thomson Enterprises. In a recent discussion, they told me that you are handling the review process. I understand that the materials I had sent to Mr. Hamill were passed along to you.

At your earliest possible convenience, I would like to meet with you to learn about your company and its public relations goals. Enclosed is some recent publicity one of our software clients received in *Hamilton* magazine's August issue. The story focused on how to choose a software supplier.

I will call you at the beginning of next week to check your schedule. Thank you, in advance, for your consideration.

Cordially,

Gene O'Connor

go/mn

encs.

Sample Letter 6.32. Letter requesting an appointment after rescheduling a trip.

[date]

Georgina S. Cowen
Bootbakers of America
4545 Razzen Way
Ft. Wayne, NJ 07008

Dear Ms. Cowen:

I have rescheduled my trip to Ft. Wayne and hope it will be possible for you to meet with me on January 22. Would it be possible for me to meet you at your office about 6 o'clock in the evening?

Please let me know if this is convenient for you.

Sincerely,

William Berry
Vice President

wb/mn

Letters of Interest

Sample Letters 6.33 and 6.34 were written as letters of interest in a project. These are sales letters whose mission is to get attractive projects for the writers' companies.

Sample Letter 6.33 is also written to a specific prospect, but here the letter writer not only introduces himself and explains what he is after, but also attempts to set up a meeting with the prospect.

Sample Letter 6.34 is a follow-up letter of interest to a prospect with whom the letter writer had met. The writer expresses a strong interest in a project discussed and encourages the prospect to send along any material he has. The writer then highlights the benefits of working with his company and closes by reiterating his desire to see the prospect's material. The letter serves not only to reinforce the writer's interest, but also to present his company as an ideal match for the prospect's work.

Sample Letter 6.33.   Letter of interest in project and request for meeting.

[date]

Dr. James Wagon
Joe Bing College
47 Bing Boulevard
Noreaster, ME 04003

Dear Dr. Wagon:

I am the program coordinator for Andoris Seminar Productions. It has come to my attention that you are an authority in the area of personnel management. We are interested in running seminars in your specialty area.

I would welcome the opportunity to discuss your program with you as well as the field of personnel management in general.

At present, I am planning to be at Joe Bing College on January 21, 20X2. Perhaps, if it is convenient for you, we could meet on campus. I will be arriving in Noreaster on January 20 and will be staying at the college's guest quarters.

I am looking forward to meeting you. In the meantime, if I can be of any assistance to you, please feel free to call upon me.

Cordially,

Martin Night
Program Coordinator

mn/ar

Sample Letter 6.34.   Strong letter of interest in project.

[date]

Mr. Paul Jensen
Sunvale Enterprise College
98 Bethany Road
Sunvale, MD 20607

Dear Mr. Jensen:

I was glad to have had the opportunity to meet with you when I was at Sunvale Enterprise last month. Thank you for sending me a proposal letter for the seminar we talked about having you run.

Your project sounds very interesting. We would like to know more about it. I understand you have some sample material prepared, which we would be interested in seeing. I would be happy to send you the comments and suggestions of our board of advisers. I trust that you will find these recommendations to be helpful as your work progresses.

Mr. Jensen, I know you are very interested in having your seminars produced. As a prospective seminar leader, you will undoubtedly consider a number of criteria in selecting whom you would like to work with in putting on the seminar. These might include sales, advertising, promotion, and content development assistance. In all of these aspects, Andoris Seminar Productions stands alone. For more than 25 years, Andoris has specialized in three things: performing extensive market analysis designed to develop a limited number of quality seminars; maintaining very high content standards built on years of experience; and reaching a maximum market for its seminars through a concentrated promotion policy.

I look forward to hearing from you and seeing your material. In the meantime, you have my best wishes for continued progress on your work. If I can be of any assistance to you, please do not hesitate to call upon me.

Best regards,

Martin Night

mn/js

Letter to Difficult-to-See Prospect

Sample Letter 6.35 was written to a prospect with whom the letter writer has been having trouble getting in touch. The writer clearly explains her predicament in the first paragraph by mentioning how many times she has tried to call the prospect. She does this in an inoffensive way by expressing her understanding of how busy the prospect must be. The writer realizes the prospect is short on time, so she wastes none of it and gets right to the point in her second paragraph. Here, she briefly explains what her company can do for the prospect. She closes by saying she will once again call the prospect to set up a meeting. But having written this letter, she has laid the groundwork for more successful results.

Sample Letter 6.35. Letter to a sales prospect who is difficult to see.

[date]

Mr. Allen Kenney
Volt & Wattage Company, Inc.
78 Alma Road
April, IA 50025

Dear Mr. Kenney:

I have tried to call you several times during this past month, but have had no success in reaching you. I can appreciate how busy you must be handling the installation of a new computer system at your company.

Palay Insurance Benefits Company is keenly aware of the heightened competition in insurance and is committed to responding with more creative and attentive servicing to corporate customers such as you. We combine the personal touch and convenience of a local insurance firm with all of the sophistication of the major insurance companies in our city.

I will call you in the near future to try to schedule a visit at your convenience. I look forward to meeting with you.

Sincerely,

Bridget Palay
Vice President

mpp

Letter to Find Decision Maker

Sample Letter 6.36 was written to a new customer to find out the decision-making process at the customer's company. The letter writer expresses his appreciation for the new business, but goes on to ask for a face-to-face meeting with the recipient and with others at the customer's company who have the power to make decisions to purchase the writer's products.

Sample Letter 6.36. Letter sent to assess who makes decisions at new customer's company.

[date]

Mr. Ralph Stewart
Chief Operating Officer
Plattsburgh Quality Paints, Inc.
43 Lorraine Terrace
Grand Forks, ND 58201

Dear Ralph:

It's wonderful news that you've decided to give us at Citadel Pigments your business. I appreciate all the time you've taken over the past several months to consider us and whether our products and people could meet your company's needs. I'm thrilled that you've chosen us. Thanks for being our advocate throughout the decision-making process.

Now that it's clear we'll be working together, I'd like to set up a meeting with you and anyone else at Plattsburgh Quality Paints who's likely to be involved in the relationship with us. Of course, working with you directly will be great, but we're also realistic that your day-to-day responsibilities as COO will demand a great deal of your attention. I'd like to get to know all the other people at your company who will be making decisions. It will be helpful to meet some of the personalities behind the squares on your organizational chart.

Perhaps you and I can meet over coffee sometime next week to talk about the various people who should be involved in the larger meeting I've proposed. I'll give your office a call to set up a time.

Once again, thank you for choosing to do business with us. I'm looking forward to a rich and rewarding partnership.

Sincerely,

Alan Gerous
Vice President

Letters Confirming Proposals

Sample Letters 6.37 through 6.39 were written to confirm sales proposals that had been made to customers. All followed some initial contact with the prospect.

Sample Letter 6.37 was written after the letter writer had a phone conversation with a prospect about his need for insurance. The writer opens by recounting the conversation and mentioning a mutual acquaintance who suggested the prospect to the writer. The next paragraph gives a capsule review of the proposal, followed by instructions to the prospect on how to go forward.

Sample Letter 6.38 was written to confirm a proposal for use of a function hall and catering facilities. The letter writer immediately acknowledges the prospect's reservation, reiterating what she has told him about her needs. He follows by explaining costs and procedures for securing the room and encloses sample menus to help her decide on her menu for the function.

Sample Letter 6.39 is written as a follow-up to action taken as a result of Sample Letter 6.38. After the customer has confirmed the room and chosen a menu, the letter writer writes to confirm the menu and instructs the reader on the procedure for informing him of an exact head count for the function. The writer, who wrote the letter shortly before the function, extends his offer of help should the reader need it before the function.

Sample Letter 6.37.   Letter confirming proposal for services.

[date]

Mr. Ed Devick
RR & Associates
56 Downside Street
Cambridge, AL 35004

Dear Mr. Devick:

I just wanted to send you a brief note to tell you that I truly enjoyed speaking with you and look forward to advising you in the area of insurance and fringe benefit planning. Tracey Hunt speaks very highly of you.

I've enclosed a proposal and application for John Jay Insurance Company for the following disability insurance coverage:

$2,900 per month benefit
60-day waiting period
Payable to age 65
Coverage in your own occupation
Cost of living adjustment, which keeps pace with inflation
Future insurance option

I feel extremely comfortable with John Jay's proposal and recommend that we apply for it. Please sign where indicated (two times) on the enclosed application and mail it back to me in the envelope provided with a check payable to John Jay Insurance Company for $733.25.

Thanks in advance for the business. I hope to meet with you in person soon.

Cordially,

Lauren Gary
Principal

LG/mn

Enclosures

Sample Letter 6.38.   Letter confirming proposal for services.

[date]

Ms. Nancy Armitage
186 Stanfield Road
Sibling, OH 43044

SUBJECT: ARMITAGE/CATTON WEDDING

Nancy, I am delighted to acknowledge a reservation for the Armitage/Catton wedding from 1 to 5 P.M. on Saturday, January 18, 20X6, in the Great London room of the Hopscotch Hotel. We will set the room for a reception, luncheon, and dance and we understand that you expect 75 guests.

The rental for the room is $800, reduced by $100 for each $1,000 you spend on food and beverages.

I have enclosed a copy of this letter that, when signed and returned to my office, will confirm your reservation. We also require that a deposit of $800 accompany your confirming copy and that it be returned within 14 days.

Full payment of your estimated bill, based on the guaranteed figure, will be required the day of the function. All payments should be made to our banquet manager prior to the start of the function in cash, certified check, or by credit card. Kindly make your check payable to The Hopscotch Hotel, Inc.

I have also enclosed our menus for your perusal and would appreciate hearing from you within three weeks about your menu selection.

We look forward to the opportunity to serve you. I can assure you that we will do our utmost to make this event a success.

DAVID L. BIXTON
DIRECTOR, SALES AND MARKETING

dlb/ajm

Enclosures

Sample Letter 6.39. Follow-up in response to confirming letter in Sample Letter 6.38.

[date]

Ms. Nancy Armitage
186 Stanfield Road
Sibling, OH 43004

SUBJECT: ARMITAGE/CATTON WEDDING

Nancy, with your upcoming function soon at hand, I am pleased to enclose the finalized copies of the menus and arrangements for your wedding for your verification. To help us proceed with the arrangements, kindly sign and return the original copy to us, making any notations or changes that you desire.

We will require that you furnish us with a guaranteed attendance number by noon two business days prior to the function. Should a count not be received, your highest estimate will be used when we determine the final bill.

We look forward to the pleasure of serving you. If, in the interim, I can be of any assistance to you whatsoever, please do not hesitate to call on me.

DAVID L. BIXTON
DIRECTOR, SALES AND MARKETING

dlb/ajm

Enclosure

Follow-Up Sales Call Letters

Sample Letters 6.40 through 6.46 were all written to follow up on a sales call to a prospect.

Sample Letter 6.40 was written to follow up on a meeting with a prospect. This letter writer briefly expresses thanks for the meeting, explains in capsule form what his company can do for the prospect, and closes by expressing a desire to work with the prospect.

Sample Letter 6.41 was written to follow up on a phone conversation. Here, the letter writer gets right to the point when he writes that he has enclosed the materials requested by the prospect in their conversation. He closes by reminding the reader of a meeting they have set up and thanks him for his interest in the company's services.

Sample Letter 6.42 was written as a follow-up to a former customer who had decided to go with the competition. The letter writer follows up a conversation he had with someone at the reader's company who told the writer why they made the shift to a new company. First the writer sets up the situation in the letter. Then he announces how his company is able to meet and surpass the competition when it comes to supplying the former customer's needs. He closes by expressing a desire to serve the reader and encourages him to call should he need any help.

Sample Letter 6.40. Follow-up letter to meeting.

[date]

Mr. Gerald Johanson, Chairman
State Oil Refinery
75 Mascot Place
Alderbine, GA 30002

Dear Mr. Johanson:

Thank you for taking time out of your schedule to meet with me at the Racquet Club last Thursday. It was a pleasure for David Pardy and me to meet with you and the other partners of your organization to discuss your company's data processing needs. I hope this is just the beginning of a solid relationship between our two companies.

As I told you at our meeting, our company specializes in servicing companies like yours. Please feel free to call on me at any time to discuss your needs. I would be glad to meet with you or your partners at your convenience.

Thank you again for the meeting. I hope to be able to work with you in the not too distant future.

Sincerely,

Alan Ross
Vice President

ar/fk

cc: David Pardy

Sample Letter 6.41.   Follow-up letter to phone conversation.

[date]

Mr. Walter B. Jingle
Christophers, Leighs & Plummers
P.O. Box 45
Menahagon, WA 98765

Dear Mr. Jingle:

I've enclosed a copy of our press kit, which you requested when we spoke on the telephone yesterday. Among other things, the press kit contains articles I've written, stories in which I've been quoted, biographies of me and our senior staff, and a client list.

I look forward to meeting you the week of October 5. Thank you very much for your interest in NES Public Relations. I'll speak with you soon.

Yours truly,

Mack Nilton

mn/mv

Enclosure

Sample Letter 6.42. Letter following up on lost sale.

[date]

Mr. Carl B. Replick
Myers and Myers, Inc.
456 Merrimac Place, Suite 4B
Williamsburg, NY 10501

Dear Mr. Replick:

Checking through my records, I noticed that you were no longer an active customer of Zyblick Office Supplies. When I called your office, I was informed that your company is now using our competitor from a few counties over. Your office manager, Zed Globonk, was refreshingly forthright in telling me how Zyblick fell short of the mark in keeping your business.

I'm pleased to tell you that we have set up a whole new line of filing supplies, which Mr. Globonk expressed a desperate need for. We feature a wide array of legal- and letter-size folders, as well as a variety of color-coded hanging folders.

I thought you'd also be interested to know that we've established same-day delivery service and overnight billing, features Mr. Globonk mentioned would really help your business. These services are not offered by any of our competitors.

Mr. Globonk told me that you make all purchasing decisions at Myers and Myers. If you need additional information from me, Mr. Replick, please feel free to call. I welcome the opportunity to serve your company once again. I will do my best to ensure your satisfaction.

Sincerely,

Robert Kemprel

rk/js

Sample Letter 6.43 was written as a follow-up to a previous sale. The letter writer opens his letter by thanking the customer for her prior business and reassuring her that his company will continue to provide quality products and services. He closes by mentioning a listing of products he has enclosed with the letter and encouraging the reader to call him should she have any questions.

Sample Letter 6.44 was written as a follow-up letter to an active customer who had attended the letter writer's exhibit at a trade show. The writer reminds the reader about the trade show and then elaborates on a new product his company is offering. He closes by expressing his appreciation for the reader's business. The letter serves not only to sell the customer on the company, but to keep him informed.

Sample Letter 6.45 was written as a follow-up to a referral made by an associate of the reader. The letter writer immediately identifies the situation by mentioning the referrer's name in the first paragraph. If the prospect recognizes the name as someone he trusts, he is more likely to read on. The writer next explains what his services are, mentions an enclosed brochure, and closes by encouraging the reader to get in touch with him.

Sample Letter 6.43.   Follow-up letter to previous sale.

[date]

Ms. Beverly T. Cole
Academy Services, Inc.
P.O. Box 3456
Latin, KY 40011

Dear Ms. Cole:

Thank you for purchasing your computer equipment at Diskquick Services earlier this year. My associates and I at Diskquick would be pleased to provide any services we can to your company, or act as a sounding board on your hardware and software needs. We do business with many professional services in the Latin area and are familiar with the challenges of operating a company such as yours.

To familiarize you with Diskquick, I enclose a copy of our latest product listings. Please feel free to call me or any of my associates on the enclosed list any time. I'll call you within the next few days to introduce myself over the phone.

I look forward to meeting you.

Sincerely,

Alan Macalester
Vice President

am/mn

Enclosures

Sample Letter 6.44.   Follow-up to exhibit visitor.

[date]

Mr. Lawrence Z. Weimer
Weimer Images
454 Main Road
Transit, PA 15001

SUPPORT MATERIAL FOR NEW PRODUCTS

Larry, at the trade show in March, we announced that we would be introducing a new line of medium-sized photography enlargers. The response we received at the show was tremendous and, in order to help you present the enlargers better, we are enclosing a selection of new sales literature.

In addition to the introduction of the new enlarger, we are making other changes. We're now better equipped than ever to respond to your needs and the needs of your customers. You may already have noticed faster handling of orders. More improvements in service are on the way!

This promises to be an exciting year for us and we're glad you're part of it.

MICHAEL KERRY
VICE PRESIDENT—SALES AND MARKETING

Enclosure

Sample Letter 6.45.   Follow-up to referral.

[date]

Mr. John Nivas
Marketing Director
Nivas, Royal, Lauten, Inc.
681 Line Hill Avenue
Norstar, MA 02129

Dear Mr. Nivas:

Beatrice Clonig suggested I write you because she thought you might be interested in the unusual services that I provide corporations.

I perform magic at sales meetings, trade shows, and corporate parties. I also work with companies to use magic in promotions and new product introductions. Magic is used to support the theme of the introductions, to strengthen the theme of the meeting, and to reinforce key marketing points and product attributes in an entertaining presentation. Each show is specially designed to highlight the client's program objectives.

I have enclosed one of my promotional brochures for your information. It should give you a better indication of my capabilities and expertise.

If you think that corporate magic might be something that Nivas, Royal, Lauten, Inc. would be interested in exploring, please do not hesitate to get in touch with me. I hope to hear from you soon.

Cordially,

Ray Fontmore

rf/jm

Enclosure

Sample Letter 6.46 was written as a follow-up to a proposal that had been sent to the customer by the letter writer.

Sample Letter 6.46.   Follow-up to a proposal.

[date]

Ms. Beatrice Jared
Jared Software Development Company
48 Charles Street
Catalonia, NH 03031

Dear Ms. Jared:

On August 20, we sent you a proposal for packing and shrink-wrapping boxes of your software. Since we haven't heard from you yet, I thought I'd use this opportunity to remind you to review the proposal, which we believe will address your needs efficiently and profitably.

Thank you very much for considering us. We look forward to working with you.

Sincerely,

Larry Douglas
Director of Marketing

Letter to Renew Contact

Sample Letter 6.47 was written to a prospect whom the letter writer knew when she was at another company. He congratulates her on the new position, reminds her who he is, and offers any help she might need in choosing services that his company provides.

Sample Letter 6.47. Sales letter to renew contact.

[date]

Dr. Lindsey Harl
Executive Vice President
Emerson, Waldo & Associates
One Divinity Place
Coopers, OH 43044

Dear Lindsey:

I was pleased to hear that you have become an associate of Emerson, Waldo & Associates. Please accept best wishes from all of us at Ambrose Trucking Company.

You may remember that we had several phone conversations when you were vice president of operations at Grimes and Grimes. Since that time my duties have changed at Ambrose Trucking Company from handling long-term fleet leasing arrangements to handling the accounts of large wholesale firms like Emerson, Waldo.

Please let me know if I can be of assistance to you or help you better serve your clients. We at Ambrose Trucking are committed to providing the quality trucking services that wholesalers require to run a successful business.

Again, I wish you continued success.

Kindest regards,

C. C. Lange
Vice President

ccl/jlb

Letter Welcoming New Client

Sample Letter 6.48 was written to welcome a new client. The letter writer opens by welcoming the client, and follows by telling him who will be handling his account, how the company will help him, and what he should expect from the company. The writer closes by informing the reader that his account representative will be calling him to set up a meeting. This brief but informative welcoming letter serves not only to remind the new client of what services the company will provide, but more importantly to assure him that the company cares enough about him to take the time to welcome him after he has already agreed to give the firm his business.

Sample Letter 6.48.   Letter welcoming a new client.

[date]

Mr. Alexander Hayes
Rightaweigh, Inc.
98 Bolivia Avenue
Cortland, NJ 07007

Dear Mr. Hayes:

We're pleased to welcome you as a new client and want to take this opportunity to thank you for your selection of Nilges and Crowbacker, CFPs, to handle all of your financial planning needs. You have chosen a firm that is committed to providing you with excellent service and superior professional counsel.

We have assigned Greta Lockin as your personal financial planner and primary liaison. Of course, Greta will work closely with our entire staff of specialists to ensure that you will receive the best guidance on all matters.

Our firm specializes in strategic financial planning to help you and your company prosper. We address your future potential as well as assess your past financial performance. What's more, we provide ancillary services that can be vital to your success, such as complete management of all your financial software needs.

As a client of Nilges and Crowbacker, CFPs, you will receive monthly newsletters with the latest tax and financial information available. You will also be invited to special seminars we regularly conduct on financial matters of interest to our clients.

Greta Lockin will be calling on you shortly to arrange an initial appointment. Should you have any further questions on any or all of our services, please do not hesitate to call Max Nilges or me.

Again, welcome to Nilges and Crowbacker.

Sincerely,

Niles Crowbacker
Principal

nc/mr

Letter Asking for Referral

Sample Letter 6.49 was written to an existing customer with whom the writer has recently met. The letter writer first takes care of business by telling the reader that his check and application have been received. Next the writer asks the reader for possible referrals who might be interested in his services. He describes the type of clients he is looking for and suggests that he call the reader to see if he is willing to recommend some people. The tone of the letter is congenial, not at all pushy. The writer makes it clear that it is entirely up to the reader whether or not to make referrals.

Sample Letter 6.49. Letter asking for a referral.

[date]

Mr. Geoffrey Spaulding
Animal Crackers, Inc.
45 Marx Drive
Chico, CA 90003

Dear Mr. Spaulding:

It was good to meet with you for lunch at the Racquet Club last week. I've received your first premium check and your application for the disability insurance policy I recommended to you. I'm glad I was able to fill your needs with this policy. I trust you'll be as pleased with this product as you have been with insurance products you have purchased through me in the past.

At lunch you mentioned that you run into a good number of small-business owners in your business dealings. If you think it is appropriate, I would welcome the opportunity to furnish these people with the same quality of service that I and my colleagues at Pacific Insurance Benefits, Inc. have supplied you.

As I mentioned to you, Pacific Insurance Benefits has been getting more and more into the area of fringe benefit and insurance planning for small-business owners. Would you consider thinking of a few business owners you know who could use my services?

I'll call you next week to see if you'd be willing to refer me to these people. A referral from you would go a long way in opening new doors for me and my colleagues.

I look forward to talking to you next week.

Best regards,

Gino Inatreck

gi/js

Letter Promoting Special Sale

Sample Letter 6.50 was written to promote the special sale of a property that unexpectedly came to market. The letter writer explains the situation and describes the property in the first three paragraphs, then closes by telling the reader how she can take advantage of the offer if she is interested. The writer clearly points out why the offer is a special one and how the reader can benefit from it.

Sample Letter 6.50.   Letter promoting special sale.

[date]

Ms. Zoe Patterson
34 Laramy Street
Apriori, UT 84003

Dear Ms. Patterson:

You now have an opportunity to step in and build a house where the preparatory work has already been done!

Due to the owner's serious illness, the construction of a house in the prestigious Township section cannot be completed. The owner would like to sell the site as is for $79,900—less than the appraised value.

The property includes a secluded one-acre lot, blueprints for a 3,400 square-foot house, all necessary building permits, a cleared home site and driveway, in-place footings, temporary water hookup, temporary electricity hookup, and $2,500 worth of building materials on the lot.

If you are interested in additional information, please call me at 999-888-8888. We plan to list the property with a real estate agency as of January 25, 20X6, so please call soon if you are interested.

Sincerely,

Max Jeffries
President

mn

Letter to Wish Existing Customer Holiday Greetings

Sample Letter 6.51 is a brief, social missive intended to relay season's greetings to a customer. The language is neutral—it is appropriate for holidays of any religious observance—and universally applicable, without sounding bland.

Sample Letter 6.51.   Letter of holiday greetings.

[date]

Mr. Walter O'Clair
99 Wausau Boulevard
Mateo, FL 32004

Dear Mr. O'Clair:

We at Packard Automotive would like to express our best wishes to you during this holiday season. We appreciate your business and look forward to serving you and servicing your automobile during the coming year.

May the upcoming year bring you and your family health and happiness and a safe and joyous holiday season.

Yours truly,

Sam Rowar

Letter to Acknowledge Anniversary of a Sales Relationship

Sample Letter 6.52 was written to commemorate an anniversary of a sales relationship. Nothing is asked for and nothing is sold; the author of this letter is simply connecting with his client in a friendly, congratulatory manner, while reinforcing what appears to be a solid business alliance.

Sample Letter 6.52.   Letter to acknowledge anniversary of a sales relationship.

[date]

Ms. Toni Tamules
Body by Toni
1247 Pearl Drive
Roswell, MA 02219

Dear Ms. Tamules:

Can you believe that it's been ten years since you first opened and we at Samson Weights walked into your fitness center to pitch our Galaxy Class Modular Weight equipment? Time sure has flown, and we're glad to see that your business has grown as big as your customers' biceps, while our relationship with Body by Toni is as strong as our namesake.

In this day of shifting business alliances, we want you to know that we are as committed to satisfying your equipment needs today as we were on Day One, and that we hope to be with you when Body by Toni celebrates its twentieth anniversary.

Congratulations on your business successes, and as always, don't hesitate to call on us when you're planning for new growth.

Sincerely,

Rodney Caballero

Public Relations Letters

Public relations is a marketing tool used by many professionals to build public awareness of their business. Sample Letters 6.53 through 6.61 are examples of public relations letters that were written for a variety of purposes.

The letter writer in Sample Letter 6.53 offers a retainer to a public relations firm after the firm made a presentation to the writer and her company. The writer is clear in her enthusiasm and requests a follow-up meeting in person to solidify the specifics of the contract between her company and the public relations firm.

Sample Letter 6.53. Letter offering retainer to public relations firm.

[date]

Mr. Leonard Rover
Rover Public Relations
34 Natick Road
Newbury, CT 06022

Dear Leonard:

I am delighted to offer you a six-month contract to serve as our public relations company.

The senior executives and I were taken with your keen insight into the issues facing our business and our industry. Your plan to help win us coverage in online, print, and broadcast media struck us as the clearest, most ambitious, and most realistic approach we had seen. Your company's background in successfully working with other artisanal food companies confirmed for us that your firm is the one that will help us at Boonton Bagel Company propel our business forward.

Please give me a call so we can set up a meeting to go over the specifics of your contract.

We're excited to have you as part of our team and look forward to working with you.

Sincerely,

Tiffany Cole, President

Sample Letter 6.54 was written as an invitation to a customer to attend an open house at the letter writer's company while the customer is in town on other business. The writer clearly lays out the details for the customer and gives him a mechanism by which to respond.

Sample Letter 6.54. Invitation to an open house.

[date]

Mr. Brian Palay
Senior Vice President
Palay Travel Services, Inc.
434 Washington Street
Boston, SC 29001

Dear Mr. Palay:

The annual convention of travel services professionals is coming up and this year it's going to be held on December 10 to 15 in Sacramento, where Leighton Ticket Printer Equipment is headquartered. I'm hoping that you'll be able to attend the convention that will give Sacramento a chance to play host to you and others in your industry.

We'd like to invite you to take a tour of Leighton Ticket Printer Equipment's manufacturing facility while you're in town. We've coordinated with the convention planners and scheduled a tour for December 12, from 8 P.M. to 10 P.M. We have food, refreshments, and entertainment planned as well as a tour of the latest in ticket-printing machinery for your industry.

I've enclosed a postage-paid reply card with this letter. Please indicate on the card whether you'll be able to attend the evening's tour. We're looking forward to seeing you in December in Sacramento.

Sincerely,

Tricia Ford
President

Enc.

Sample Letter 6.55 is written as an invitation to the press to attend an annual professional conference. (Such invitations are commonly sent out as emails. This letter is easily adapted to an email by using the text of the letter as the email message to your intended recipient.) This letter clearly establishes what is being promoted. The writer first makes the invitation, elaborates a bit on what can be expected at the conference, mentions special services that will be available to the press, and closes by encouraging the reader to respond soon to take advantage of local accommodations.

Sample Letter 6.56 was written to promote the formation of a new company. The writer directs his letter to a member of the press, suggesting a possible story.

Sample Letter 6.55.   Letter inviting press to conference.

[date]

Ms. Nancy Kenworthy, Editor
Hamilton Financial Journal
54 Garland Drive
Hamilton, CA 90005

ANNUAL CONVENTION OF THE NATIONAL INVESTMENT ADVISORS GROUP

Ms. Kenworthy, you are cordially invited to be the guest of the National Investment Advisors Group at its Tenth Annual Convention and Exposition on October 5 to 8 at the World Trade Pavilion in Bilink, Idaho. Please join us, as our guest, for all of the educational and general sessions, the exhibitions, and all scheduled meals. A special reception to honor the media is scheduled for Tuesday, October 6. Registration will be in the press room at the World Trade Pavilion.

Some 2,000 investment advisors are expected. The four-day event features three general sessions and more than 100 education sessions in 10 major subject areas conducted by key industry leaders. The exhibition features more than 300 financial product and service companies. Detailed information is featured in the enclosed brochure.

Keynote speakers include Alice Nyquil, one of the nation's leading commentators on investments, and a four-person panel debating the future of the investment advisory industry. The closing session will feature Timothy Thomas, the leading commentator on personal finance in the country.

Interviews can be arranged during the week with speakers, industry leaders, attendees, and NIAG officers to meet your editorial needs and deadlines. My staff and I will be glad to help you line up any interviews we can.

To better ensure your preference of accommodations and rates, please complete the enclosed registration form and return it to me by August 30.

The 20X5 NIAG Convention and Exposition is filled with more information on the investment advisory industry than you will find anywhere else. We look forward to hearing soon that you can be with us.

PAMELA A. HOAN
PUBLIC RELATIONS DIRECTOR

PAH/trw

Enclosure

Sample Letter 6.56. Letter introducing company.

[date]

Mr. John Hill, Editor
Local Business Chronicle
P.O. Box 3452
San Anamant, CA 90007

Dear Mr. Hill:

When the Sibling International Commerce Club opened last summer at the Sibling International Center on San Anamant Wharf, it was yet another significant indication that San Anamant has truly become a city of international scope. *Local Business Chronicle* readers might be interested to know that membership in the Sibling International Commerce Club opens new international opportunities to them as well.

San Anamant's Sibling International Commerce Club joins more than 50 other clubs throughout the world in offering a host of business and social amenities to members. These clubs have become "homes away from home" for frequent business travelers, places where not only can they relax and enjoy fine food and spirits, but also where they can arrange for translator services, receive discounts at hotels, and have access to temporary office space and secretarial services. These reciprocal memberships at clubs in nearly every major commerce center throughout the world offer central staging areas to conduct both business and personal affairs while on the road.

Because the global marketplace is shrinking daily, we thought a profile of the Sibling International Commerce Club and its activities would provide valuable information for your readers.

Thank you, in advance, for your consideration of an article on the Sibling International Commerce Club. I'll call you next week for your feedback.

Sincerely,

Alan Harlan

ah/mn

Sample Letter 6.57 was written as a general announcement to all customers of a company's decision to merge with another company. The letter begins with the announcement of the merger and swiftly reassures the customer that the service she is accustomed to will continue and even improve as a result of the new corporation. The second paragraph is dedicated to an explanation of the benefits of the merger, and the close includes an offer of further information and assistance, as the writer includes the phone number of her company's customer relations manager.

Sample Letter 6.57.   Letter announcing a merger of two companies.

[date]

Ms. Anna Persel
2531 Saxon Hill Road
Dorbabble, MA 02139

Dear Ms. Persel:

We are writing to inform you that your neighborhood video store, Videodrome Inc., will be merging with Magneto Video Corporation in February 20X3. We want to assure you that the efficient, friendly service you have come to associate with Videodrome will not only continue, but expand with the new merger. As a way of thanking you for being such a valued customer, please accept our gift of six free rentals that you may use any time over the next year.

By joining the best parts of both our companies, we will be able to provide you and your family with even more enjoyable benefits. In addition to a free membership, we will offer you a frequent renter club card. After renting twelve DVDs, you will receive the thirteenth rental free. We also promise to always have one staff member dedicated to helping you find the movie that perfectly fits your mood, no matter what it is. In addition, every time you rent a DVD, you will automatically be enrolled in a free giveaway. If selected, you will be entitled to a wide range of complimentary rentals and refreshments.

We know that you have many options, online and otherwise, when it comes to renting films. We recognize that you and a devoted clientele continue to appreciate having a physical store that caters to your unique film-rental needs. We appreciate your business and want you to know that we look forward to continuing to serve your entertainment needs in the future. Should you have any questions, concerns, or suggestions about the upcoming merger, please don't hesitate to contact our customer relations manager, George Bushwacker, at 1-800-321-7839.

Sincerely,

Mahalia F. Simone

Sample Letter 6.58 was written to a business acquaintance by someone who decided to form his own business. The letter writer announces his new business in the first paragraph, follows that with a brief description of the type of work the business does, and closes by encouraging the reader to meet with the writer if he is ever in the writer's area. While the writer is not making any direct sale with the letter, he is building an awareness that may pay off in the future.

Sample Letter 6.59 was written to accompany information that a professional organization was offering as an educational tool to consumers. The letter writer sets up the reasons for the need for the information in paragraphs 1 and 2, follows with a description of the material enclosed with the letter, and closes by offering to set up interviews with members of the professional group should the reader want to pursue this information.

Sample Letter 6.58.   Letter announcing the formation of a new business.

[date]

Mr. Samuel Johnson
19 Court Road
Lichfield, GA 30004

Dear Sam:

In August I left my position as manager of consulting at Boswell and Boswell, Inc. to establish my own consulting business. I would like to take this opportunity to pass along my business card and to tell you a little bit about my business.

My practice will deal with automating accounting firms and small businesses. My services will focus on three primary areas:

- Consulting services to CPA firms on use of computers in audit, tax, and management; client computer consulting; and special financial analysis.
- Consulting services to small businesses that are considering automation.
- Training seminars on specific software packages including: Excel, Word, PowerPoint, and Outlook.

The last four months have been quite rewarding professionally. Business has taken me to New York, Boston, and Europe.

If you are in the New York or Boston area and would like to get together, please call.

Sincerely,

Robert Lang
Principal

rl/js

Sample Letter 6.59.   Letter accompanying industry information.

[date]

Mr. Jacob Wirth
Wirth & While Journal
45 Boston Place
Nashville, MA 02139

HELPING INVESTORS COPE WITH STOCK MARKET CRASH

The aftereffects of the recent stock market plunge have left investors confused and uncertain over both the economy's future and their own financial situations. Frankly, investor confidence has been shaken.

What can investors do now to calm their fears and restore optimism to their financial outlook?

This question and others are answered in the enclosed background information, which provides practical advice for investors in coping with their finances. The information comes from the National Investment Advisors Group (NIAG), the 10,000-member professional organization in the investment advisory industry.

Overall strategies are provided in this material to help investors protect and build their investments to better prepare them to meet their short- and long-term objectives.

Leading professionals in the investment advisory industry are available to talk about what investors can and should be doing now to meet their immediate and long-term goals. If you would like more information or to arrange an interview with an investment advisor, please do not hesitate to call me or Athena Chin at 212-555-6767.

PAMELA A. HOAN
PUBLIC RELATIONS DIRECTOR

PAH/trw

A good public relations tactic is to keep abreast of prospective customers' status in the professional market. The writer of Sample Letter 6.60 used the occasion of the reader's new position as an excuse to not only congratulate the reader but also to briefly promote the writer's services. The letter clearly focuses on the congratulations, but by briefly reminding the reader about the writer's capabilities, he increases the chances that should she need such services, she will remember his company.

Sample Letter 6.60. Letter congratulating customer on promotion.

[date]

Ms. Pamela Chin
Seimor & Simons
45 Tewksbury Road
Alexandria, MI 48028

Dear Ms. Chin:

Congratulations on being named an associate at Seimor & Simons. While I realize that you are limited in the amount of insurance business you handle for clients, I would be glad to help you in any way I can.

Savin Hill Benefits Group tailors insurance programs for professionals like you. We also have a fast response time for any business referrals.

Good luck with your new responsibilities. I hope I can be helpful to you with any service you need or question you have.

Sincerely,

Albert Flynn
Vice President

af/cc

In Sample Letter 6.61, the letter writer makes a clear, direct request to an editor that a correction be made to an article that was published on the recipient's website. The writer points out the specifics of the error and asks for immediate attention to correct the mistake. (This letter can easily be adapted to be sent as an email by using the text of the letter as the body of your email to the recipient.)

Sample Letter 6.61. Letter requesting a correction to an article.

[date]

Ms. Tess Palay
Editor
Fortuitous Fortunes Web News
34 Analysts Place
Franklin, MA 02555

Dear Ms. Palay:

While we appreciate the article you ran about our company, Boonton Bagel Bakers, on your website, we regret that the article featured a major error. Your writer stated that we are a not-for-profit company and that all of our profits go to endangered species organizations. Each of those facts is incorrect. We are neither a not-for-profit nor do our profits go to such organizations.

We have no idea where your writer got the idea that either of these facts were true, but we request that you publish a correction to the article on your website as well as change the existing posted article or take it down from your site.

As you can appreciate, we would hate to give your readers the idea that we are presenting our business as something that it is not.

Thank you for your immediate attention to this issue. We trust that you will make the correction to your website as quickly as possible.

Sincerely,

Tiffany Cole, President
Boonton Bagel Bakers

bc/dw

CHAPTER 7

Customer service letters

Customer service letters are some of the most important letters you will write. Serving the needs of customers is a sure way to capture their loyalty to your business. Even when sticky issues such as complaint resolutions or price increases arise, handling these issues with respect for the customer is crucial in maintaining the integrity of the business and in achieving desirable results.

All of the customer service letters in this chapter were written with the customer in mind. Many were designed to win over or strengthen the loyalty of customers. Others were crafted to achieve a desired goal without alienating existing customers.

Many of the letters in this chapter can be sent as emails or as attachments to emails. Some company policies regarding handling customer disputes and resolution will require writing formal letters. But the content, whether written as a formal letter or an email, will not vary greatly. For those letters in this chapter that can be adapted to emails, it's simple enough to copy the text of the sample letter into the text of your email.

Complaint Resolution Letters

Sample Letters 7.1 through 7.8 were all written to deal with complaints made by customers. Sample Letter 7.9 was written by a customer after several attempts to resolve problems.

Sample Letter 7.1 was written to acknowledge receipt of a customer complaint. The letter writer acknowledges the complaint in the first paragraph, informs the customer that a credit will be issued to her account while the complaint is being investigated, and finally lets her know how to get in touch with her customer service department if she has any further questions.

Sample Letter 7.2 was written to a customer who had complained about an incorrect billing that appeared on his charge account statement. In this letter, the letter writer explains what further information the customer service department needs to explore the discrepancy. In the first three paragraphs the writer clearly spells out the steps the customer should take to help speed up the investigation. The writer closes by thanking the customer for his help and encourages him to call if he has any questions while the problem is being cleared up.

Sample Letter 7.3 was written to inform a customer that all the information necessary to resolve a complaint had not been received. The letter could be written as a follow-up to the information requested in Sample Letter 7.2. The writer recaps the complaint, explains that the temporary credit is being rescinded, and asks the customer to call if he has any other questions. The reference line on this letter matches the one on Sample Letter 7.2, indicating they both refer to the same account.

Sample Letter 7.1. Letter acknowledging receipt of complaint.

[date]
A-564-654567-90000

Mrs. Alison Q. Rumpole
546 Haversford Drive
Massapequa, NY 17310

Subject: Incorrect Charge Query

Dear Mrs. Rumpole:

You recently inquired about the charges on your monthly bill from Henderson & Henderson Department Store. We have written the store management to try to resolve the discrepancy. As soon as we receive their reply, we will write you again.

While we are conducting our investigation, we are issuing a temporary credit on your charge account for $86.81.

If you have any questions or if we can be of further service, please call me or another customer service representative at the telephone number listed on your monthly billing statement.

Cordially,

(Mrs.) Leslie T. Waters
Customer Service Manager

ltw/jls

Sample Letter 7.2.   Letter instructing customer on procedure to clarify billing.

[date]
A-456-8765-87777

Mr. Simon F. Wallace
43 Douglas Road
Far Hills, PA 29534

Dear Mr. Wallace:

In order to trace the payment of $20.95 you recently called us about, we need a copy of the front and back of your cancelled check. If the information on the copy is not readable, please handwrite it so that it is legible.

If your check has not yet cleared, simply stop payment on it and send us a replacement check. We have enclosed a return envelope for your convenience.

While waiting for this matter to be resolved, we are issuing a temporary credit to your charge account. If we do not receive a copy of your cancelled check by December 7, we will remove the temporary credit.

We appreciate your help in resolving this situation quickly. If you have any questions or if we can be of further assistance, please call me or another customer service representative at the telephone number listed on your monthly billing statement.

Cordially,

(Mrs.) Leslie T. Waters
Customer Service Manager

ltw/jls

Sample Letter 7.3. Letter notifying customer that necessary information for complaint resolution was not sent. Could be sent as follow-up to Sample Letter 7.2.

[date]
A-456-8765-87777

Mr. Simon F. Wallace
43 Douglas Road
Far Hills, PA 29534

Dear Mr. Wallace:

You recently called us about the payment for $20.95 not credited to your charge account.

When we could not locate the credit, we asked you to send us more information. Since we have not received the necessary information from you, we are removing the temporary credit we had issued to your account.

If you have any questions or if we can be of further service, please feel free to call me or another customer service representative at the telephone number listed on your monthly billing statement.

Cordially,

(Mrs.) Leslie T. Waters
Customer Service Manager

ltw/jls

Sample Letter 7.4 could also be sent as a follow-up to Sample Letter 7.2, but here the letter writer agrees with the customer's complaint and attempts to resolve the issue. The writer addresses the problem immediately in the letter, explaining what caused the problem, lets the reader know how it will be resolved, and apologizes for the mishap. The letter is short, but clarifies the problem and is intended to set the reader's mind at rest.

Sample Letter 7.4. Follow-up to Sample Letter 7.2, agreeing with customer's complaint.

[date]
A-456-8765-87777

Mr. Simon F. Wallace
43 Douglas Road
Far Hills, PA 29534

Dear Mr. Wallace:

We have found that we inadvertently applied your payment of $20.95 to another charge-account holder's account. We have now transferred it to your account, and it will appear on an upcoming statement.

We apologize for any inconvenience this may have caused.

If you have any questions, or if we can be of further service, please call me or another customer service representative at the telephone number listed on your monthly billing statement.

Cordially,

(Mrs.) Leslie T. Waters
Customer Service Manager

ltw/jls

Sample Letter 7.5 acknowledges a customer's complaint while firmly restating company policy and clearly indicating the impossibility of meeting the customer's request. However, the author attempts to retain the customer's allegiance by offering a discount on future products, before cordially closing with the expectation that the customer will respect company policy.

Sample Letter 7.5. Letter acknowledging complaint and indicating company policy.

[date]

Ms. Lisa Cubalot
186 Havanah Place
Atlanta, GA 30044

Dear Ms. Cubalot:

Enclosed with this letter please find, in wrap, the block of Stilton cheese that you returned to us late last week. Unfortunately, we have a very strict policy against the return of any food products. Because of obvious health and freshness issues, none of our food is refundable.

We're sorry that you did not enjoy our cheese. However, on the order form in our catalog, it clearly states that the sale of all perishable items is final. Because we value your patronage, we will gladly provide you with 25% off of your next Cheese Louise! order. Just mention this letter, and my name, when you call.

I know that you respect our return policy, and we appreciate your future business.

Thank you,

Jim Walker
Customer Service Associate Manager

encl.

Sample Letter 7.6 was written in response to a customer's complaint, which appears to be unfounded. The tone is formal; the apology is qualified and limited to a generic apology for the customer's dissatisfaction. The writer closes with a promise to look into the matter further, while promising future contact from the Customer Service Department.

Sample Letter 7.6. Letter acknowledging unfounded complaint.

[date]

Frank Armitage
2881 Hidden Lake Lane
Chesterland, MO 63055

Dear Mr. Armitage:

Not only is your letter, dated January 28, extremely rude, it is also quite inaccurate. According to your statement, one of our West Branch Sales Associates spoke obscenities to you and your wife while you were in line.

I apologize if you had an unpleasant shopping experience in our store; however, the employee you have charged with inappropriate behavior was not working on the day of your visit. In addition, we have no sales receipts for the items that you state were purchased. I am continuing to look into this matter, but I have to admit some reservations on our behalf.

A representative from our Customer Service Department will be contacting you shortly. Please call our store if we can help further.

Sincerely,

Hugh G. Printz
Store Manager

Sample Letter 7.7 was written to disagree with a customer complaint. In the first paragraph of the letter, the letter writer refers to the complaint and disagrees with the customer about a product defect. The writer then explains to the reader that he may return the product for a refund if he is dissatisfied with it for any reason, and closes by explaining the appropriate procedure for future complaints.

Sample Letter 7.7. Letter disagreeing with customer.

[date]

Mr. Elmore T. Holstein
56 Trueblood Terrace
Minerva, WA 98010

Dear Mr. Holstein:

In response to your letter of May 12 about your purchase of Dandy Wanda's Clam Sauce, while we appreciate your concerns, I assure you that we have taken all necessary steps to ensure that the product meets the highest nutritional standards.

If you are dissatisfied with this product, however, we will be pleased to refund your money for your purchase.

For future reference, please direct any specific concerns about return of products to the store from which you purchased the goods.

Cordially,

James T. Lardley
Customer Service Manager

jtl/jl

Sample Letter 7.8 is a more detailed complaint resolution letter written to clear up some problems the client had with the company's services. The letter writer begins by apologizing for the displeasure, then details the problem, explaining how it occurred. The writer proceeds to offer a solution to the problem, telling the client that the company will pay for any problems that were caused by his error. He also clearly spells out how much cost there will be to the client as a result of the suggested resolution. He then asks that the client call him to give him the go-ahead with the approach he has recommended.

Sample Letter 7.8.   Complaint resolution letter.

[date]

Ms. Millicent Conroy
Conroy & Smyrna, Inc.
678 Boxford Street
Taylor, NJ 07015

Dear Millicent:

I am sorry that you are not pleased with the copies of your company press clips that we sent you. Alice Farning, from your office, sent me a copy of each press clip. After reviewing them for context, here are my suggestions.

Four of the clips are fine. They are enclosed with this letter. There is nothing missing from the clips, nor is anything taken out of context.

Six of the clips are out of context. As I explained, these copies were made from my portfolio boards. They are a compilation of quotations your company received, highlighted for our presentation purposes. For your purposes, I agree, they should be complete articles in case a client or prospective client decides to read one.

I have the originals for all of the articles. To make a complete set, we must copy 23 additional pages, 500 copies of each page. We also must consider that the longer pieces have advertisements surrounding the editorial content. I recommend that we hire a paste-up person to cut and paste the pages, thus combining columns and eliminating the advertisements. This will lessen the number of pages and make for better presentation. I will get an estimate for this work if you agree that this is the way to go. Then I'll know exactly how many pages will have to be copied, and I can get a final quote.

We have spent $595 plus tax for the initial group of 5,000 copies. Farran Public Relations is responsible for paying $210 for the initial 6 pages that weren't acceptable. We will also pay for those 6 pages to be redone. This leaves an additional 17 pages, 500 copies each (8,500 x 7 cents), before any advertisements are removed and columns combined by a competent paste-up artist. While the number of pages will be reduced by this process, the artist's time will be an additional cost.

Millicent, I'm sorry to waste your time with these details. But my responsibility to your company is to get approval on any expense beyond our fee. These expenses for copying could total as much as $800 to $1,000 for the project. I don't want to proceed without your authorization.

This project is not a simple copy job. It requires careful thought and organization to provide Conroy & Smyrna, Inc., with effective presentation materials. We emphasized the value it will provide your company through third-party credibility. It will be well worth our efforts, and should help to provide your company with a competitive edge, especially in new-business situations.

Please give me a call about how you'd like to proceed. I appreciate your patience and understanding. I am confident this project will prove to be a rewarding investment.

Sincerely,

Mack Nothrop
Account Executive

mn/pb

Encs.

Sample Letter 7.9 was written to express extreme dissatisfaction with a company's behavior. It does not request any further action and does not make any attempts to resolve a problem; rather, it outlines, in great detail, the steps the customer has taken in the past to address a problematic situation and closes with a condemnation of the company's ineptitude. The writer's barely restrained disgust is revealed through his specific references to the healthcare provider's mistakes and misinformation. Enclosures support this author's case for the company's negligence.

Sample Letter 7.9. Complaint letter written after frequent attempts to resolve problem.

[date]

Mr. Gene Russel
Customer Service Supervisor, Billing Division
Alpha-Omega Healthcare
P.O. Box 1125
Blue Bell, PA 15022

Mr. Russel:

I am writing to you to clear up a persistent and frustrating problem that I have had with Alpha-Omega Healthcare. Last week I received the enclosed letter from your Provider Payment Department, informing me that you are unable to pay a claim for diagnostic services performed on my wife, Lois Ketchum, at the Wycliffe Clinic/Department of Radiology and Oncology on April 15, because you do not have a referral from my primary care physician for those services. I do not need a referral for these services, and Alpha-Omega's own Contract Holder Group Agreement, a legally binding contract, specifies this.

The diagnostic service my wife had performed last month was a hysterosalpingogram (HSG). If you will reference your own Infertility Services Agreement, effective January 1, 20XX, you will see that the hysterosalpingogram is a procedure that is covered by your company without a referral. In case you do not have ready access to your own legal documents, I have enclosed a copy of this contract and have highlighted the pertinent information for your ease. You will kindly note that the HSG test, item number D.6 on your Infertility Services Agreement, does not need a referral if diagnostic services are performed by a participating provider. Dr. Carpenter at Wycliffe Clinic is such a provider, and her office did perform the HSG for diagnosis only.

Pardon my writing at such length, but my wife and I are increasingly frustrated with your company. We have been exceedingly conscientious about following your insurance agreements and referral procedures. My wife has spoken to many representatives in your member services departments in an attempt to find out precisely what benefits we were entitled to receive. When those staff members were unable to assist her, she spoke to supervisors in an effort to get a copy of your coverage contracts. On several separate occasions, she was told that either no such document existed, or that she could not receive a copy of it. Finally, a supervisor sent her a copy of the coverage contract. We have not had any services performed that are not listed under the Direct Access Specialist Benefits section, and the only services we have had performed were for diagnostic purposes only. We understand that treatment of infertility is a separate issue from diagnosis, and that certain treatment procedures are not covered by your company. Alpha-Omega does not seem to understand its own policies, and we have had to pay the price in lost time, mounting aggravation, and emotional duress.

You can rest assured that we will be changing our insurance company as soon as humanly possible; I would not recommend Alpha-Omega to anyone unless I had a personal vendetta against them. We will also be filing a formal complaint with our state's Commissioner of Insurance.

Infertility is an emotionally draining and sensitive medical problem. Alpha-Omega's involvement in this process has been marked by incompetence, insensitivity, and misinformation, and has made a difficult time more troubling. Shame on you.

Harry Ketchum
ID# BBC6D3LA

3 Enclosures

Apology Letters

Sample Letters 7.10 through 7.19 are all examples of letters of apology.

Sample Letter 7.10 is a general letter of apology written to express regrets over a problem caused to a customer. Because of the general nature of this letter, it is easily tailored to any situation where a letter of apology is needed.

Sample Letter 7.11 was written to express apologies about an employee's rudeness. The letter writer acknowledges the customer's complaint, apologizes for the treatment he received, stresses that it does not reflect the typical quality of service of the company, indicates the rude employee has been reprimanded, and closes by again apologizing for the inconvenience.

Sample Letter 7.12 is an apology for a product defect. The letter writer expresses regrets over the customer's having had to return the product, but assures him that the product will be repaired or replaced to the customer's satisfaction. The writer continues by mentioning the outstanding reputation of the particular product and extends an offer of assistance if there are any other questions.

Sample Letter 7.13 was written to apologize for damaged goods that a customer received. The author acknowledges that the company was clearly in the wrong but manages to salvage both the company's business reputation, by mentioning that this kind of incident is unprecedented, and the customer relationship, by offering to replace the damaged goods free of charge.

Sample Letter 7.14 was written to apologize for a delayed shipment. The letter writer tells the customer when she can expect the product and then explains what caused the delay. He continues to apologize for the inconvenience and explains that the company has taken an extra effort to get the replacement shipment there on time.

Sample Letter 7.10.   General letter of apology.

[date]

Mr. Harold T. Harigold
56 Yorkshire Terrace
Columbus, MI 48029

Dear Mr. Harigold:

Please accept our deep and sincere apologies. On behalf of the Hoodle Company, I wish to express our regrets and assure you that all efforts have been made to rectify your situation.

Please call or write me personally if you have any further questions or comments about this situation. Thank you for your kind understanding.

Sincerely yours,

James Elwood
Customer Service Manager

je/jl

Sample Letter 7.11. Letter apologizing for employee's rudeness.

[date]

Mr. Zach Rendell
56 Biscayne Drive
Florina, FL 32008

Dear Mr. Rendell:

I am writing in response to your letter of May 15, 20X8, in which you described your frustrations in dealing with one of our employees.

I apologize for the treatment you received and want to assure you that it does not reflect the quality of service we strive to maintain. I have spoken with the employee and am confident this will not occur again.

Please accept my apology. We appreciate your business and look forward to continuing our relationship in the future.

Sincerely,

Barbara T. Blazen
Customer Service Manager

BTB:jk

Sample Letter 7.12.   Letter apologizing for product defect.

[date]

Mr. Harold P. Winkle
67 Yorkey Place
Fenway, NE 68012

Dear Mr. Winkle:

We regret that you had to return the stereo system you purchased from our Sherman Oaks store because of a defect. We assure you that your system will be repaired or replaced as soon as possible.

The Z-186X system is one of the finest available, and the Z Company one of the most reputable and quality conscious. The Hoodle Company stands behind these products and will take whatever steps are necessary to guarantee your satisfaction with this product.

Please call my office if you have any further questions about this problem.

Sincerely,

James Elwood
Customer Service Manager

JE/jl

Sample Letter 7.13.   Letter apologizing for damaged goods.

[date]

Mr. James Matz
164 Myrtle Street
Kensington, London
England W8 6QT

Dear Mr. Matz:

We just received your letter, dated May 19, regarding the two defective picnic tables that were delivered to your home. Please accept our most sincere apology.

I can assure you that in eight years of business, this is our first notice of a damaged order. The majority of our products ship to residents of the domestic United States. And, of course, with an international order, we try to take special precautions with shipping. However, as we now know, the unexpected can occur.

We have already shipped two replacement tables, with the hope that these will be delivered in perfect condition. We will not charge you for the shipping. Thank you for purchasing your new cedar picnic tables from our company.

Yours very truly,

David Bleumeyer
President

Sample Letter 7.14. Apology for delayed shipment.

[date]

Ms. Carol P. Hunneycutt
Haskins, Haskins & Sony, Inc.
34 Radcliff Road
Cambridge, KY 40013

Dear Ms. Hunneycutt:

I have seen to it that the computer tables you ordered from us on May 1 have been loaded on our truck. The shipment should arrive in Cambridge by Thursday of this week.

After receiving your letter of May 15, I checked our warehouse and found that the original shipment of computer tables was mistakenly returned to us. I apologize for the error and hope that this replacement shipment will reach you in time to meet your needs.

Ms. Hunneycutt, I realize that we cannot make up for the inconvenience the delivery mishap caused you. I hope that this rush shipment will make up for some of it.

Please call me if you have any questions or problems. Again, sorry for the delay.

Best regards,

Armand L. Newport
Vice President

aln/jls

Sample Letter 7.15 was written to apologize for a delay in responding to a request for service. The writer explains the reasons for the delay and promises to service the customer by a specific date. In closing, the writer attempts to interest the customer in a sales plan that might prevent this type of service delay from happening in the future. The close is upbeat and promising.

Sample Letter 7.15.   Letter apologizing for service delay.

[date]

Mr. Ed Sharp
215 Kilgo Circle
East Topeka, GA 30077

Dear Mr. Sharp:

Our company recently received your letter asking for service for your outdoor safety lighting system, the OpticLight Millennium System, and I write to apologize for our delay in responding to your request. Frankly, the holiday season is a busy one for those of us in the lighting business, and this season was made worse by the resignations of two key lighting technicians.

However, we have hired new personnel, and within the next three weeks we will be sending out a team to inspect and refurbish your bulbs, wiring, alarm system, and motion detectors. I hope that this will meet your safety needs.

According to your consumer history with us, you have been purchasing OpticLight products for more than two years now. Could I interest you in the Platinum Protection Plan? This plan is our top-of-the-line service plan, and it would ensure regular and timely service of all OpticLight products, written reminders of key dates in your service calendar, discounts on installation of new equipment, and an extended warranty on any lights in our new Millennium Line, all for one fixed price. I have included a promotional pamphlet on the Platinum Protection Plan for your convenience.

Thank you for your patience, and we will see you within three weeks.

Sincerely,

Anne Michaels
Service Supervisor

Encl.

Sample Letter 7.16 was written to a customer who was overcharged after she returned a product. The letter writer takes full responsibility and tries to keep the letter's tone friendly by explaining her company's fallibility.

Sample Letter 7.17 is a short, direct apology for a billing error. The letter writer explains that he's enclosed a copy of the corrected bill and hopes that the customer was not too inconvenienced by the mistake. It's short and to the point and gives the customer the results he wanted.

Sample Letter 7.16.   Letter apologizing to a customer for an overcharge.

[date]

Ms. Lisa Tarry
Purchasing Director
Savin Hill Couriers
186 Grampian Way
Newtonville, WA 98909

Dear Ms. Tarry:

We like to think of ourselves as flawless when it comes to customer billing and service. But, as you point out in your letter of March 14 citing discrepancies in your bill, we have made an error in how much we owed you for return of merchandise.

Please forgive us. Even with our state-of-the-art customer billing software, it seems we are still fallible. I have spoken to the appropriate people, who have assured me that they've discovered the underlying problem and corrected it. Regardless, the mistake is inexcusable and I will do everything I can to make sure it doesn't happen again.

I am enclosing a check for the amount we owe you. Should you have any problems or need any service in the future, please do not hesitate to call on me.

Sincerely,

Toni Wel
Account Manager

Encl.

Sample Letter 7.17. Letter apologizing to a customer for incorrect billing.

[date]

Mr. Henry Kramer
43 Douglass Road
Far Hills, OR 97024

Dear Mr. Kramer:

I've enclosed a corrected statement of your account with us. I am truly sorry about the incorrect charges that appeared on your bill.

We do our best to ensure the accuracy of all of our accounts by double-checking all of them, but somehow we still make mistakes from time to time. I hope our error did not cause you too much trouble. We value your business and look forward to serving you flawlessly in the future.

Sincerely,

Uri Amherst
Customer Service Manager

Enc.

Sample Letter 7.18 was written to apologize for a billing error. The author quickly gets to the point and then clearly states the steps he is taking to resolve the problem. In addition to applying a credit to the customer's account, the author encloses a revised and corrected invoice for the customer's records, before closing with his contact information for further assistance.

Sample Letter 7.18.   Letter apologizing for billing error.

[date]

Mr. James White
White & Sons Hardware, Inc.
1581 Leabrook Lane
Naperville, IL 60038

Dear Mr. White:

As per your request, I have reviewed the White & Sons Hardware account. According to our records, the correct cost of three hundred Slam Bam titanium hammers is $2,975.00.

Thank you very much for contacting me about this error. We certainly apologize for any inconvenience, and we have already credited to your account $326.00. In addition, enclosed with this letter is an updated and accurate invoice.

We appreciate your continued business and look forward to working with you in the future. If you have any questions or concerns about this matter, please don't hesitate to call me. My telephone number is 404-876-5415.

Sincerely,

Jacob Coleman
Accounts Payable Representative

encl.

Sample Letter 7.19 was written to inform a customer of an item's unavailability. The tone is apologetic. The author concludes by refunding the customer's payment and by enclosing a current catalog to encourage future purchases.

Sample Letter 7.19.   Letter apologizing for out-of-stock product.

[date]

Ms. Henrietta Packard
1103 Ramona Drive
San Pedro, TX 75609

Dear Ms. Packard:

We recently received your order number 110-2680-3 for a Collector's Edition Mixed Exotic Nuts Gift Tin, advertised in our winter catalog for $32.95 for the five-pound size.

I regret to inform you that the item you ordered is no longer in stock. There was high demand for this product and we sold our entire stock quickly. Your order, which arrived April 27, was not placed in time to secure the Gift Tin.

Enclosed is your check, uncashed, and a copy of our summer catalog. I hope that this updated catalog will contain something that interests you. If so, please don't delay— order now! We appreciate your business and look forward to serving you in the future.

Sincerely,

Mac D'Amia
Customer Service Representative

2 encs.

Letter Acknowledging Order

Sample Letter 7.20 was written to acknowledge an order and explain how it will be shipped. The letter writer clearly explains how much of the order is being shipped and how much has been back-ordered, and thanks the customer for his business.

Sample Letter 7.20. Letter acknowledging an order.

[date]

Mr. Simon Legyern
Legyern Cabinetmakers, Inc.
45 Merrimac Trail
Williamsburg, CO 80045

Dear Mr. Legyern:

Thank you for your order of 12 cases of wood glue from our company. The invoice for $288 is enclosed.

A portion of your order—8 cases—was shipped out this morning and should reach you within 10 days. We regret that to fill your order, we depleted our stock and must order the remainder of the glue from the manufacturer. You should receive the remainder of your order within 2 weeks. We apologize for the delay, but as a result of a special bulk rate we offered on this particular type of glue, we sold much more than we had anticipated. We are, of course, offering you the same savings that were featured in the sale.

Thanks for your order. We look forward to doing more business with you in the future.

Sincerely,

Kate Narconi

kn/js

enc.

Letters Correcting Wrong Shipment

Sample Letters 7.21 and 7.22 were written following incorrect product shipments. In Sample Letter 7.21, the letter writer immediately explains that the correct product is being shipped by express. He apologizes for the error and asks the customer to return the incorret product at his convenience and at the company's expense. Sample Letter 7.22 is a variation on that theme.

Sample Letter 7.21. Letter correcting shipment of wrong merchandise.

[date]

Mr. Robert R. Noren
Big Bank School
56 Teller Place
Island, HI 96700

Dear Mr. Noren:

We've shipped two cases of The Commercial Accounts Kit to you by overnight express mail. These forms will replace the shipment of The Retail Accounts Kit we sent you by mistake.

We apologize for the error we made in shipment. Your order for two cases of the forms was clear in stating the amount, title, and date on which you needed the forms for use in teaching your commercial accounts seminar on January 5, 20X3.

I am pleased that the correct forms will arrive in time for you to use in your seminar. When you have time, will you send The Retail Accounts Kits back to us? We will, of course, pay for the shipping charges, and have enclosed a shipping label that will bill directly to our company's account.

Again, I apologize for any inconvenience we may have caused. I hope this year's sessions go well.

Sincerely,

Merlin L. Nesgas

mln/jls

Enc.

Sample Letter 7.22.   Letter apologizing for an incorrect shipment.

[date]

Mr. Robert Johnson
Hazelnut Books
P.O. Box 3452
Soul, MT 59005

Invoice #15248

Dear Mr. Johnson:

What can I say? We made a mistake in refusing to accept the carton of books you returned to us that we had indeed incorrectly shipped to you in the first place. I can understand your frustration with us and I apologize for the inconvenience we've caused you.

Please return the carton of books to us once again and I will personally see that you are credited for the returned books and reimbursed for all of the shipping charges you incurred.

Again, please accept our apology for the mishap. We value your business and look forward to many more years of a fruitful relationship.

Sincerely,

Dave Iberia
Customer Service Manager

Product or Service Information Letters

Sample Letters 7.23 through 7.26 are examples of product or service information letters.

Sample Letter 7.23 was written in response to a customer's request for a duplicate copy of his charge account records. The letter writer explains that he has enclosed the copies and offers any help he may be able to give to the customer.

Sample Letter 7.24 informs the customer that the entire amount of product he ordered is not in stock and that partial payment is being returned.

Sample Letter 7.25 was written to inform the customer that the product offered is out of stock, but the letter writer suggests a substitute for the desired product. The writer explains that the substitute has been used by many others who also use the primary choice product. He asks that the customer let him know if she'd like the substitute product in place of the original order.

Sample Letter 7.26 was written to inform a customer about the reasons for the damage to a shipment of products the company made to the customer. The letter writer takes the blame for the damage to the shipment, offers a solution to the problem, and thanks the customer for his patience.

Sample Letter 7.23. Letter responding to customer's request for information.

[date]
A-354-29

Mr. Alexander Campbell
Authentic Bagels Company
14 Pendleton Road
Scots, PA 15012

Dear. Mr. Campbell:

The records you requested are enclosed. Because of the technical difficulties we have in processing microfilm, I am unable to provide better quality copies.

I am sorry for any inconvenience this may cause. If I can be of any further assistance, please call me or another customer service representative on our toll-free number, 800-555-4444.

Sincerely,

Ambrose Kemper
Customer Service Representative

jls

Enclosure

Sample Letter 7.24. Letter informing customer item is out of stock.

[date]

Mr. Jackie Mustang
Whist, Inc.
98 Primiano Place
Rockefeller, MA 02234

Dear Mr. Mustang:

I hope your shipment of garland arrived in good shape. Since we did not have the full quantity you ordered, I am enclosing a check for $8.76 to cover the difference.

I'm looking forward to seeing you in November at the dealer's show in Penob City.

Yours truly,

Kate Peterson

kp/jb

enc.

Sample Letter 7.25. Letter suggesting substitute for an out-of-stock item.

[date]

Ms. Alicia T. Hansdale
67 Utica Road
Ithaca, CT 06045

Dear Ms. Hansdale:

Thank you for your recent order for 500 Acmeplus 320 thumb drives. Unfortunately, that item is out of stock.

In the past, many of our customers have used our All-Star 782 thumb drives in place of Acmeplus 320s, and have found them completely satisfactory.

I would be happy to send you the All-Star thumb drives on a no-risk trial basis. If you don't find them completely to your liking, simply return the unused thumb drives and we will refund your money.

Please let me know if you would like to try the All-Star product. If you do, I'll ship them out immediately.

Thank you for your order. I look forward to hearing from you.

Sincerely,

Mark E. Mathews
Account Representative

mem/jk

Sample Letter 7.26.   Letter apologizing for damaged shipment.

[date]

Mr. Alan T. Quizone
Back Bay Secretarial Services, Inc.
306 Dartmouth Street
Trenton, PA 15043

Dear Mr. Quizone:

After receiving your letter today, I instructed my warehouse foreman to load a new shipment of computer tables onto one of our trucks to be sent to you. You should have the tables by the time this letter reaches you.

The damage to the first batch of computer tables was almost undoubtedly the result of the poor handling it received from the shipping service we used. We will arrange to pick up the damaged tables from your office at a time that is convenient for you.

I apologize for the inconvenience this matter has caused you. I am sure that the computer tables you receive on the second go-round will meet with your approval.

Thank you for your patience.

Sincerely,

Oscar E. Renter
Account Executive

oer/mln

Thank-You Letters to Customers

Sample Letters 7.27 through 7.31 were all written to thank customers. Sample Letter 7.27 was written to thank a customer for a testimonial about a company's products. Sample Letter 7.28 thanks a customer for a referral to a prospective customer. Sample Letter 7.29 thanks a customer for supporting a new business. Sample Letter 7.30 thanks a customer for continued business support. Sample Letter 7.31 thanks a customer for repeat business.

All of the letters express sincere thanks to the customer for a different reason. But in each, the letter writer lets the customer know how important the customer is to the company. Thank-you letters to loyal customers can go a long way in ensuring that their loyalty will continue for some time to come.

Sample Letter 7.27.   Letter thanking customer for a testimonial.

[date]

Ms. Nancy Lang
Business Enterprise College
186-A Storming Hill Road
Grampian, PA 15056

Dear Ms. Lang:

Thank you very much for the kind words you said about Andoris Company. Your testimonial lets us know that we are doing something right and that our customers appreciate it.

Rarely does someone take the time to write us about the good job she thinks we are doing. We appreciate the time you took to express your pleasure.

I am glad that the software that we sold you fits the bill perfectly for your work on account management. We think the software is among the best—if not *the* best—easy-to-use software available today for account management.

Thanks again for your kind words. If we can be of help in the future, we'd consider it a pleasure to serve you.

Sincerely,

Manuel L. Narciega
President

MLN:jls

Sample Letter 7.28. Letter thanking customer for a referral.

[date]

Mr. Jeffrey R. Krauss
Krauss Associates
25 Huntington Avenue, Suite 408
Boonton, NJ 07005

Dear Mr. Krauss:

Thanks for referring me to Kate Paul, who you thought might be in need of insurance planning. I called on Kate last Wednesday and enjoyed meeting with her and her partner at Kate Paul & Helen Louise Enterprises, Ltd.

You were quite correct in assessing Kate's insurance situation. I am sure my firm can meet her insurance needs and help her plan for the future.

Thank you for calling Kate ahead of time to let her know I'd be calling on her. She told me how positive you were about my services. That endorsement from you was a tremendous boost to my credibility before I even walked in the door.

Thanks again for the referral and your kind words.

Sincerely,

Greg B. Luzinski
Principal

gbl:jlh

Sample Letter 7.29.   Letter expressing appreciation for support.

[date]

Mr. Edward J. Cole
Baning Consulting Group
301 Morlan Road
Bethany, WV 26032

Dear Mr. Cole:

The time has simply flown by, but on July 31, Parpubris Company will celebrate five years in business. We're proud of the office equipment and office design services we've provided and the reception we've received in the marketplace, all in five short years.

Much of the credit for our success has resulted from the support of loyal customers like you who have consistently come back to us to place orders. It's friends like you who have put Parpubris on the map as the supplier of office equipment and design services to businesses throughout the tri-state area.

Thank you for your support over the last five years. We plan to continue to provide the products and services that have satisfied you in the past. We look forward to a prosperous future made possible by customers who've stuck with Parpubris since our beginnings.

Thanks again.

Best regards,

Mary L. Neals
President

mln/jls

Sample Letter 7.30.   Letter thanking new customer for business.

[date]

Mr. Dave Wallace
Parthenon Products
45 Allenton Road
Washington, D.C. 20001

Dear Dave:

I wanted to let you know how much we at NES Products, Inc., appreciate your business and the opportunity to be able to serve you. I hope that this is the beginning of a long and beneficial relationship for both you and NES Products.

If there is anything I can do for you and Parthenon, please give me a call. When you're in the area, make sure to drop in and say hello.

Sincerely,

David St. Simon
Sales Representative

dss/mn

Sample Letter 7.31.   Letter thanking customer for repeat business.

[date]

Ms. Rachel Victoria
39 Tide Place, Suite 654
Boonton, NJ 07005

Dear Ms. Victoria:

I wanted to take the time to thank you for your repeat business. I want to make sure that you know how high a value we at Graham Products place on our relationship.

We are trying to do a good job for you and will always welcome your suggestions. If you like our service and products and the way we do business, we hope you will recommend us to your friends and acquaintances. If not, we hope that you will tell us why.

Please feel free to call upon us whenever we can be of service. We want you to feel that Graham Products is always responsive and eager to give you the best service and products in the business.

Yours very truly,

Miles Cannon
President

mc/mn

Letter to Lapsed Customer

Sample Letter 7.32 was written to a customer who had not visited the company for some time. Nowadays it's easy to keep track of customers and their buying habits. This comes in handy, particularly in service businesses where regular visits (for example, automotive tune-up or accounting services) are common. The letter writer here gives the customer an easy method of responding to the query.

Sample Letter 7.32. Letter to customer inquiring about customer's absence.

[date]

Mr. Albert Dowlin
45 State Road
Prime, RI 02805

Dear Mr. Dowlin:

It's been some time since you've visited us for service here at Palmer Automotive Guys. We hope it was nothing we did that is keeping you from bringing your car in for regular service. If it is because of something we did, please let us know and we'll try to make it up to you.

Please fill out and mail back to us the postage-paid customer feedback card I've enclosed. If you've got specific gripes or concerns about our service, I'll give your comments my immediate attention.

Sincerely,

Simon Alterone
Customer Service Manager

enc.

Pricing Letters

Sample Letters 7.33 through 7.35 all deal with pricing of products. All three letters clearly lay out the issues and leave little doubt in the customers' minds about how the company is planning to deal with these particular pricing questions.

Sample Letter 7.33 announces to a retail customer that the wholesaler will be raising its prices on goods. The letter includes a list of products and the percentage price increase to which they will be subjected.

While the primary purpose of Sample Letter 7.34 is to announce a freeze on price increases, the writer takes the opportunity to introduce several new products to a company's line. The letter serves not only as a customer service letter, but also as a sales letter.

Sample Letter 7.35 informs a customer that the product he desires is in stock and that quantity discounts on the merchandise are available. He asks the customer to let him know how much of the product he would like and how he would like it shipped.

Sample Letter 7.33.   Letter informing customer of a price increase.

[date]

Mr. Paul Vanice
Vanice Camera Shop
96 Pauline Drive
Oshkosh, WI 53056

PRICE INCREASE ON BLACK-AND-WHITE PHOTOGRAPHY PRODUCTS

Mr. Vanice, effective February 26, 20X2, we will be raising prices on black-and-white products by the following percentages:

PAN F, FP4, HP5, PAN films all types	3.6%
XP-1 film except 36 exposure	3.6%
XP-1 film 35mm, 36 exposure	12.0%
Bornesprint paper	5.0%
Bornesobrom paper	8.0%
Multigrade II, Multigrade FB, Bornespeed papers	4.0%
All liquid chemicals	3.5%

We are happy to announce that all film and paper powder chemicals will be significantly reduced in price. Watch your price list for details. New catalog pages will be mailed to you before February 26.

We at Bornes Photo Corporation would like to thank you for your past support and wish you continued success this year.

MAURY SIMONS
VICE PRESIDENT, MARKETING

MS/js

Sample Letter 7.34. Letter notifying customer that prices will not be raised.

[date]

Ms. Zoe Jeffries
Laramy Equipment Company
34 Main Street
Apriori, UT 84003

Dear Ms. Jeffries:

Just a quick note to send you the 20X5 Extendacord price list. Please note that we have held last year's prices. We will continue to do so for as long as possible.

Extendacord, Inc., has a new look and several new cords and covers for home appliances. We have redesigned the fold-a-way cord, wrap-a-round cord, and retractable cord. Three new additions to our line of appliance covers are the Heatshield 1000, the ProTouch, and the Keepitwarm Mit. We have also enhanced the entire Extendacord look with colorful accents on all of our products.

You can see all of this for yourself in the enclosed Extendacord catalog or during the February Home Appliance Show in Salt Lake City. Come visit us in booth B-444.

See you in Salt Lake City.

Cordially,

Keye Quinn
National Sales Manager

kq/mn

encs.

Sample Letter 7.35. Letter informing customer about volume discount.

[date]

Mr. Ambrose Kemper
Kemper Construction Company
Box 8765
Encino, AR 71665

Dear Mr. Kemper:

Thank you for your inquiry about our drywall products. We do have drywall in stock. It can be shipped from here or directly from Little Rock. The cost per sheet is $39 plus $20 for crating. If you order 40 sheets or more, the price will be less.

I understand that you are interested in buying 15 sheets. Delivery time for an order of this size usually averages two to three days. I should also mention that Washington Freight System does allow a 50% discount on freight charges. This is a considerable savings. The cost to ship 15 sheets would be approximately $207.50 less 50%, or $103.75.

Once you decide how much drywall you need and how you'd like it shipped, please get in touch with me. We look forward to filling your order.

Yours truly,

Max Martinson
Vice President

mm/sf

Change-in-Location Letters

Sample Letter 7.36 was written to inform customers of a change in location of repair services. The letter clearly and briefly gives the customer the information she needs to continue to use the services.

Sample Letter 7.36. Notice of change in location.

[date]

Ms. Zelda Jeffries
Laramy Equipment Company
34 Main Street
Apriori, NJ 07036

Subject: New National Service Update

Dear Ms. Jeffries:

We are pleased to announce that as a result of our recent expansion into our new facilities in Boonton, New Jersey, we are now performing all repairs of household appliance products sent directly to New National at the following two locations:

New National Corporation   New National Corporation
312 West Main Street   43 Lorraine Terrace
Boonton, NJ 07005   Far Way, NJ 07072
ATTN: Appliance service   ATTN: Appliance service

The only exceptions to this policy are discontinued products for which parts are no longer available. If we receive an appliance that we are unable to repair due to lack of parts, we will return it to you unrepaired, at no charge.

An estimate of repair costs will continue to be sent to you for approval prior to the start of any repair. To save repair time, preapprovals will be honored if a letter of authorization accompanies the product.

Thank you for your cooperation and support. We remain committed to providing you with the finest service available.

Cordially,

Martin North
Director of Operations

mn/lh

When a business location closes, it's often good to let existing customers know of the closure, partly out of courtesy and partly to let them know if another branch is available at which they can shop. Sample Letter 7.37 accomplishes both tasks by being direct with the reader while also being clear in how much the recipient's patronage has been appreciated.

Sample Letter 7.37. Letter notifying customer that store will be closing.

[date]

Mrs. Vivian Basket
456 Fascinating Lane
Cambridge, GA 30087

Dear Mrs. Basket:

We are sorry to let you know that the Bayonne Tramlaw Store will be closing on Tuesday, September 11.

We value your business and hope that the closing of this branch will not diminish your loyalty to our company. Our Denville location, just 8 miles away, remains open and thriving. We hope that we will be able to count you among the customers at that branch.

Thank you for continuing to shop with us. We trust that we will be able to count you among our customers for years to come.

Sincerely,

Lynda Less
Vice President, Customer Service

ll/zr

Project Status Letters

Sample Letters 7.38 through 7.41 all involve questions of project status.

Sample Letter 7.38 requests a response to a project proposal. It is a brief letter written as a follow-up to a phone conversation. The letter writer gives the reader a cutoff date by which she would like to have a response and explains why time is of the essence.

Sample Letter 7.39 was written to inform a client about the status of services provided to the client. The letter writer clearly details all of the work she has done for the client and asks the client to indicate whether or not he is pleased with the results.

Sample Letter 7.40 informs a client about the status of contracts that were to be sent him. Because the letter writer is taking longer than she thought she would have to in ironing out the details of the contracts, she sent this letter to assure the client the matter is under control.

In Sample Letter 7.41, the letter writer quickly lists some of the work done to date on the client's account, and asks for a reaction to the work done.

Sample Letter 7.38.　Letter asking for response to project proposal.

[date]

Ms. Nancy Kenworthy
56 Yount Street
Berkeley, CA 90021

Dear Ms. Kenworthy:

It was good to speak with you earlier today. Sheila Morlan and I are eager to go forward with the screenplay of *The Man Who Lived in the Adirondacks*. Therefore, I must ask that I hear from you within the next three weeks—no later than Monday, November 24—about any possible revisions to the agreements I sent you. If we have not heard from you by then, I would like all of Sheila's materials returned to me so that we can pursue our own efforts.

Nancy, considering the amount of time that has passed on this project, I'm sure that you understand our concern. I look forward to hearing from you and getting the agreements signed very soon.

Best regards,

Pamela Yale

py/ph

cc: Sheila Morlan

Sample Letter 7.39.   Letter to client about status of project—services rendered to date.

[date]

Mr. George Dendins
Dendrinos Fish House
1966 Jim Lewis Drive
Boonton, NJ 07005

Dear Mr. Dendins:

I spoke with Alan Prestige, a freelance writer for *The Daily Mail*, and sent him the materials he needed to do a review. He planned to eat at Dendrinos Fish House last night.

Let me tell you about the other things I did for Dendrinos Fish House in July. I have, on a number of occasions, spoken to Regina Wheaton, food critic for *The Blaze*, about your expansion plans. Simon Grimes interviewed Deena Dendrinos for the October issue of *Boonton* magazine. Although the restaurant may not be mentioned in that story, this is a good way to introduce Simon to Dendrinos. He works in the features department, which is responsible for the annual "Best and Worst" listings. The other day I spoke with Marvin Allens about a story he's doing for *The Daily Mail* in September. It's a guide to restaurants in the Boonton area. Dendrinos will be included.

I'll keep you posted on my progress with all of these people.

You mentioned the menu award Dendrinos received. I would be glad to send out a release with accompanying sample menus to the local press and national trades. Information must be timely and salient to even stand a chance of getting publicity. Let me know the details as soon as possible.

I know you were disappointed about not being anointed as Boonton's best fish house in July's *Boonton* magazine. I was too. All I can say is: I know you'll be around for a long time to come. Your day will come; I'm sure.

I believe that covers the work we've done to date. I think my time was well spent. Quite a bit was accomplished in this past month. The results of it all will come later.

Let me know if you are pleased with our work so far. I look forward to hearing from you.

Sincerely yours,

Mary Nilthonson
Account Executive

mn/js

Sample Letter 7.40. Letter to client about status of project—
pending contracts.

[date]

Mr. James Louis
312 Lathrop Avenue
Boonton, NJ 07005

Dear Mr. Louis:

I just wanted to let you know that the changes I am requesting in your new contract with Doris Corporation are more extensive than I had expected, and that it will take a bit longer than I predicted to get them down to you for your signing. I'm finishing up negotiations with Zoe North now, though, so it shouldn't be too much longer.

Thanks for your patience.

Best regards,

Beverly J. Carlson

bjc/ejc

Sample Letter 7.41. Letter about status of project, including samples of work to date.

[date]

Mr. Zack Romance
Romance & Romance, CPAs
54 Quickness Drive
Encino, WA 98045

Dear Mr. Romance:

We're off to a good start. I've enclosed some of the things we've been working on. Please look them over and give us your feedback. Here's what's enclosed:

- Samples of sales materials, including rough sketches for brochures and collateral material
- Marketing program memorandum—a draft of a memo that will come from you and Jim about marketing plans for the company and the employees' role
- AICPA release—for your approval, then for release to the local and trade press
- Biographical information sheet—for employees to fill out to aid our internal publicity program

I met with Alice Glipstein from your office this morning. I am assigning her the duties you and I had previously discussed, such as preparing your information package and serving as a marketing/publicity liaison.

I look forward to hearing your reaction to the status of our work so far.

Sincerely yours,

Melvin Nierce

mn/js

encs.

Product-Handling Letter

Sample Letter 7.42 was written to a customer informing him of proper handling procedures for a company product. The letter writer clearly states the purpose of the letter, instructs the reader that the information on handling is enclosed, and asks that it be passed on to the appropriate person within the firm.

Sample Letter 7.42.   Letter giving handling procedures for product.

[date]

Mr. Loren Ray, Director
Humana, Humana & Kramden
45 Eufala Drive
Huntington, MA 02245

Dear Mr. Ray:

Enclosed is a material safety data sheet for propane gas that we supply to all of our customers. This information is part of our program to provide you with the health, safety, and environmental protection information that is necessary for the safe handling of propane.

Please direct this information to the person in your firm responsible for health and safety matters as well as to all employees handling propane. If additional material safety data sheets are required, or if you have any questions about the safe handling of our product, please call me at 323-555-7654.

Thank you very much for your business.

Sincerely,

O. C. Dillard
Operations Engineer

ocd/rgj

Enclosure

Letters Announcing Personnel Changes

When personnel changes will directly affect a working business relationship, clear communication in advance of the change goes a long way toward maintaining a smooth transition. Sample Letter 7.43 is from a supervisor to a client. It is direct, encouraging, and brief, and introduces not only the new account representative but also the idea that the new rep will write to introduce himself.

Sample Letter 7.43. Letter introducing a new account representative (from supervisor).

[date]

Lucas Evans, President
Gym-Tastic Exercise
1500 Venice Boulevard
Laguna, CA 30043

Dear Mr. Evans:

As you know, your current account representative, Olga Kolesnikov, has decided to leave us here at Top Flyte to pursue her dream of working at the circus. As of July 1, the representative handling Gym-Tastic Exercise's account will be Ellis Mannon.

Mr. Mannon has been with Top Flyte for six years, and served as Olga's mentor when she joined us. I know that you were pleased with her support and attention to detail; I am sure that you will be equally satisfied with Mr. Mannon's oversight of Gym-Tastic's account.

Mr. Mannon will be writing to you personally to introduce himself. Rest assured that the transition between account managers will be seamless. You can expect the same high level of care and dedication from him that you got from Olga.

Very truly yours,

Christopher P. Dugan
Vice-President of Sales

CPD/bjc

Sample Letter 7.44 is a follow-up from the supervisor's letter of introduction. The fact that Mr. Mannon followed up on Mr. Dugan's letter is itself a reassuring gesture to the potentially anxious client. The tone of the letter is confident and enthusiastic: the writer's goal is to present himself as competent and supportive. While it's appropriate for the writer to include some details about his background and qualifications, it's not necessary to reproduce a complete résumé in this context.

Sample Letter 7.44. Letter introducing a new account representative (from new representative).

[date]

Lucas Evans, President
Gym-Tastic Exercise
1500 Venice Boulevard
Laguna, CA 90043

Dear Mr. Evans:

My supervisor, Chris Dugan, recently wrote to inform you that I will be managing Gym-Tastic Exercise's account as of July 1, 20X8. I am eager to begin working with Gym-Tastic, and have already held extensive debriefings with Olga Kolesnikov, your current account representative, to learn the ins and outs of your company in order to support you as fully as possible. Although I know you enjoyed an excellent working relationship with Olga, I am confident that I can provide a comparable level of support.

I have extensive experience in the exercise industry, working my way up from floor trainer at the Dumbbell's chain of gyms in Stockton, California, to Director of Marketing and Research for Bounceback Latex Industries. In addition to a B.A. in Exercise Physiology from U.C.L.A., I earned my M.B.A. from Stanford with a focus on Small Business Management. My experiences on the gym floor and in the classroom have provided me with both a practical and a theoretical understanding of your industry.

After working at Bounceback for seven years, I was hired by Top Flyte in 20X2. I left Bounceback, where I held an executive position, for Top Flyte, where I have been in Sales for the last six years, because Top Flyte affords me the opportunity to work with small businesses like yours more directly. Olga has told me great things about you and your company, and I know that we will work well together to meet Gym-Tastic's needs.

I will call you this week in order to set up a meeting to review your company's existing account, your goals for Gym-Tastic, and my thoughts on how I can best help you achieve your vision. If you have any questions or concerns in the meantime, please give me a call at (310) 555-1331.

Sincerely,

Ellis Mannon
Account Representative

Subscription Response Letters

Sample Letters 7.45 through 7.49 were written in response to subscriber inquiries. Whether the letter writer is addressing a complaint or a positive inquiry, the writer treats each subscriber with courtesy, providing all of them with the information they need.

Sample Letter 7.45 was written to respond to a subscriber who wanted to know why a renewal notice was sent out so early in his subscription period. The letter writer acknowledges the question and clearly spells out the publication's policy on renewal notices.

In Sample Letter 7.46, a subscriber is offered either a refund or an extension to make up for an overpayment.

Sample Letter 7.47 was written to a customer to respond to an inquiry about back-issue sales. The letter writer clearly spells out the pricing structure for back issues and informs the reader that some issues will be facsimile copies, not originals. By explaining this to the reader, she diminishes the chances of a disappointed customer.

Sample Letter 7.48 was written in response to a subscriber inquiry about why a refund for a cancelled subscription has taken so long to be sent. The letter writer explains the holdup, apologizes for the delay, and assures the reader he will expedite the refund.

Sample Letter 7.45. Letter responding to question about subscription renewal notice.

[date]

Mr. John T. Larry
65 York Place
Plattsburgh, PA 15205

Dear Mr. Larry:

Thank you for your recent note about your renewal notice. The reason you received a renewal notice well before your expiration date is simple economics. Anyone in the subscription business learns two facts about renewals very quickly. First, the average subscriber needs several renewal notices before he or she actually resubscribes.

Second, renewal notices sent prior to the expiration of the current subscription are far more effective than those sent after expiration.

Putting these facts together results in a series of renewal notices beginning well before expiration to allow sufficient time between notices.

If you do not wish to renew in advance, you may wait until closer to your expiration. We will continue to send you notices.

Thank you for your interest in *Business Life*. We look forward to continuing to serve you.

Best regards,

Harriet Tibbits
Publisher

ht:js

Sample Letter 7.46. Letter notifying subscribers of a price decrease.

[date]

Mr. John R. Reynolds
67 Truscott Lane
Hudson, NJ 07010

Dear Mr. Reynolds:

Originally, we offered Parriston Company customers like you a subscription to *The Review* for $87 a year. We have now reduced that price to $75 per year. Therefore, we would like to offer you the opportunity to extend your subscription for an additional 6 months—6 extra issues at no charge.

If you prefer, we will send you a refund check for $12. Simply check off the appropriate box on the enclosed questionnaire and mail it back to us in the enclosed postage-paid envelope.

Thank you for your interest in *The Review*. We look forward to continuing to serve you.

Yours truly,

Glenda Allen
Publisher

ga/js

encls.

Sample Letter 7.47.   Letter responding to question about back issues.

[date]

Mr. Larry T. Lester
67 Farway Road
Bolovin, MS 39194

Dear Mr. Lester:

Thank you for your letter inquiring about back issues of *The Armchair Reader's Review*. We have a limited supply of back issues. The cost of back issues is $7.00 per copy. With any order that exceeds 9 copies, this price is reduced to $6.50 per copy.

If we have the issue in stock, we will send you the actual printed issue. We will mail facsimile copies of the issues, however, if we are out of stock. The same price will be charged for these copies. We want people to understand our back-issue policy, since some people would rather not receive a facsimile.

We have enclosed a postage-paid envelope for your convenience in mailing your check. We've also enclosed an index to help you decide which back issues you'd like to receive. We regret that we cannot bill you for any back issues. Therefore, please be sure to include payment.

We look forward to serving you.

Best regards,

Yvette Nelson
Publisher

yn/js

encs.

Sample Letter 7.48.   Letter written in response to cancellation and refund query.

[date]

Ms. Letitia T. Ryan
56 Tyscott Road
Tucker, NH 03035

Dear Ms. Ryan:

We have sent your request for cancellation of your subscription to *The Review* to our subscription service department and have requested your refund from our accounting department. Both requests were forwarded on April 15, 20X6. Upon checking with our accounting department, however, we have found that your refund check is just now being processed.

Please accept our apologies. As soon as we receive your check from the accounting department, we will immediately forward it to you.

Sincerely,

John Nelson
Associate Publisher

JN:js

Sample Letter 7.49 was written to respond to a subscriber who claimed that he had never ordered the publication and so was cancelling his subscription. The letter writer expresses his concern over the reader's claim. He explains that a copy of the order card with the reader's signature is enclosed, and offers this as the reason the subscription was sent. The letter writer then offers to continue sending issues to the subscriber with no obligation until the first invoice, at which time the subscriber can cancel the subscription.

Sample Letter 7.49. Letter written as a follow-up to subscriber who cancelled saying he never ordered subscription.

[date]

Mr. Jack T. Wags
65 Yucaman Place, Apt. 5A
Boonton, NJ 07005

Dear Mr. Wags:

You recently returned an invoice for a year's subscription to *Home Life* marked "cancel." The reason given for the cancellation was that you had never subscribed.

I am writing you because I am concerned about our reputation. We are very proud of our long history of service to subscribers and do not want any misunderstanding to damage our standing with you. As you can see from the enclosed order card we received from you, we did have reason to believe you ordered a subscription. We are not in the practice of billing people for subscriptions without an order. Not only would that be ethically and legally wrong, it also would not make economic sense.

As a result, I have not cancelled your subscription. I will continue to send you copies of *Home Life*. If you still wish to cancel because you don't like the publication, you are under no obligation to pay for these copies. They are yours to keep. I am sending them so that if you do wish to continue your subscription, you won't miss any issues.

On the enclosed postage-paid card are spaces to check whether you would like to continue your subscription or still cancel it. Please check the appropriate space and return this card to me.

Thank you for considering *Home Life*.

Sincerely,

Alan Tempor
Publisher

AT:JS

Encl.

Letters to Stockholders

Sample Letters 7.50 through 7.61 were all written to stockholders or prospective stockholders. Sample Letter 7.50 was written to a prospective investor in the letter writer's company. He clearly states why he is writing and details just enough specifics on the company to get her to read the materials he's enclosed and to set up a meeting to talk about investing.

In Sample Letter 7.51 the writer acknowledges a new shareholder, to whom he is sending an annual report.

Sample Letter 7.52 was written to accompany a proxy statement. The letter writer explains the issues that will be covered at the company's annual meeting and urges the reader to complete and send in the proxy whether or not she attends the meeting.

Sample Letter 7.53 was written to announce an annual meeting to shareholders and to request the completion and return of the enclosed proxy statement. Sample Letter 7.54 was written as a follow-up to Sample Letter 7.53 to remind the shareholder to send in her proxy statement. In Sample Letter 7.55, the letter writer acknowledges receipt of the shareholder's proxy statement.

Sample Letter 7.56, in which the writer invites stockholders to the annual meeting, is a variation of the letter featured in Sample Letter 7.52.

Sample Letter 7.57 was written as a letter to accompany an annual report. The letter writer clearly explains that the annual report is enclosed, writes enthusiastically of the company, and encourages the reader to review the annual report and call the company with any questions. Sample Letter 7.58 is a shorter version of a cover letter for an annual report. It states simply that the annual report is enclosed, makes a brief positive remark about the company's status, and encourages the reader to follow up if he or she has questions.

Sample Letter 7.59 was written to accompany a balance sheet sent to stockholders. The letter clearly states what the balance sheet features and what it does not feature.

Sample Letter 7.60 was written to accompany an offering memorandum for stock. The letter writer clearly explains that she is enclosing the requested materials and tells the reader which forms to fill out and send back.

Sample Letter 7.61 is a letter of confidentiality sent to a client who is interested in acquiring a company. The letter clearly details its intent and instructs the reader on the appropriate procedure to take in completing the confidentiality agreement.

Sample Letter 7.50.   Letter to prospective investor.

[date]

Ms. Yuuki Long
56 Forester Place
Miami, MI 48024

Dear Ms. Long:

I am president of Boonton Bagel Bakeries. David Palay suggested I get in touch with you about a unique opportunity to invest in our company.

We are a closely held private company. Our chief business is supplying bagels to restaurants and hotels throughout the Midwest. The demand for our product over the past five years has been tremendous. It continues to grow rapidly, which has resulted in a need for us to expand our bakery operations. We are looking for investors who can help us finance the facility expansion we need to meet demand.

My partner, Edmund Kohlberg, and I founded Boonton Bagel Bakeries five years ago. The company was built on the idea of providing the best bagel in the region at the best possible price. We've focused mostly on wholesale markets and have been very successful by providing customers with quality goods and reliable deliveries. I have enclosed a partial list of the various restaurants and hotels with whom we do business.

The demand for our bagels has grown, which means we either have to expand our bakeries or turn down orders. We decided that the most profitable way to expand our bakeries is to find investors. In addition to our customer list, I have enclosed our audited financial statements for the past five years as well as a copy of our business plan, which includes a profile of our history, operations plan, and key management.

After you've had a chance to review the materials, I'd enjoy meeting with you to talk about the specifics of any investment you might be interested in making in Boonton Bagel Bakeries. Please give me a call to set up a meeting at your earliest convenience.

Sincerely,

Frank Grimes
President and Cofounder

Encs.

Sample Letter 7.51. Letter acknowledging new shareholder.

[date]

Mr. Lester Louis
67 Cornell Boulevard
Alfred, ND 58022

Dear Mr. Louis:

I'd like to welcome you as a new shareholder in Authentic Bagels Company. As president and CEO, I am committed to the growth of the company, which will ensure that your investment in us is profitable.

I encourage you to read the enclosed annual report. Our annual shareholders' meeting is held every November 1, and I hope you will attend so we might have the opportunity to meet in person.

If you have any questions, please do not hesitate to call on me. I or a member of my staff will see to it that your questions are answered promptly and completely. Thank you for investing in Authentic Bagels Company.

Sincerely,

Harold T. Almond
President and CEO

Enc.

Sample Letter 7.52.   Letter accompanying proxy for annual meeting of stockholders.

[date]

Ms. Lauren J. Palle
54 Lincoln Drive
Grand Forks, ND 58021

Subject: Notice of Annual Meeting

Dear Ms. Palle:

The annual meeting of stockholders of Dover Company will be held at Boonton Bandwagon Hall, 324 Lathrop Avenue, Boonton, New Jersey, on Wednesday, April 27, 20X8, at 11:00 A.M. Stockholders will consider and act on the following matters:

1. Determination of the number of directors and election of directors for the ensuing year
2. Ratification of the selection of Rosenblatt, Talbnesor & Company as auditors of Dover Company for the current year
3. Any other matter that may properly come before the meeting or adjournment

Whether or not you attend in person, it would be appreciated if you would fill in and sign the enclosed proxy and return it promptly in the enclosed envelope. If you attend the meeting, you may, of course, vote your shares even though you have sent in your proxy.

Sincerely,

Mel Posner, Clerk

mp/js

Enclosure

Sample Letter 7.53. Letter announcing annual meeting to shareholders and requesting proxy statement.

[date]

Ms. Annmarie Long
45 Savin Hill Terrace
Grampian, CA 90045

Dear Ms. Long:

The board of directors, management, and I invite you and our other shareholders to attend the annual shareholders' meeting of Authentic Bagels Company at 8:30 A.M. on Thursday, November 1, 20X5, in the second-floor auditorium at Authentic Bagels Company's main building on 456 Bialy Road in Comstock, California.

I have enclosed an agenda for the meeting. Please note that we have many important issues to cover. These issues are explained in detail on the proxy statement, which is also enclosed.

I encourage you to try to attend the meeting. If you can't attend, please return a completed and signed proxy so it can be voted as you wish.

Sincerely,

Harold T. Almond
President and CEO

Encs.

Sample Letter 7.54. Letter reminding shareholder to send in proxy statement.

[date]

Ms. Annmarie Long
45 Savin Hill Terrace
Grampian, CA 90045

Dear Ms. Long:

Please remember to complete, sign, and return the proxy statement I've enclosed by October 25, 20X5. The annual meeting of Authentic Bagels Company will be held on November 1. We will need to have a vote or proxy from at least half our shareholders with voting rights to take any action.

We encourage you to attend the annual meeting in person. If you can't, however, would you please complete, sign, and return your proxy? You'll find another copy of the proxy statement enclosed in case you've misplaced the one we sent you on September 24, 20X5.

Thank you for your continued support of Authentic Bagels Company.

Sincerely,

Harold T. Almond
President and CEO

Enc.

Sample Letter 7.55. Acknowledgment of receipt of proxy statement.

[date]

Ms. Annmarie Long
45 Savin Hill Terrace
Grampian, CA 90045

Dear Ms. Long:

Today we received your completed and signed proxy statement, which we will use to vote your shares at the November 1 annual shareholders' meeting of the Authentic Bagels Company. Thank you for taking the time to return the proxy to us and for your continued interest in and support of the company and its future.

Sincerely,

Harold T. Almond
President and CEO

Sample Letter 7.56. Letter inviting stockholders to annual meeting.

[date]

Mr. Alan Palay
45 Twilite Road
Simmons, AL 35056

Dear Mr. Palay:

You are cordially invited to attend the 20X8 annual meeting of stockholders of Parris Company on Thursday, April 28, 20X8, at 11:00 A.M. at Boonton Bandwagon Hall, 324 Lathrop Avenue, Boonton, New Jersey.

The formal business to be considered and acted upon by stockholders at this meeting is the election of directors and the ratification of the selection of the company's certified public accountants. These matters are described in detail in the accompanying Notice of Annual Meeting and Proxy Statement. We will also use this opportunity to report to you on Parris's 20X7 performance and outlook for the future.

It is important that your shares be represented whether or not you are able to be there in person. I urge you, therefore, to register your vote now by completing, signing, and returning the enclosed proxy card promptly.

All stockholders will receive a report of the meeting in the mail.

Sincerely,

Mary Nachez, President

mn/js

Enclosures

Sample Letter 7.57.   Letter accompanying annual report.

[date]

Mr. Ryan D. Kenney
45 Trander Road
Elipses, NJ 07056

Dear Mr. Kenney:

Enclosed is the MR. WONDERFUL Public Partnerships' Annual Report for 20X4. It contains important information about your investment.

I am very proud of the enclosed report because it clearly demonstrates that the limited partnerships formed by MR. WONDERFUL are producing and performing as anticipated.

We live in an economic environment that is becoming increasingly complex due in part to tax reform, deficits, and globalization of financial markets. It is, therefore, very gratifying to me to see the positive results of a simple investment concept: the free and clear ownership of commercial real estate properties producing monthly spendable income. For your information, we have reproduced a table on the back of this letter that summarizes the success of these public programs.

As our financial world becomes more complicated, the necessity of sound financial planning increases. I urge you to update your financial plan and review your long-range goals with your professional financial planner.

If you or your financial planner have any questions or need further information on the enclosed annual report or our continued investment programs, please feel free to call our investor/broker relations staff at the toll-free numbers listed below.

Yours truly,

B. R. Roenshoot
President

brr/mnn

Enclosures

Sample Letter 7.58.   Short cover letter to annual report.

[date]

Mr. Lawrence D. Braden
Parks, Bryans, Alans & Sims
67 Gotshald Drive
Arcade, ME 04056

Dear Larry:

You might find Arris Company's 20X7 annual report interesting. With a lot of hard work and good luck, the company had an excellent year. We are looking forward to continued progress.

Please give me a call if you have any comments.

Sincerely,

Maury Noblesse
President

mn/js

Enclosure

Sample Letter 7.59.   Letter to stockholders accompanying balance sheet.

[date]

Mr. Paul W. Hudson
LKTY, Inc.
991 Hampton Road
Newfork, NH 03033

ARRIS COMPANY ANNUAL BALANCE SHEET

Mr. Hudson, we have compiled the accompanying balance sheet of Arris Company as of December 31, 20X4, and the related statements of income and expense and changes in financial position for the year then ended in accordance with the standards established by the American Institute of Certified Public Accountants.

A compilation is limited to presenting in the form of financial statements information that is the representation of management. We have not audited or reviewed the accompanying financial statements and, accordingly, do not express an opinion or any other form of assurance on them.

At management's election, these financial statements were prepared for their internal use and therefore do not necessarily include all of the disclosures required by generally accepted accounting principles. If the omitted disclosures were included in the financial statements, they might influence the user's conclusions about the company's financial position, results of operations, and changes in financial position. Accordingly, these financial statements are not designed for those who are not informed about such matters.

SIMON NIELSON, C.P.A.

sn/js

Enclosures

Sample Letter 7.60.   Letter offering memorandum for stock.

[date]

Mr. Thomas Alexander
Franroad and Libersmidt Corp.
45 Hope Park
Trintonite, NJ 07085

Dear Mr. Alexander:

I am enclosing the two confidentiality letters and a confidential memorandum on Fleitschmidt & Co. that you requested in our telephone conversation today. As I explained to you, the management of Fleitschmidt has recently become concerned about the level of stock held by certain investors. Therefore, management is pursuing a course that allows it the opportunity to control who its partner may be.

The management team at Fleitschmidt has positioned the company in the microcomputer and peripherals market. We have a strategy for the future that we would like to implement and are selectively approaching a few companies that we feel may help us enhance and accelerate that strategy.

Please sign and return one of the confidentiality letters. We would then like your thoughts on this opportunity after you have had a chance to review the memorandum. Since time is an issue, I look forward to hearing from you soon.

Best regards,

Rowena Guitterez
Vice President

rg/ms

Enclosure

Sample Letter 7.61.   Letter of confidentiality.

[date]

Mr. Thomas Alexander
Franroad and Libersmidt Corp.
45 Hope Park
Trintonite, NJ 07085

CONFIDENTIALITY AGREEMENT

Mr. Alexander, in connection with your possible interest in acquiring Fleitschmidt & Co., Nilges Investment Bankers, Inc., and Fleitschmidt will be furnishing you with certain materials that contain information about Fleitschmidt that is either nonpublic, confidential, or proprietary in nature. Such information, in whole or in part, together with analyses, compilations, studies, or other documents prepared by Fleitschmidt or Nilges Investment Bankers, to the extent such analyses, compilations, studies, or documents contain or otherwise reflect or are generated from such information, is hereinafter referred to as the "Information," and the existence of any negotiations or discussions between us will also be considered "Information." In consideration of furnishing you with the Information, you agree with Nilges Investment Bankers and Fleitschmidt that:

1.   The Information will be kept confidential and will not, without prior written consent of Fleitschmidt, be disclosed by you, your agents, or your employees, in any manner whatsoever, in whole or in part, and will not be used by you, your agents, or your employees, other than in connection with the transaction described above. Moreover, you agree to transmit the Information for the purpose of evaluating your possible

interest in acquiring Fleitschmidt to those who are informed by you of the confidential nature of the Information, and you will cause such agents and employees to comply with the terms and conditions of this Agreement. In any event, you will be responsible for any breach of this Agreement by your agents or employees.

2.   The Information, including analyses, compilations, studies, or other documents prepared by you, your agents, or your employees, will be held by you and kept confidential and subject to the terms of this Agreement, or destroyed.

3.   In the event that you or anyone to whom you transmit the Information pursuant to this Agreement becomes legally compelled to disclose any of the Information, you will provide Fleitschmidt with prompt notice so that Fleitschmidt may seek a protective order or other appropriate remedy and/or waive compliance with the provisions of this Agreement. In the event that such protective order or other remedy is not obtained, or if Fleitschmidt waives compliance with the provisions of this Agreement, you will furnish only that portion of the Information that is legally required and in so doing you will not be in violation of this Agreement.

The foregoing restrictions do not apply to Information that is or becomes part of the public domain without your fault.

In accepting the Information, you are aware of the importance of maintaining security surrounding all discussions in order to preclude the possibility of premature disclosure to third parties, including Fleitschmidt's customers.

If the above terms are in accordance with your understanding of our agreement, please sign the enclosed copy of this letter and return the copy to us.

ROWENA GUITTEREZ
VICE PRESIDENT

rg/ms

Enclosure

Accepted by: _____
This_____ day of, _____ [year]
By: _____

Letter Dealing with Unreasonable Customer

When dealing with unreasonable customers, cordial telephone conversations are often the first line of defense. However, occasionally two parties simply cannot work things out in person and it becomes necessary to deny a request formally. Sample Letter 7.62 is a good example of an unreasonable request. The writer alludes to specific instances of the past relationship and the recipient's prior unreasonableness, all while maintaining a cordial tone.

Sample Letter 7.62. Letter denying an unreasonable customer request.

[date]

Ms. Millicent Catellier
Pets-a-Million
13 Nueva Buena Avenue
Harrison, NJ 07098

Dear Ms. Catellier:

I regret to inform you that we will be unable to supply you with the eleven additional flavors of dog biscuit that Pets-a-Million has requested. We have re-engineered our bakeries twice already to accommodate your desire for Pets-a-Million to offer "Prosciutto," "Caramel Glaze," and "Eggs Benedict" flavored dog biscuits; the new flavors of "Monkfish," "Beurre Blanc," and "Lingonberry" are, we feel, extremely esoteric and unnecessary flavors for dogs. The market relevance of these gourmet biscuits is minimal and not cost effective for our company.

While we fervently desire to continue supporting your chain of pet stores in their mission to provide central New Jersey's pet owners with savory and unique comestibles for their canine companions, we cannot meet your company's request in this instance. If you have further questions about our decision or its effect on our business relationship, please don't hesitate to call me at my extension, listed above on the letterhead.

Sincerely,

Edgerrin Coleperson
Customer Service Representative

CHAPTER 8

Credit and collection letters

"Neither a borrower nor a lender be" might have been words Polonius could live by in Hamlet's Denmark, but such philosophy simply doesn't work in today's society. In the United States, credit has become a standard way of doing business. We buy our homes and cars on credit, start businesses on credit, stock our stores on credit, and so on. In the world of credit, the lender has to be particularly careful about the borrower's ability to pay back funds.

The letters in this chapter arm the lender with a variety of credit and collection letters that can be used to ensure that a solid relationship is built with a borrower. Should that relationship falter, the letters are here to help the lender recoup the money that was lent. There are letters here that can also be used to help any businessperson set up credit arrangements with a company with which it does business.

The letters in this chapter will not help a businessperson avoid being a borrower or lender. But they just may make the roles a little bit easier to handle.

Many companies will continue to handle credit and collection issues through formal correspondence. While most of the letters in this chapter would be sent in letter form, they could easily be adapted to emails or as attachments to emails. For those letters in this chapter that can be adapted to emails, it's simple enough to copy the text of the sample letter into the text of your email.

Letter Requesting Commercial Credit

Sample Letter 8.1 was written to a company with which the letter writer wanted to establish a business relationship. Fully aware that he will have to set up credit arrangements with the firm, he requests that the reader send him the forms that he will need to complete to establish commercial credit.

Sample Letter 8.1. Letter requesting commercial credit.

[date]

Mr. Renatto Kim
Kim Metal Products, Inc.
P.O. Box 3456
Tuscany, WV 26039

Dear Mr. Kim:

After an extensive market survey, we have determined that your company's rolled steel products best meet manufacturing specifications required by our automobile factory. But before we begin placing orders—which we anticipate will occur on a quarterly basis—I am writing to inquire about your terms for granting commercial credit.

Since there is probably specific information that you require before establishing a credit account, perhaps it makes the most sense for you to send me the forms we should fill out.

I look forward to hearing from you, and to establishing a credit relationship with your company.

Sincerely,

Lee I. Larroquette
Purchasing Manager

LIL:wlg

Credit Information Letters

Sample Letters 8.2 and 8.3 both involve credit information. The letter writer of Sample Letter 8.2 is writing to thank a customer for his order and to request that he fill out some standard credit information forms. The letter is courteous, brief, and clearly written.

Sample Letter 8.3 was written to send credit information that was requested. It could be sent as a response to Sample Letter 8.2. The letter writer wastes little space. He simply explains that he is enclosing the necessary materials.

Sample Letter 8.2. Letter requesting credit information.

[date]

Mr. Morton P. Stovak
VA Hospital
177 Varoom Street
Rockaway, NJ 07056

Dear Mr. Stovak:

Thank you for your recent order of prosthetic devices from Snug Fit Products, Inc. I note that this is the first order you have placed with our company, so let me take this opportunity to express our gratitude as well as to pledge our every effort to serve you in the future.

Before we can ship your order, however, there is some standard credit information we need. I have enclosed three forms that I would like you to complete. Once we have these completed forms, we can set up your credit account and expedite your order with the least possible delay.

Sincerely,

Carmine D'Amato

cd/wg

encls.

Sample Letter 8.3. Letter sending credit information.

[date]

Mr. J. Lee Jumbuck
Matilda Corporation
12 Swagman's Way
Sydney, HI 96745

Dear Mr. Jumbuck:

Enclosed in triplicate is the credit information that you requested. I trust that this data will satisfy any concerns you may have about our creditworthiness, and that it will lead to the establishment of a credit account for our organization.

Cordially,

Gajan Matoussamy

gm/wg

encs.

Letters Announcing Credit Policy Change

Sample Letter 8.4 was written to announce a credit policy change. The letter writer clearly announces his letter's purpose in the opening paragraph and offers a reason for the change in credit policy. He goes on to explain the specific changes and expresses appreciation to the reader for his continued support.

Sample Letter 8.4.   Letter notifying customer of credit policy change.

[date]

Mr. Hiram T. Louis
Louis Construction Company
43 Treadway Drive
P.O. Box 4536
Newport, CA 90065

Dear Mr. Louis:

After many years of service to you, we are forced to change our credit terms effective February 26. Because of the increase in the cost of capital, changes in manufacturers' terms, and the general cost of doing business, I'm afraid we have no choice.

Our new terms are: 2% discount if paid within 10 days from date of invoice and net 30 days from date of invoice. The terms for all contracts are net 30 days from date of invoice, no retainage. A late finance charge of 2% (minimum charge $1.00) per month will be assessed on that portion of any account beyond 30 days. This is an annual percentage rate of 24%.

We appreciate your past patronage and trust you will understand and support our decision. We look forward to continuing to satisfy your building material needs for many years to come.

Sincerely,

BIG-TIME BUILDING SUPPLY

Dean Wheton
Credit Manager

dw/hs

Sample Letter 8.5 was written to a customer not specifically to announce a credit policy change, but rather to gently inform him that the company is going to enforce its current credit policy. The letter writer takes the time to explain why it's important for the customer to shorten the length of time he takes to pay his bills.

Sample Letter 8.5. Letter to valued customer who is a slow payer.

[date]

Mr. Stanley Orinski
Accounts Payable Department
Fortune Toe Spindle Works, Inc.
43 Rye Place
Sideline, NE 68098

Dear Stanley:

In an effort to make our business as efficient as possible, Dave Matthews, our chief financial officer, has been reviewing all of our books, including our customers' payment histories. Dave asked that I write you this letter because he noted that Fortune Toe Spindle Works' bills are typically paid in 90 days. I've been asked to see if we might be able to convince you to go to a payment schedule of 30 days, maybe slipping to 45 days when you need to.

As you can probably guess, not having the money owed us within a month makes it difficult for us to operate the business and pay our own bills on time. In addition to having to pay our vendors in 30 to 45 days, we need to be current with overhead costs and salaries. The amount you owe us that's 45 or more days past due is $325,000. In another two weeks, it will jump to $375,000. While our financial strength allows us to cover for receivables due to us, because you are one of our biggest customers the size of the outstanding receivables concerns Dave Matthews.

We really value our relationship with Fortune Toe Spindle Works and know that we can continue to flourish in the future. I trust that you'll find Dave's request for faster payments reasonable. Give me a call if you've got a question or need any clarification.

Sincerely,

Ron Paulus
Regional Sales Manager

Returned-Check Letters

Sample Letters 8.6 through 8.8 were written as a result of returned checks. Sample Letter 8.6 was written from the debtor to the creditor informing him that his check had been returned. After telling the creditor this fact, the letter writer apologizes, offers to reimburse the creditor for any penalty charges, and assures the creditor this will not happen again.

Sample Letter 8.7 was written to a debtor about a returned check. The letter writer states the facts in the first paragraph and explains what action he would like the debtor to take to resolve the problem.

Sample Letter 8.8 was written to address a returned check where the customer has an excellent credit history with the writer. The tone of the letter is comforting and helpful.

Sample Letter 8.6. Letter to creditor about returned check.

[date]

R. R. Shirley
Fly-By-Night Air Express
7201 Parisite Boulevard
Mesa, AZ 85034

NOTIFICATION OF RETURNED CHECK

Mr. Shirley, we were just notified that the check we made out to you on March 15 (check number 2237 for $14,675) was returned by our bank for insufficient funds.

We are terribly sorry for the inconvenience this has caused you, and would like to reimburse you for any penalties you have incurred because of the returned check. We have subsequently made a deposit to our account sufficient to cover this draft, so please instruct your bank to redeposit the check.

Please be assured this will never happen again.

JASPER T. JONES
CONTROLLER

JTJ:wlg

Sample Letter 8.7.　Letter notifying customer about returned check.

[date]

Ms. Joan B. Yennek
56 Malden Place
Medford, WY 82045

Dear Ms. Yennek:

New Bank of Medford has returned your check #454 made out to Kemper Office Supplies, Ltd., for $565 to us. The check was stamped "NSF," indicating insufficient funds.

We have enclosed a postage-paid return envelope in which you can send us a certified check, money order, or cashier's check for the $565. We ask that you do this as soon as you receive this letter.

If the lack of funds resulted from a mix-up at the bank, we encourage you to clear up this matter. If you are having some financial difficulty in meeting your monthly debt obligations, please call us to let us know. We'd like to work with you to come up with a solution. In either case, it's crucial that you call or write us immediately so that you can maintain your good credit standing.

Sincerely,

Alan T. Kicksad
Credit Manager

atk:jls

enc.

Sample Letter 8.8. Letter to customer indicating insufficient funds.

[date]

Ms. Judy Evans
The Sewing Station, Inc.
154 Lombard Avenue
Akron, OH 43099

Dear Ms. Evans:

We have received your check (#681) in the amount of $9,875.00 for our invoice #539-K-146. Thank you for your very quick payment.

Unfortunately, our bank has notified us regarding an overdraft in your account, and we are unable to accept your payment. Because your account is in such good standing, we have decided not to charge you for the error.

Please contact your financial manager as soon as possible. I am sure that this matter can be corrected. Don't hesitate to contact me if you have any questions.

Thank you,

Even Chadbourne
CCA Stationary Limited
Account Manager

Credit Reference Letters

Sample Letters 8.9 through 8.11 were written to get credit information from references. Sample Letters 8.9 and 8.10 clearly ask for the information they need, providing blank spaces for the recipient to fill in.

Sample Letter 8.9.   Letter sent to credit reference.

[date]

Ms. Beverly J. Coleman
Pink Flamingo Trading Co., Inc.
88 Latin Academy Road
Fenway, MA 02132

Subject: Credit Reference for Amlemper, Inc.

Dear Ms. Coleman:

Ambrose L. Kemper, president of Amlemper, Inc., has given us your company's name as a credit reference. Mr. Kemper has requested credit privileges for his company at Wharton Office Supply, Ltd.

Would you kindly answer a few questions for us about Mr. Kemper? There are two copies of this letter enclosed. Please complete, sign, and return one copy in the postage-paid envelope provided.

What kind of credit terms did you give Mr. Kemper? _____
_____

How punctual was Mr. Kemper in making his payments? _____
_____

Do you have any reservations about Mr. Kemper's financial responsibility or stability?
_____

Thank you for your time. We will make sure that your comments are treated confidentially.

Sincerely,

Alan L. Shoester

als/jls

encs.

Sample Letter 8.10.   Letter requesting employment information for credit applicant.

[date]

Ms. Trudy P. Reindollar
Director of Personnel
Farout Enterprises, Inc.
45 Trustme Lane
Far West, FL 32045

VERIFICATION OF EMPLOYMENT OF MAXWELL L. SIDNEY

Ms. Reindollar, Mr. Sidney has made an application for a charge account. He has used you as a credit reference. Your prompt reply will be appreciated by us and your employee. It will be held in strict confidence.

1. Is the applicant employed by your company? _____
   If answer is no, please complete the following:
   a. Date applicant left: _____
   b. Reason for leaving: _____
2. Base salary per hour _____ per week _____ per month _____ per year _____
   Is all or part of salary in the form of a bonus or commissions? _____
   Overtime earnings? _____
3. How long has the applicant been employed by your company? _____
4. What position does the applicant hold? _____
5. Are the applicant's services satisfactory? _____
6. What is the probability of the applicant's continued employment? _____
   Other remarks? _____
   _____

Please sign and date the enclosed copy and return it to me. Thank you for your assistance.

RACHEL A. GRIMES
VICE PRESIDENT

rg/lg

enc.

Acknowledged by: _____

Date: _____

Signature and Title: _____

Sample Letter 8.11 was written as a brief but direct request for information on a prospective client's credit history. After a short explanation, the writer politely and specifically asks for potentially helpful details and indicates the inclusion of a more detailed form.

Sample Letter 8.11.   Letter asking for client's credit history.

[date]

Account Management Representative
Nouveau Riche Bank
1010 Scott Boulevard
Monserrat, MI 48029

Dear Sir or Madam:

Mutual Machine Cast, of 88 Sanders Street, Detroit, has listed your bank as a reference on a recent application for a company card. Their business indicated that they kept accounts with you from January 18, 199X, through November 30, 200X.

Their request for a credit limit was for $50,000. Can you give us any information as to Mutual Machine's credit history, promptness in payment, average monthly balance, and particulars surrounding the termination of their account? Specific information about the terms of your lending contract with them would be especially helpful. We have enclosed a copy of Mutual Machine's credit application, was well as our company's form for you to complete. We will keep any and all information you provide us strictly confidential.

Thank you for your cooperation. Please call me at 706-607-9934 if you have questions.

Sincerely,

Tess Collegian

enc.

Letter Denying Credit

Sample Letter 8.12 was written to deny credit to someone who had requested it. The letter writer acknowledges the request for a credit line, but then informs the customer why it cannot be set up. The writer clearly explains the reason credit has been denied and suggests that the customer reapply at a later time, should the circumstances change.

Sample Letter 8.12.   Letter denying credit.

[date]

Mr. Alan T. Hinsdale
Hinsdale, Hinsdale, and Wanda, Inc.
43 Turnstable Road
Elmira, NY 16032

Dear Mr. Hinsdale:

Thank you for taking the time to apply for credit at Square Office Supplies, Ltd.

I'm sorry to inform you that we are unable to grant you the credit line you requested. We are grateful for your interest in our office supplies store and welcome your business, but I am afraid that your current debt situation suggests that your ability to take on additional monthly payments could put you in difficult financial straits.

When you have paid down some of your outstanding debt, or your cash flow situation changes, we would be glad to reconsider your credit application. We will, of course, welcome the opportunity to provide you with quality products and services and continue to do business on a cash basis.

Cordially,

William W. Donohoe
Credit Manager

wwd:jls

Letters Granting Credit

Sample Letter 8.13 was written to inform a customer that he has been granted credit. The letter writer welcomes the customer, announces that his credit line has been approved, and then goes on to describe his company's services, the amount of the credit line, and the name of the reader's account representative. The letter's tone is enthusiastic and helpful.

Sample Letter 8.13. Letter granting credit.

[date]

Mr. Bertrand R. Levine
Levine's Lumber Land
P.O. Box 567
Richmond, SD 57001

Dear Mr. Levine:

Welcome! Your account at Nilges Wood Supply has been approved. We are proud to have you as a customer.

Nilges Wood Supply is a 50-year-old company, with 85 stores in nine Midwestern states. We supply a complete line of building products to our customers, including millwork, plumbing, electrical, paint, kitchen supplies, bath supplies, hardware, and tools. As a leader in this industry, we strive to provide the best service possible to our customers. Our goal is to be your most valuable supplier. Customer satisfaction is our number-one priority.

Your approved credit line is $2,000. Monthly statements are mailed on the first or second working day each month. A service charge is added to past-due balances that are not paid by the 25th day of the billing month.

We at Nilges Wood Supply welcome the opportunity to serve you and look forward to a long and prosperous relationship.

Your branch manager is Sheila McGulicuty. Her telephone number is 890-555-8765.

Yours very truly,

Larry E. Nilges
Vice President—Credit Sales

len/jls

Sample Letter 8.14 was written to offer retail credit to a customer who had filled out an application when she was in one of the company's stores.

Sample Letter 8.14.   Letter offering retail credit to a customer.

[date]

Ms. Michaela Edwards
44 School Street
Latin, MD 20687

Dear Ms. Edwards:

Thank you for taking the time when you were in our Dover, Delaware, store to fill out a credit card application. We wanted you to know that just before Thanksgiving a new Stationery Plus superstore will open at the Dunkin Shopping Mall near you. At the new location, you'll be able to purchase all of the stationery and office products you need, often at deep discounts for our preferred credit card holders.

We're enclosing your credit card so that you can use it for immediate savings on opening day of our new Stationery Plus store in your area. All you need to do is sign the back of the card, read over the booklet we've enclosed on how the card works, and present it to any cashier at the store for your purchases. Your card number will automatically qualify you for any special sales.

We'll notify you with the exact day of the opening and specific sales information as we get closer to the date. Your credit card account is open now and can be used at any Stationery Plus location. We look forward to doing business with you.

Sincerely,

Bo Divise
Founder and President

Enc.

Sample Letter 8.15 was written to clearly outline the terms of a rental arrangement. After a cordial introduction, the author moves to the specific terms of the rental agreement, concluding with an explanation of the special conditions being imposed.

Sample Letter 8.15. Letter outlining credit terms of rental arrangement.

[date]

Pastor Ronnie Doyle
First Baptist Church of Carrollton
136 Oglethorpe Street
Carrollton, GA 30088

Dear Pastor Doyle:

Thank you for your recent decision to let Lackey Audiovisual handle the audiovisual needs for your "Revive Us, O Lord" conference this coming March. We share your optimism that this gathering will help bind members of our community closer together during these trying economic times.

The equipment listed on the attached sheet is being rented to you for the full two-week duration of the revival. At the end of that time, you may purchase the equipment outright. Credit terms will be as follows. There will be no interest charged for the first three months. Thereafter, the interest rate will be 14.9%, provided that you pay the minimum current due by the stated deadline. Should you ever fail to make the minimum monthly payment by the stated deadline, the interest rate will revert to 19.8%.

Enclosed you will also find a credit application form. I suggest that you complete and return it now. That way, if you decide to purchase the audiovisual equipment at the end of the revival, your approval will already be in place. We ask that at least two of the deacons of the church—who are not related to you or to each other—co-sign the credit application.

I apologize for any inconvenience this may cause. We look forward to serving you.

Yours truly,

Harlan Lackey

2 encs.

Letter Raising Credit Limit

Sample Letter 8.16 is a brief letter informing a credit card customer that his credit limit has been raised. The letter writer makes the announcement in the first paragraph and thanks the customer. Then she closes the letter.

Sample Letter 8.16.   Letter extending higher credit limit.

[date]

Mr. Loren T. Hinsdale
45 Alabama Place
Indian River, CO 80021

Dear Mr. Hinsdale:

Congratulations! Your credit card line has been increased to $2,600. Thank you for using our credit card. We have increased your line of credit so you can make more convenient credit card purchases.

We appreciate your business and hope you enjoy this extra purchasing power.

Sincerely,

Carla B. Torsolini
Credit Manager

cbt:jls

Letter Clearing Disputed Items

Sample Letter 8.17 was written to inform a debtor that items he disputed in his credit file have been deleted. The letter writer offers to send the debtor or any of the debtor's creditors a copy of the corrected report, and closes.

Sample Letter 8.17.   Letter informing customer that disputed items have been deleted from his credit file.

[date]

Mr. Jaime Chin
36 Levittown Place
Hopscotch, NY 10045

Dear Mr. Chin:

We have deleted the information you disputed about your credit rating from our files. We have put a copy of your letter disputing these items in our files.

You have the right to make a written request that we send a copy to anybody you specifically designate who has received a consumer report containing the deleted or disputed information within the preceding two years for employment purposes or within the preceding six months for any other purpose.

Yours truly,

Colman Ling
Credit Manager

cl/bl

Stop-Payment Letter

Sample Letter 8.18 was written to a bank to ask it to stop payment on a check. The letter writer clearly indicates to whom the check was made out and how much it was made out for. He asks that the bank debit his company's account for the penalty charge.

Sample Letter 8.18.   Stop-payment letter.

[date]

Mr. Leonard R. Coshatt
Large Bank
2666 Barbour Lane
Lugo, AL 35045

Dear Mr. Coshatt:

Please issue a stop-payment order on our company check number 722-311, written on June 30, 20X4, to Earle B. Lockwood Sod Farm for $2,545.

Please debit our account for the $15 fee assessed for issuing this stop-payment order.

Sincerely,

Ernest T. Bream

etb/wlg

Collection Letters

Sample Letters 8.19 through 8.29 are examples of collection letters.

Sample Letters 8.19 through 8.23 are a series of letters that can be used in sequence for collection purposes. This series features a first, second, third, fourth, and final overdue notice for payment due. While maintaining a level of decorum, the letters become increasingly less patient, until the final notice that the account will be turned over to a collection agency.

Sample Letter 8.24 is a brief collection letter that was sent along with a bill. The letter writer clearly explains to the reader how to figure out the amount due. This letter was written from a wholesaler to a retailer that purchased goods.

Sample Letters 8.25 and 8.26 are also examples of a series of collection letters. Sample Letter 8.25 was written as a second notice on charges due on an account. The letter writer states the amount overdue and expresses concern that the reader appears to be having financial difficulty. The writer offers to help the reader deal with the overdue payment problem. Sample Letter 8.26 was written to the same person after no response was received to Sample Letter 8.25. The writer is less sympathetic and explains that he has had to notify various credit agencies about the delinquency. He offers some hope to the reader by explaining he can clear up his credit rating by filling out the enclosed reply card and making payment arrangements.

Sample Letter 8.19. Letter serving as first reminder after monthly statement.

[date]

Mr. Kyle T. Reading
Bolivian Import Merchants, Inc.
56 Trinity Place
Detroit, IL 60065

Dear Mr. Reading:

This is to inform you that we have not received the payment of $650 that appeared on our billing statement of June 8, 20X7. If you have already made the payment, please disregard this notice.

If there is any question about your bill, please call my office immediately.

Thank you for giving your prompt attention to this matter.

Sincerely,

Mark Hoddlecoock
Credit Manager

jl

Sample Letter 8.20.   Letter serving as second overdue notice.

[date]

Mr. Kyle T. Reading
Bolivian Import Merchants, Inc.
56 Trinity Place
Detroit, IL 60065

Dear Mr. Reading:

We are still waiting for the payment of $650 due since June 8, 20X7.

Failure to resolve this matter may result in the suspension of your credit privileges and can jeopardize your credit rating.

Sincerely,

Mark Hoddlecoock
Credit Manager

jl

Sample Letter 8.21.   Letter serving as third overdue notice.

[date]

Mr. Kyle T. Reading
Bolivian Import Merchants, Inc.
56 Trinity Place
Detroit, IL 60065

Dear Mr. Reading:

Your account is overdue for $650, as we previously noted in our correspondence. We have had a long and pleasant business relationship in the past and hope to continue this relationship in the future.

If there is any reason you cannot make full payment on this account, please call my office immediately to discuss a new payment schedule.

Unless we hear from you, we will be forced to take other steps to remedy this problem. You will thereby be jeopardizing your credit rating.

I look forward to hearing from you this week.

Sincerely,

Mark Hoddlecoock
Credit Manager

jl

Sample Letter 8.22.   Letter serving as fourth overdue notice.

[date]

Mr. Kyle T. Reading
Bolivian Import Merchants, Inc.
56 Trinity Place
Detroit, IL 60065

Dear Mr. Reading:

Despite three previous reminders about the $650 overdue on your account since June, we have received no response from you.

As previously noted, we will be pleased to discuss a revised payment schedule in order to help you resolve this matter. Unless we have heard from you within 5 days, however, we will find it necessary to turn your account over to a collection agency.

We thank you for turning your attention to this matter immediately.

Sincerely,

Mark Hoddlecoock
Credit Manager

jl

Sample Letter 8.23.   Letter serving as final overdue notice.

[date]

Mr. Kyle T. Reading
Bolivian Import Merchants, Inc.
56 Trinity Place
Detroit, IL 60065

Dear Mr. Reading:

As of this writing, we have received no response to correspondence about payment of $650 due since June 20X7.

Therefore, we must send this final notice to inform you that your account will be turned over to a collection agency if full payment is not received by November 15, 20X7.

We urge you to give your prompt attention to this matter.

Cordially,

Mark Hoddlecoock
Credit Manager

jl

Sample Letter 8.24.   Short initial collection letter.

[date]

Mr. Peter T. Nobless
Nobless Hardware Store
P.O. Box 5432
Roanoke, GA 30021

Dear Mr. Nobless:

Enclosed you will find a statement with your September 20X7 charges. Please subtract any payments you have made that are not reflected on this bill, and remit the remainder promptly.

If you have any questions concerning your bill, I will be glad to help.

Sincerely,

Lois T. Handley
Credit Manager

lth:ltg

enc.

Sample Letter 8.25.   Letter serving as second notice on charges due.

[date]

Mr. Thomas T. Dialon
76 East Coast Drive
Sudbury, VT 05056

Subject: Credit Charges Due

Dear Mr. Dialon:

Is something wrong? A few weeks ago we sent you a notice that your charge account payment was past due for $575. In spite of this notice, we have received no payment from you. You should be acting now to preserve your good credit rating.

We will be understanding if there is a reason why you have not been able to make the payment. Call me to explain the circumstances. We always make every effort to accommodate our customers who are encountering financial difficulties, as long as they cooperate with us.

If you fail to either bring your account up to date or contact us to make some new arrangements, however, we will be forced to turn the matter over to our collection department and instruct them to inform the various credit reporting bureaus about your delinquent status.

Sincerely,

Simon L. Gree
Credit Manager

mls

Sample Letter 8.26. Follow-up to no response to second-notice collection letter in Sample Letter 8.25.

[date]

Mr. Thomas T. Dialon
76 East Coast Drive
Sudbury, VT 05056

Subject: Credit Charges Due

Dear Mr. Dialon:

The payments on your charge account have become seriously delinquent. The credit manager of Bixley Department Store has turned your account over to us, the Collections Department.

You have already been sent a late payment notice, followed by a letter from our credit department requesting payment. Both of these polite requests have remained unanswered. We have also attempted to reach you by telephone, but have had no success.

Because you have been unresponsive to those efforts to bring your account up to date and to preserve your good credit rating, we have notified various consumer credit reporting agencies of your present delinquent status. We now intend to take every legal recourse we can to collect from you the entire amount you owe, plus whatever late charges and legal fees we incur.

It's still not too late to clear up this matter. You can still pay the amount you owe and start restoring your credit rating at Bixley Department Store by coming in personally, calling us, or using the enclosed postage-paid reply card to make arrangements for payment.

You must respond immediately or we will have to take corrective action against you.

Sincerely,

H. N. Hart
Supervisor, Collections Department

mls

enc.

Sample Letter 8.27 was sent as a follow-up collection letter to a debtor who had sent in payment, but was still delinquent on his account. The letter writer thanks the reader, but explains the delinquency that remains. He asks that the reader call to arrange an equitable payment schedule.

Sample Letter 8.27. Follow-up collection letter.

[date]

Mr. Carl D. Weaver, Controller
Busalami Department Stores
28 Huntington Avenue, Suite 507
Brookline, MI 48056

Dear Mr. Weaver:

Thank you very much for sending March's payment on Purchase Order #0254. However, payments for January, April, May, and June are still outstanding. Copies of the outstanding invoices are enclosed.

Could you please call us with a proposed payment schedule? It is important that we be able to anticipate our cash flow situation.

Sincerely,

Maxwell L. Nitten

mln/jls

encls.

Sample Letter 8.28 is a collection letter that was sent by a law firm after the creditor failed to collect money due from the debtor. The writer is clear and pointed in his language. He recaps the delinquency problem and closes by giving a payment due date, after which he will take legal action against the debtor.

Sample Letter 8.28. Collection letter from a law firm.

[date]

Querilous Office Supply, Inc.
43 Rustballic Road
Simondale, KS 66025

Attention: Mrs. Evelyn Z. Querilous

Subject: Balance Owed to Welan Rubber Stamp Company, Inc.

Dear Mrs. Querilous:

This law firm has been hired by Welan Rubber Stamp Company, Inc., to collect the balance that you owe it. We understand that as of November 25, 20X7, the balance owed was $2,354.65, reflecting charges for products sold by Welan Rubber Stamp Company, Inc. to Querilous Office Supply, Inc. We further understand that you wrote a check to our client dated November 10, 20X7, in payment of the balance; payment was subsequently stopped on the check; and the check was returned to our client for insufficient funds.

This letter is being written to demand that you make full payment of the balance by Wednesday, January 18, 20X8. If payment is not made by that time, we will take appropriate legal action to collect the amount due.

Cordially,

Wesley T. Harding, Jr.

wth/wlg

cc: Mr. Simon B. Welan
    R. Stephen Levitz, Esq.

Sample Letter 8.29 was written to a customer who was sent a collection letter by mistake. The letter writer apologizes and quickly takes responsibility for the mistake.

Sample Letter 8.29. Letter to customer who received collection letter by mistake.

[date]

Mr. Brisbane T. Hackett
34 Lowell Avenue
Tarrytown, MI 48024

Dear Mr. Hackett:

Thank you for calling us earlier this week to let us know that we had incorrectly sent you a collection letter last week. We've checked our records and you are indeed correct. We made a mistake.

We're so very sorry. We have corrected our records and will work hard to ensure that no similar mistakes occur in the future. We will also make sure that your credit rating has not been adversely affected by our mistake. I apologize for any inconvenience our mistake caused you.

Sincerely,

Barbara Landau
Collections Manager

Credit-Suspension Letter

Sample Letter 8.30 was written to suspend a customer's credit after no response was received to earlier collection efforts. This letter could be written as a follow-up to the collection letters featured in Sample Letters 8.19 through 8.23. The letter writer informs the debtor that he has had to turn the account over to a collection agency and that his credit privileges have been suspended. He offers hope that credit privileges may be reinstated if the matter is resolved.

Sample Letter 8.30. Letter suspending further credit. Follow-up to Sample Letters 8.19–8.23.

[date]

Mr. Kyle T. Reading
Bolivian Import Merchants, Inc.
56 Trinity Place
Detroit, IL 60065

Dear Mr. Reading:

We regret to inform you that the Hoodle Company has found it necessary to turn your account over to the Coin Collection Agency for collection of the $650 you have owed since June 20X7.

We must further inform you that all of your credit privileges with the Hoodle Company have been revoked.

Please resolve this matter immediately so that we may reinstate your credit privileges and continue our business relationship.

Cordially,

Mark Hoddlecoock
Credit Manager

jl

Letter Reinstating Credit

Sample Letter 8.31 was written after a delinquent customer paid the amount due on his account. The letter writer thanks the customer for his payment and announces that credit has been restored. This letter could be written as a follow-up to any of Sample Letters 8.19 through 8.23 after delinquent payment has been received.

Sample Letter 8.31. Letter reinstating credit. Follow-up to Sample Letters 8.19–8.23.

[date]

Mr. Kyle T. Reading
Bolivian Import Merchants, Inc.
56 Trinity Place
Detroit, IL 60065

Dear Mr. Reading:

Thank you for payment of $650 on your account. We are pleased to inform you that the Hoodle Company has reinstated your credit privileges.

We look forward to continuing our business relationship and providing you with all of your office supply needs.

Best regards,

Mark Hoddlecoock
Credit Manager

jl

Letters Accepting Partial Payment

Sample Letters 8.32 and 8.33 are acknowledgments of partial payment on a delinquent account.

Sample Letter 8.32 thanks the debtor for payment, tells him how much is still due, and reminds him that the remainder must be received for credit to be reinstated.

Sample Letter 8.33 is written to acknowledge partial payment and confirm that a new payment schedule has been arranged.

Sample Letter 8.32. Letter accepting partial payment.

[date]

Mr. Kyle T. Reading
Bolivian Import Merchants, Inc.
56 Trinity Place
Detroit, IL 60065

Dear Mr. Reading:

Thank you for partial payment of the $650 owed on your account. Please note that your balance is now $500, overdue from June 20X7.

While we appreciate this partial payment, it is essential that complete payment be received by November 15 in order for us to reinstate your credit privileges and continue our business relationship.

Sincerely,

Mark Hoddlecoock
Credit Manager

jl

Sample Letter 8.33.   Letter accepting partial payment.

[date]

Mr. Kyle T. Reading
Bolivian Import Merchants, Inc.
56 Trinity Place
Detroit, IL 60065

Dear Mr. Reading:

We received partial payment of $150 after you called us about your account and arranged a new payment schedule. We trust that this mutually agreed upon schedule will result in complete and timely payment of the $500 still due on your account.

Thank you for the partial payment. Please call my office if you have any questions about your account.

Sincerely,

Mark Hoddlecoock
Credit Manager

jl

Letter Acknowledging Payment

Sample Letter 8.34 was written to a customer after he had paid up all past invoices. The letter writer acknowledges payment, then recounts the new payment schedule he has arranged with the customer.

Sample Letter 8.34.   Letter acknowledging payment.

[date]

Mr. Carl E. Twonby
The Riverboat Steakhouse
654 Pacific Avenue
Carlsbad, IA 50032

Dear Mr. Twonby:

I received payment for all of the past invoices. Thank you very much.

We have two months left on our initial contract. Beginning with August, I will bill you at the end of each month. That way, I'll be able to adjust our fee to the work performed. The figure will not exceed the $1,700 we agreed upon earlier. Let me know if this meets with your approval.

Sincerely,

Mark L. Blinke

rp

Letter About Deposit Due

Sample Letter 8.35 was written to a prospective hotel guest to remind him that a deposit is due on a room he has reserved.

Sample Letter 8.35. Letter reminding customer that deposit is due.

[date]

Mr. Simon T. Harsdale
45 Trustworthy Drive
Penobscot, IL 60021

Dear Mr. Harsdale:

Please refer to our acknowledgment of your request for reservations dated November 7, 20X6. As you will note, a $125 deposit per room is required to secure your reservation. This deposit was due within 10 days of the date of the acknowledgment of your reservation.

To date, we have not received your deposit and are eager to make your reservation definite. Please forward your remittance by return mail in the postage-paid envelope provided or telephone immediately to let us know your plans. Our toll-free number is 800-555-4545.

We are looking forward to hearing from you.

Cordially,

Beverly G. Krauss
Reservations Manager

bgk:lls

enc.

Letter to Lender to Renegotiate Payment Terms

In Sample Letter 8.36, the letter writer writes to the bank from which he has borrowed money to renegotiate repayment terms. The letter writer is clear and lays out a proposed repayment plan tied to the unexpected cash-flow needs of the business.

Sample Letter 8.36.   Letter to bank when payment is past due on loan balance.

[date]

Mr. Max Nilges
Vice President
County and State Bank
6 Tristam Place
Montclair, MA 02104

Dear Mr. Nilges:

Last year, we were granted a loan from County and State Bank for $250,000. We agreed to pay back the loan in 48 monthly payments. For the past 12 months, we've met our payments without exception. We work hard to stay current with all of our financial responsibilities and to keep our credit rating as strong as it is.

Now, I must ask your assistance in helping us meet some unexpected costs. Two months ago, our building was involved in a freak traffic accident in which a city bus crashed into the building and damaged the outside structure and most of our interior reception area. Our insurance covers most, but not all, of the repair expenses. On top of that, one of our key customers is being hurt by the current downturn in the economy and has stretched its payments out to 60 days for the next several months.

Our own business is very healthy and we continue to be both profitable and well regarded for our quality customer service. To help us pay for the building repair and to redouble our collections efforts, would you consider allowing us to postpone our payments for the next three months, after which time we'll get back on schedule?

We've appreciated your commitment and support to our business over the years and trust that you will understand and accommodate our request. Thanks very much.

Sincerely,

Jerry Oloff
President

Letter from Customer About Billing Error

Sample Letter 8.37 was written by a customer to clear up an error in billing. The writer's tone is polite and not accusatory, and the mention of the company's original price, as quoted on the enclosed fax, lends support to her claim that the company, not the customer, is in the wrong. The writer closes with a request for further contact and an expeditious solution to the problem.

Sample Letter 8.37.   Letter from customer about billing error.

[date]

Asher Tameling
SupraTRAX Incorporated
129 Portland Street
Wheaton, IL 60192

Dear Mr. Tameling:

On July 5 I placed an order for 50 SupraTRAX Ho Hiawatha boy train sets and was told that the total cost came to $3,560.00.

I just received an invoice from your company requesting a payment of $4,180.00. There must be some error. I have enclosed a copy of the fax from your Customer Service Department that quotes the lower price.

Please contact me as soon as possible so that we can clear up this matter. The train sets are in wonderful condition. We will be happy to supply you with a check as soon as you provide us with an accurate invoice.

Sincerely,

Sarah Costner
Store Manager

enc.

CHAPTER 9

Letters to vendors and suppliers

This chapter contains examples of letters that are commonly written to vendors and suppliers. The occasion for writing these letters varies from something as simple as placing orders to issues that must be carefully handled, such as complaints about salespeople or products. The letters here serve as models for professionals to use in their own dealings with vendors and suppliers.

Unless a formal proposal is required and you're writing a formal letter to accompany that proposal, many of the letters in this chapter can be sent as emails or as attachments to emails. For those letters that can be adapted to emails, it's simple enough to copy the text of the sample letter into the text of your email.

Letter Dealing with a Request for Proposal

Requests for Proposals, or RFPs, frequently go out to prospective vendors as a call for business. The RFP can be a specific and often complex document, one that lists requirements, specifications, and budgetary restraints. Letters that accompany these RFPs can vary in their own specificity, but should at a minimum indicate an enclosed document and offer further assistance, if needed. Sample Letter 9.1 is a straightforward example of such a letter.

Sample Letter 9.1.   Letter accompanying an RFP.

[date]

Jeff McCutcheon
iFab, Inc.
4000 N. Michigan Road
Jonesboro, MA 02123

Dear Mr. McCutcheon:

One of the goals for us here at the Falmouth Civic Center is to increase the number and quality of playgrounds in our city. As an organization, we have set the ambitious goal of redesigning our existing three city playgrounds and building three new sites around the downtown area, replete with water elements, challenging but safe climbing environments, and multi-age play structures.

To help us meet our goal, we need a qualified and capable company to oversee the design, construction, and installation of these playgrounds and all related equipment. We admire iFab's experience in metalwork, fabrication, and custom design for creative enterprises in the region. Of particular interest to us was your recent installation of the "Bats" pavilion at the Metropole City Zoo.

We would very much like you to consider responding to our initial Request for Proposal, enclosed. The deadline for submission of proposals is Friday, December 1, 20X3. Our committee will meet on December 8 to review proposals, and notifications to those companies approved for promotion to the second round of applications will occur on January 3, 20X4.

If you have further questions about the project, the RFP, or the proposal requirements, please call me at (508) 555-5415. I look forward to receiving your submission.

Sincerely,

Michaela Coleman
Chair, Buildings Committee

mc/ldf

encl.

Letters Involved with Presentations

Sample Letter 9.2 is written to a sales rep, requesting that she make a sales presentation. The letter writer is clear in what she is asking as well as clear in how she will follow up to confirm the recipient's availability and willingness to make the sales presentation.

Sample Letter 9.2. Letter requesting a sales presentation.

[date]

Dr. Whitney Lighthouse, President
Precision Physician's Equipment
45 Scalpel Avenue
Point Medic, NJ 07550

Dear Dr. Lighthouse:

At Outdoor Doctor Pavilions, we are interested in providing our trade show customers with the latest in medical equipment options. Recently, your company was referred to us as one that might have the sort of unique products ideally suited to our customers.

Our semi-annual conferences, where all of our sales force gathers, take place in August and March. We were hoping you could find time in your schedule to attend our conference in March to make a sales presentation about your products to our sales force.

The conference takes place from March 4 through March 7. If you could let us know of your availability and willingness to make a sales presentation, we will work with you to accommodate your schedule.

Please call me at 617-555-2217 or email me at md@odp.com to let me know of your availability.

Sincerely,

Mary Dock
CEO, Outdoor Doctor Pavilions

md/nm

Sample Letter 9.3 acknowledges someone who made a sales presentation to the letter writer's business in response to a Request for Proposals. The letter makes clear that no decision has yet been made about the contract recipient, but also lays out a rough timeline for when a decision might be expected.

Sample Letter 9.3.   Letter acknowledging a sales presentation made after an RFP.

[date]

Mr. Lucas Evan David
Fighting Designers, Inc.
164 Turtle Lane
Stonevillege, MA 02188

Dear Mr. David:

Thank you very much for the design presentation you made today for the Python Flying Bridge project.

We have now received presentations from the short list of vendors we developed in response to our RFP. We do not anticipating hearing any more presentations.

Once we have decided on a vendor, we will be in touch with you. We anticipate that the deliberation process will take us roughly three weeks.

Thank you very much for your presentation as well as your patience as we make this choice that is critical to the future of our project.

Sincerely,

Liam Nephewson
CEO, PFP Partners

LN/js

cc: Graham Cleese

Letters Dealing with Vendor Bids

Letters awarding contracts to vendors should be short, but enthusiastic, as they set the tone of a positive working relationship between business partners. This type of letter will usually come at the end of an application process that has established a degree of familiarity between correspondents. The award of a contract also signals the progression of the relationship to a new level. The details of the contract will be hammered out in future correspondence.

Sample Letter 9.4. Letter awarding contract to a vendor.

[date]

Ms. Tess Freiman, Creative Director
Fuchsia Design, Inc.
Harbor Farms Road
Lightning, TX 75090

Dear Ms. Freiman:

Thank you for your proposal for the redesign of the Junior Apparel campaign in Righteous! Girlswear's midwest region stores. Your vision for displaying our pre-teen line of clothing was dramatic and cost effective, and we are pleased to inform you that we have decided to award Fuchsia Design the contract to create all related display materials for our Righteous! Junior Apparel line.

Our Marketing Director, Elsa Zlotnikoff, will call you in the next few days to go over the terms of the enclosed contract. We here at Righteous! Girlswear look forward to working with you in the coming months. Congratulations again on a successful proposal.

Sincerely,

James Rothberg

JR:ejc

encl.

Depending on the terms of a request for a bid, you may be required to notify losing bidders that you have awarded your business to another company. At any rate, it is courteous to respond to unsuccessful bidders: doing so may keep future business channels open. This type of letter can be short and sweet, complimentary but direct.

Sample Letter 9.5.   Letter notifying losing bidder.

[date]

Grady Rogers
Nor-Cross Enterprises
5300 Marietta Drive
Baltimore, MD 20601

Dear Mr. Rogers:

Thank you for your recent bid to manufacture and distribute Hi-Ball's new product, The BuddhaBall™. Your proposal was thoughtful and met our minimum requirements for cost and quality, taking into consideration our warehousing and distribution guidelines.

However, another company delivered a proposal that was more cost effective than Nor-Cross Enterprises' bid, and we have decided to award the contract to that company. We do appreciate your efforts on our Request for Proposal, though, and we will certainly keep you in mind for future business ventures.

Sincerely,

Mike Branigan

MB/js

Letter Placing Order

Sample Letter 9.6 was written to place a simple order with a company. The letter writer clearly spells out what he wants to order, listing the product names, quantities, and total cost. He also indicates that he is enclosing a check for the order, and instructs the reader where to ship his order.

Sample Letter 9.6.   Letter placing order.

[date]

Mr. Maxwell North
Andoris Publishing Company
23 Lathrop Avenue
Boonton, NJ 07005

Dear Mr. North:

Please send me the following books advertised in your Fall 20X7 catalog:

5 copies of *The Commercial Loan*	$245.00
6 copies of *Banking Dictionary*	294.00
3 copies of *Bank Selling Directory*	105.00
Total	644.00
Less 10% discount on 10 or more books	64.40
Amount due:	$579.60

I have enclosed a company check for $579.60. Please send the order to me at: Big Bank Company, 186-A Grampian Road, Gloucester, New Jersey 08343.

Thank you for your assistance.

Sincerely,

Larry T. Edsel
Training Director

lte:jls

enc.

Letter Requesting Distributor's Name

Sample Letter 9.7 was written to a company to request the name of a distributor in the letter writer's area. The writer explains that he came across the product at a trade show. He asks for the name of a local distributor so he can purchase the product.

Sample Letter 9.7.   Letter requesting name of dealer or distributor.

[date]

Mr. Carl T. Pernicks
Vice President
Advanced Copiers In Offices, Inc.
76 Troden Road
Troden, CT 06056

Dear Mr. Pernicks:

I picked up your business card and a brochure for your company's copiers when I was at the Annual Office Supply Trade Show in Anaheim. I am very interested in buying a Mark-VG564 Copier, advertised on page 5 of your brochure.

Can you please send me the name of a distributor in my area? I would like to examine the machine to see if it is capable of meeting my business needs.

Thank you.

Sincerely,

Alan T. Rylees

jls

Letter Seeking Information About Product

Sample Letter 9.8 was written by someone whose office was in the process of evaluating a variety of copiers to make a purchase decision. The letter writer explains this situation and asks the reader to send information on his product. The writer briefly explains the type of office she runs so the reader might get an idea of her office's needs.

Sample Letter 9.8. Letter requesting information about product.

[date]

Mr. Vladimir Puchefsky
Vladimir's Copy Machines
45 Orange Road
Trinstale, MI 48056

Dear Mr. Puchefsky:

We are in the process of updating our copier equipment. Will you please send us information on the price, capabilities, and availability of your office line of copy machines?

Byron Public Relations, Inc., is a 50-person public relations company. We currently have two copy machines, which we plan to trade in. Because of the volume of copying our company does, we are considering purchasing four copy machines.

Please send us the information we need to evaluate whether or not your firm can supply us with the copiers we need.

Thank you very much for your help.

Sincerely,

Leigh Simons
Office Manager

ls/js

Letter Asking About Quantity Discounts

Sample Letter 9.9 was written to a business to request information about quantity discounts on a product the letter writer is interested in buying. The writer identifies the product, explains how many copies he would be interested in purchasing, and asks if the reader can give him quantity discount prices on the purchase. He closes by letting the reader know when he'd need the first of the product shipments so the reader will know that he would like to make a decision about the purchase soon.

Sample Letter 9.9.   Letter asking about quantity discounts.

[date]

Mr. Nathan T. Bloom
Dover Products Company
312 West Main Street
Boonton, NJ 07005

Dear Mr. Bloom:

On a recent trip from New York to Boston, I picked up a copy of Jason Lang's book, *Marketing Financial Advisory Services: A Hands-On Guide*, at an airport bookstore.

I speak on the subject of financial services marketing frequently. After reading Mr. Lang's book, I thought it might make an excellent course book for some of the seminars I run. Do you offer quantity discounts on your books? If I were to order copies, my first order would be for a minimum of 100 books. My seminars are run quarterly, so I would probably order 300 more copies throughout the year.

Please let me know if you can offer me a discount on this large purchase. I have a seminar coming up the first week of November and need to make a decision soon about which text I will use.

Thank you for your help.

Sincerely,

Brandt T. Higginbottom

bth/jls

Letters Complimenting Vendors

Sample Letters 9.10 and 9.11 were written to compliment vendors. The writer of Sample Letter 9.10 took the time to write about the quality service he had been getting from his sales representative. A letter like this does a lot to build goodwill with the sales representative and with the vendor.

Sample Letter 9.11 was written to compliment a vendor on the job he had done. The letter writer is particularly pleased with the service that the vendor has provided and lets him know. He clearly indicates that part of the success of his company's product is due to the vendor's services. Like Sample Letter 9.10, this type of complimentary letter goes a long way toward building goodwill and a solid relationship with the vendor. It also helps the vendor since it will give him something to show to others who might be interested in using his services.

Each of these letters could easily be sent as an email instead without making any significant changes to the text of the messages.

Sample Letter 9.10.   Letter praising supplier's representative.

[date]

Mr. Richard H. Unimant
Branch Manager
Best Copy Service
412 Santiago Drive
Wonderland, NJ 07020

Dear Mr. Unimant:

I recently renewed our service contract on our copy machine for the third consecutive year. Our lasting business relationship has prompted me to write this letter.

I want to compliment your company on its most important asset—your service representative, Peggy Fection. Peggy is a superior individual. She is always prompt, courteous, and diligent. Her work is quick and professional and it cures whatever ails our tired old copying machine. She instills a quiet confidence in your company, which is one of the reasons we continue to do business with your company. When we decide to upgrade our copying system, we will call upon your company for further assistance.

People like Peggy are hard to find. It's not often I take the time to write a note like this, but she's been so consistently outstanding that I just couldn't help myself.

Best regards,

Max Nightson

amb

Sample Letter 9.11. Letter complimenting supplier of services.

[date]

Mr. Brady D. Omram
Omram Design Studios
45 Andover Place
Breakstone, MT 59025

Dear Mr. Omram:

Now that we've got our product—the Sunshield Sport Glasses—rolling off the production lines, I thought it appropriate to write you a note. Everyone in the company from the chairman of the board on down is extremely excited about the product. Your design of our packaging is above and beyond anything we ever expected.

I think we can credit Omram Design Studios' design approach with the success. Rather than designing a pretty box, your team created an "environment" for our product that truly communicates how special we feel the product and company behind it are.

The environment is being translated directly into a success at the wholesale and retail levels. When we started the project, Boonton Optical Company, Inc., was fairly new in the sunglass business. We did approximately $120,000 worth of business in sunglasses last year. Currently this year, after only three months of selling, we have actual sales of more than $500,000, and expect to hit $1.5 million before the year is over.

Since the product line, sales force, and advertising have remained the same, it looks like the packaging is communicating the right message to the retail trade.

Once again, thanks for a great effort. We are anxious to begin work on the next project. We like the way Omram Design Studios communicates Boonton Optical's products to the trade and the public.

Sincerely,

Zed B. Grusinki
Marketing Director

fwd

Letters Clearing Up Billing Errors

Sample Letter 9.12 was sent to a vendor to clarify a billing error made by the vendor. The letter writer is stern, yet not insulting. He identifies the cancelled check he is enclosing to verify payment and suggests that the vendor should be sure an invoice has not been paid before it threatens to turn over matters to a collection agency.

Sample Letter 9.12.   Letter to vendor clearing up billing error.

[date]

Ms. Patricia S. Paly,
Customer Service Department
P.O. Box 3452
Grand Forks Office Supply Company, Inc.
Albion, NM 87045

CLARIFICATION OF BILLING ERROR

Ms. Paly, I have enclosed a copy of the front and back of our check that was used to pay your invoice numbered 3352217. If you look at the copy of the back of the check, you will note that your company endorsed this check and that it was processed by your bank on January 5.

I would suggest that your company evaluate the procedures it uses for processing payments on its accounts receivable. It seems to me that you should correct your problems prior to sending past-due notices that threaten to turn your customers over to a collection agency.

I trust that the enclosed copy of our check will clear up your processing error and put our account back on the paid-up status.

JAMES LONG
CONTROLLER

jl:rl

enc.

Sample Letter 9.13 was written to a vendor who had shipped the wrong mix of products to the letter writer. The writer lays out the problem clearly and spells out the solution he would like from the vendor.

Sample Letter 9.13. Letter to vendor to straighten out incorrect order received.

[date]
Order #: 2488458

Mr. Loren Gary, Warehouse Supervisor
P.O. Box 3452
Eufaula Spacel Gardening Supply
Hanover, MA 02133

Dear Mr. Gary:

On April 15 we sent an order to you for several garden supply products that we planned to use for our annual Patriotic Days Sale, which runs from Flag Day on June 14 until Independence Day on July 4. Included on the list of items we ordered were one dozen large birdbaths at $600 for the dozen. We specifically ordered four in red, four in white, and four in blue.

This morning we received the shipment and were disappointed to find that all of the birdbaths you sent us were white. No letter of explanation accompanied the shipment.

We are returning eight of the white birdbaths to your attention by air freight. Please ship us the four red and four blue birdbaths we originally requested from you with our purchase order numbered 2488458.

Our Patriotic Days Sale begins on June 14 and we'd really like to have all of the bird-baths in stock before then. Thank you for giving your immediate attention to this order and resolving the mistake.

Sincerely,

Greg Gold, Chief Buyer

Letters Complaining to Vendors

Sample Letters 9.14 and 9.15 are examples of letters that were written to complain to vendors or suppliers.

Sample Letter 9.14 was written to a supplier of a business product. The letter writer clearly establishes his complaint and suggests the solution the reader should take. He explains that he would like to discuss the problem with the wholesaler since he has never had such a problem with the vendor before. The letter is clear and leaves no doubt about what the problem is and how the writer expects it to be resolved.

Sample Letter 9.15 was written to a vendor to complain about one of his sales representatives. The letter writer clearly explains that the sales representative is breaking the writer's company policy by directly approaching employees. After warning the sales representative and finding the situation has not changed, the writer finds it necessary to write the vendor to complain about the situation. The letter writer asks that the vendor speak to the sales representative to get him to stop breaking company policy.

Sample Letter 9.14. Letter complaining about unsatisfactory products.

[date]

Mr. Lawrence E. Tribune
Tisk-a-Disk, Inc.
43 Software Center Turnpike
Framingham, NH 02256

Dear Mr. Tribune:

For the last several months, my customers at the store have been returning Tisk-a-Disk thumb drives. Never before have I had such a problem with one of your products. The complaint is the same for virtually all dissatisfied customers: The casing for the thumb drive falls apart soon after the thumb drive cover is removed.

Imagine the trouble this situation can cause my customers, Mr. Tribune. What if they lose valuable data that they have stored on these thumb drives? Have you been getting similar complaints from other retail outlets? Perhaps the latest shipment of thumb drives I received is an isolated case of poor craftsmanship. If not, then I will have to discontinue carrying your thumb drives and stock another company's.

I've shipped to you what I had remaining in stock of thumb drives. There are 100 packages with 10 thumb drives each, which makes a total of 1,000 thumb drives. I am returning these since I am concerned the same unraveling problem might occur. Since the wholesale price is 69.5 cents a thumb drive, please credit my account for $695.

Please call me when you've assessed this problem and let me know Tisk-a-Disk's plans for correcting the situation. I look forward to hearing from you in the next couple of days.

Cordially,

Justin L. Raisch

jlr/nls

Sample Letter 9.15.   Letter complaining about sales representative.

[date]

Mr. Oscar B. Crum
Crum Notepads, Inc.
467 Scholarly Way
Tuskin, AL 35045

Dear Mr. Crum:

As you are probably aware, *The Armchair Reader's Review* orders a significant amount of supplies from your company. We are pleased with the quality of the products, particularly the reporters' notebooks you manufacture. But I am writing you because of difficulty I am having with your sales representative assigned to our territory, Mack McIntyre.

While we do make frequent purchases from your company, we have time and time again requested that Mr. McIntyre deal directly with our office manager for product ordering. We have asked that he call to set up an appointment before arriving on the scene. On many occasions, Mr. McIntyre has simply shown up at our offices. Often, even when he has already met with the office manager, he approaches our writers and editors directly to encourage them to buy your products.

I must ask that Mr. McIntyre follow the procedure we have clearly outlined for him to use in approaching us for orders. His method of "cutting through the red tape" eats up our writers' and editors' valuable time. By having our office manager handle the ordering, we have centralized that function. I am sure you can understand why this procedure is important to us.

While we let Mr. McIntyre know about the appropriate procedure when he first took on this sales territory, he has continued to fail to follow it. Many of our editors and writers are up in arms about the disruption and continue to complain to me about his direct sales approaches.

We are very pleased with your products. We are also pleased with the speed and efficiency with which you handle orders. We are not looking to make life difficult for Mr. McIntyre. We simply ask that you speak to him about following the procedure that we have established here.

Cordially,

Kate McGuffie

km/js

cc: MN

Letter Cancelling Contract

Sample Letter 9.16 was written to cancel a contract with a supplier. The letter is short, but the letter writer clearly explains that his company would like to cancel a contract coming up for renewal. He closes by requesting that the machine that was contracted out to his company be removed as soon as possible.

Sample Letter 9.16.   Letter to vendor cancelling contract.

[date]

Mr. Richard H. Unimant
Branch Manager
Best Copy Service
412 Santiago Drive
Wonderland, NJ 07020

Dear Mr. Unimant:

We do not plan to renew our contract for the use of a Copier 14X40 copying machine. The contract expires June 20 of this year.

The copying machine is located at our downtown office in Melrose. We would like to have the machine removed at your earliest possible convenience.

Sincerely,

Phlange A. Indelible
Office Manager

PAI:jls

Letter Firing Vendor Because of Economic Conditions

Sample Letter 9.17 was written to a vendor to explain why the writer would not be using the company's services anymore. The reason for the firing was that business was off for the letter writer. The writer's tone is friendly but clear, expressing regrets that for the time being he can no longer do business with this vendor.

Sample Letter 9.17.   Letter firing a vendor.

[date]

Mr. David Epstein
Sales Manager
Pompton Paper Products
Wooster, ID 83230

Dear David:

I know you're well aware that sales have been soft lately for us. Well, this has caused us to reexamine the profitability of all of our vendor relationships. Because the costs of your goods are much higher than other paper product suppliers we do business with, we are going to terminate our current relationship with Pompton Paper Products.

Our decision reflects our determination to get our gross margins in better shape and in no way reflects badly on the service we've received from your sales representatives nor on the quality of your goods. The professionals at Pompton Paper Products are among the most helpful and informed with whom we do business.

I am really hopeful that economic conditions change so that we're able to do business with Pompton Paper Products again. Until then, please know that we've appreciated the service you've given us over the past eight years and are grateful for all the help you've given us in establishing ourselves as the leading retailer of stationery supplies in the Southwest.

Sincerely,

Jeffrey Anne
Vice President

CHAPTER 10

Personnel letters

A large volume of correspondence flows through the personnel department of every major business. Smaller businesses may also find their mailboxes and outboxes stuffed with personnel-related letters. Whether they are written by the business or by a prospective employee of the business, when personnel-related letters are written effectively they can do a good deal to enhance the credibility of both the business and the prospective employee.

Personnel letters may not secure business, but they will help ensure that you hire the best possible candidate for a job and maintain a good relationship with that candidate once he or she is on board. If you are looking for a job, some of the letters in this chapter can be used as models for selling yourself to a prospective employer.

Many other personnel matters call for written communication, but usually not in letter form. Such issues as organizational changes, labor relations activities, changes in benefits, office closings, and other in-house matters are most often addressed in memorandums distributed to employees in the workplace. Since letters are rarely sent in these cases, they are not covered here.

Many of the letters in this chapter can be sent as emails or as attachments to emails. But formal letters offering employment or terminating employees are still largely sent as conventional letters. And some companies specify whether they want to receive correspondence through email or letters sent through the mail. For those letters in this chapter that can be adapted to emails, it's simple enough to copy the text of the sample letter into the text of your email.

Job Interview Request Letters

Sample Letters 10.1 through 10.5 were written by prospective employees to request job interviews.

Sample Letter 10.1 was written in response to an advertisement the letter writer had seen. The writer refers to the advertisement, mentions a bit about her background that is appropriate to the advertised position, asks for an interview, and gives the reader information about how to reach her during the day. She also indicates that she has enclosed a résumé for the reader's perusal.

Sample Letter 10.2 was written to request an interview after the letter writer had had a brief conversation with the addressee. The writer asks that his application be considered for a specific open position, gives the reader some information about his past work experience, and asks that his résumé be routed to the appropriate people at the company.

If either of these two letters were sent as an email, you would be sure to mention "the *attached* résumé" rather than "the *enclosed* résumé." This holds true for any other letter from this or any other chapter that contains an enclosure: in an email, you would refer to it as an attachment.

Sample Letter 10.3 was also written as a follow-up to a conversation, but here the letter writer is not applying for a specific position. Instead, she is asking that the addressee give her any advice on seeking a position at his company. She thanks him for the talk they had, mentions her professional background, asks if he might be able to refer her to any appropriate person within his company, and mentions when she will try to call him again.

Sample Letter 10.1.   Letter requesting job interview based on advertisement.

[date]

Mr. Jacob L. Rudman
Parris Sheet Metal Company
312 West Main Street
Boonton, NJ 07005

Dear Mr. Rudman:

Enclosed is my résumé, which I am sending in response to your advertisement on *The Boonton Chronicle*'s website for a production engineer.

I am currently employed at Heavy Sheet Metal Company as one of three production engineers. I have complete responsibility for the sheet metal fabrication process from beginning to end. As you can see from my résumé, I have been a production engineer for the past five years.

Please feel free to call me at my office during the day or at my home in the evening. Both numbers are listed on my résumé. I will call you on Tuesday, January 17, to arrange a convenient time for us to meet if I have not heard from you before then.

I look forward to speaking with you.

Sincerely,

Marie L. Dow

enc.

Sample Letter 10.2.   Letter requesting job interview as follow-up to phone conversation.

[date]

Ms. Elaine Longworth
Personnel Director
Primary Textbooks Company, Inc.
One Parkway Plaza
Brighton, OR 97065

Dear Ms. Longworth:

Please consider my application for the humanities editor position in the college division at Primary Textbooks, which we discussed during our brief phone conversation earlier this week.

As you can see from my enclosed résumé, I have been at Andoris Publishing Company for four years. The work I have done there and at Andover Parris and Cromwell & Fitch seems to mesh well with the qualifications Primary Textbooks desires in a college editor. I would welcome the opportunity to make a move into a larger publishing house with Primary Textbooks' reputation.

Please forward my résumé to the appropriate people, and give me a call should you need more information from me.

Thanks for your consideration. I look forward to hearing from you.

Sincerely,

Max Birney

enc.

Sample Letter 10.3.   Letter requesting job advice.

[date]

Mr. Orin P. Hikep
Vice President
Franing, Transcome & Lewis Company
12 Broadway
Boonton, NJ 07005

Dear Mr. Hikep:

Enclosed is the copy of my résumé that I mentioned I would send you when we talked earlier today. I appreciate your taking the time to look at it. If there are any suggestions you can make to improve it, I would be very grateful.

As you can see, I've been at Hungadunga & McCormick for almost four years. The firm is a small typesetting company, which has offered many opportunities for me to develop skills in composition. I now feel that it is time for me to move to a larger company that will offer me more of a chance to move into a management position.

If you know of any opportunities at Franing, Transcome & Lewis, please let me know. Feel free to pass on my résumé to the appropriate division. I am also sending a copy of my résumé to Larry Fenner in your personnel department. I spoke briefly with him about a position at your company.

I know that you are very busy, Mr. Hikep, and I just want to thank you again for agreeing to look at my résumé and for being willing to help. I'll call you after Thanksgiving to see if you have any suggestions.

Sincerely,

Carol Nesin

enc.

Sample Letter 10.4 was written to request a job interview on the basis of a referral. The letter writer makes it clear in her first paragraph that she is writing at the recommendation of a mutual acquaintance who told her the reader's company was seeking to fill a position. She goes on to tell the reader a little bit about her background, and closes by asking for an interview.

Sample Letter 10.4. Letter requesting job interview on the basis of referral.

[date]

Ms. Kimberly Duachim
Pulverize Products, Inc.
23 Reply Place
Biloxi, MO 63025

Dear Ms. Duachim:

I am sending my résumé to you on the recommendation of Lawrence Kernel of Splendid Paper Corporation. Lawrence told me that you were accepting applications for a product manager. From Lawrence's report, your company sounds very attractive to me. I would be interested in talking with you to learn more about your company and the position.

For the past four years, I have been at Quile Investment Products, Inc. Before that, I was at Laramy Products, Inc. The work I've done at these companies has given me a wide range of experience and an opportunity to develop skills that are essential to a product manager.

I would welcome the opportunity to talk with you or to answer any questions about my background and career that you might have. You can reach me during the day at 999-555-5555.

Thank you for your consideration.

Sincerely,

Gladys T. Namelock

enc.

Sample Letter 10.5 was written to thank a prospective employer for a job interview. He thanks the reader, goes on to express his pleasure at having met him and others at the company, and mentions the fact that he would welcome the opportunity to work at the company.

Sample Letter 10.5. Letter thanking prospective employer for job interview.

[date]

Mr. George Penelope
Assistant Personnel Officer
Boonton Life Insurance Trust
34 Old Boonton Road
Boonton, NJ 07005

Dear Mr. Penelope:

Thank you very much for the opportunity to talk with you on May 25. It was a very enjoyable experience, and I also learned a great deal about the responsibilities your job opening entails.

My conversation with you, along with my conversations with Mr. Hoelsch and Ms. Sivad, reinforced my opinion that Boonton Life Insurance Trust is a company that I would like to work for. I feel that Boonton Life Insurance Trust offers an opportunity for professional as well as personal growth. For these reasons, I would very much like to be a part of the personnel division.

Thank you again for your time. I am looking forward to hearing from you soon.

Sincerely,

David A. Inacca

Letters Accompanying Résumés

Sample Letters 10.6 and 10.7 were both written to accompany résumés sent to a prospective employer.

Sample Letter 10.6 was sent to follow up a meeting with the addressee. The letter writer reminds the reader where they met, goes on to give some information about his professional and academic background, and closes by asking that he and the reader meet to discuss employment prospects.

Sample Letter 10.7 was written to accompany a résumé. Here, the writer's purpose is to introduce himself to a prospective employer. He mentions some of his professional and school-related experience, and expresses an interest in meeting with the addressee at his earliest convenience.

Sample Letter 10.6. Letter accompanying résumé from recent graduate.

[date]

Mr. King L. Smythe
Boonton Life Insurance Trust
34 Old Boonton Road
Boonton, NJ 07005

Dear Mr. Smythe:

Several weeks ago, I was invited to stop into your department to fill out an application for a position with Boonton Life Insurance Trust. On my way out, I had the opportunity to speak with you for a few minutes on the elevator. You mentioned at the time that there were no openings available to match my interests, but that you would keep me in mind for any openings in the future. As I told you when we spoke, I am a recent graduate of the New Jersey State University with a Bachelor of Science degree in finance and I am interested in an entry-level position in life insurance sales.

Throughout my four years in college, I maintained consistently high grades in my business courses as well as in my elective courses. I feel that the courses I have taken have strengthened my analytical skills and provided me with a sound background in the financial system.

In addition to my academic work, I have also held various jobs in the past six years to help finance my education. Through my work experience and my involvement in extra-curricular activities at school, I have developed a sense of responsibility and a deeper understanding of dealing with people. I feel that these qualities, along with my sincere interest in insurance as a career, will make me an asset to Boonton Life Insurance Trust.

At your convenience, I would like to get together with you to learn more about career opportunities at Boonton Life Insurance Trust and also to discuss my career interests in greater detail. Will you please get in touch with me so that we can arrange an interview? I can be reached during the day at 201-689-4623 or by email at ned_lared1@gmail.com.

Thank you for your consideration.

Sincerely,

Ned Lared

Enclosure

Sample Letter 10.7. Letter accompanying résumé from a person seeking to change jobs.

[date]

Mr. Sidney T. Fairview
Data Center Manager
Arlington Products, Inc.
43 East Third Street
Montville, NJ 07045

Dear Mr. Fairview:

I am a young data processing manager in the market for a new, more challenging position in a data processing environment that is conducive to career advancement and personal growth. I am willing to relocate.

I have gained my experience at JLS, Inc., of Levittown, Pennsylvania. JLS, Inc., is a service bureau providing financial institutions in the United States and Canada with automated trust management systems including online data access, daily file updates, and periodic report generation. JLS, Inc., maintains one of the largest data center operations in this region of the country.

I enclose my résumé for your review and consideration. I have also included an expanded version of my résumé to highlight some of the responsibilities and some results of my work in the positions I have held. If you would like further details or clarification of my experience, I would be more than happy to supply anything further I can. I am anxious to meet with you to discuss possible career opportunities at Arlington Products, Inc., at your earliest convenience.

Thank you for taking the time to review my credentials. I look forward to the possibility of discussing my professional career with you in the near future.

Cordially,

Larry E. Mahaffey

Enclosures

Sample Letter 10.8 was written to introduce a candidate's application for a job. While the formal application often takes place through a personnel department, occasionally it is useful to make key staff members and decision makers aware of the intention to apply for a position. This candidate immediately relates his qualifications for the position, linking the facts of his résumé, which he has enclosed, into a coherent narrative. It is critical that the application letter be intriguing, forceful, and error-free, since it is the first contact with a potential employer and the old cliché is true: you never get a second chance to make a first impression. The writer closes by expressing his hopes for an interview and allowing for future correspondence.

Sample Letter 10.8.   Letter of application.

[date]

Mr. Paul Haeuptle, Principal
Vermilion High School
10643 Firelands Road
Cuyahoga, OH 43074

Dear Mr. Haeuptle:

I am writing to apply for a position in the English Department at Vermilion High School. I received an M.A. in teaching from Emory University, a master's in theological studies from Harvard University, and a B.A. in English from Bethany College. I am currently certified in the state of Georgia to teach English in grades 7–12, and I hold an In-Field certificate in Gifted Education and endorsements in Advanced Placement

Literature and Composition, Advanced Placement Language and Composition, and the International Baccalaureate Program.

For the last five years, I have been employed as a teacher in Georgia. This year has been a particularly strong one for me, as my colleagues recognized my dedication and commitment to excellence by nominating me Norcross High School's Teacher of the Year and my students nominated me for Who's Who Among American Teachers, 20X5. I have taught Honors tenth grade, College Preparatory eleventh grade, and Gifted eleventh-grade English. Additionally, I taught Advanced Placement Literature and Composition to seniors last year; in my first year teaching this course, my students passed with a three or higher at a rate 5% above the national average. At the end of last year I was asked to implement an eleventh-grade Advanced Placement Language and Composition course for the 20X7–20X8 school year.

I would be very interested in speaking with you at greater length about a position teaching English at Vermilion High and the ways I might contribute to your community. I am enclosing a hard copy of my résumé and a copy of my Georgia certificate and endorsements. Copies of my undergraduate and graduate transcripts are being sent under separate cover, as are my references.

I look forward to hearing from your office soon, and I hope that we can arrange an interview sometime this month.

Sincerely yours,

Leigh Weeks

encl.

Even the most meticulous employer needs a reminder now and then; Sample Letter 10.9 is a follow-up letter to gently prod the recipient into replying to the writer's initial letter of application. The first paragraph states the particulars of the original letter—its date, contents, and purpose—and then the writer applies subtle pressure to respond by announcing his presence in the employer's vicinity and some specific dates for a possible meeting. By including his phone number, the close hints that a courtesy call at the least is expected.

Sample Letter 10.9.   Follow-up to letter of application.

[date]

Mr. Paul Haeuptle, Principal
Vermilion High School
10643 Firelands Road
Cuyahoga, OH 43074

Dear Mr. Haeuptle:

I sent you a letter of application and résumé on March 1, 20X8, applying for the position of English teacher at Vermilion High School, but I have yet to hear from your office that you have received my correspondence.

I am very interested in the prospect of working at Vermilion, with its diverse student body and a faculty committed to excellence. I will be relocating to Cuyahoga this summer and will be in your vicinity the third week in April. I would like to meet with you about the opening in your English Department. Could you please inform me whether you have received my application materials? I would be happy to resend any information you may need or submit further materials in support of my application. You may reach me at my home number, 404-265-6897. I look forward to hearing from you soon.

Sincerely,

Leigh Weeks

Letter Withdrawing Candidacy for a Position

The letter writer of Sample Letter 10.10 had applied for a position. She has learned unofficially that she will not receive the position. Rather than wait and get a formal rejection letter, the writer takes herself out of the running for the job.

Sample Letter 10.10.   Letter to prospective employer in which writer asks to be removed from list of job candidates.

[date]

Ms. Joan Maside
Personnel Director
Alaning Wendell Screwbolt Company
12 Rivermore Drive
Chestnut, NJ 07009

Dear Ms. Maside:

Over the past month or so, I've let you know how interested I am in the director of quality assurance position you have open at your company. You've been kind enough to let me know that I'm seriously being considered as a candidate. For that reason, I wanted to let you know as soon as I reached my decision that I no longer be considered a candidate at this time.

Here at Savin Hill Machine Works, I am in the midst of developing and implementing several projects for the company. It's important to me and to my employer that I get these projects on track and make sure they get done. Because so much of my time has gone into these projects, I feel it is best for me to stay put in my current situation for the time being.

Thank you for all the time and support you've given me over the past several months. I am hopeful that our paths will cross again in the near future.

Sincerely,

Georgina Krauss

Letters Responding to Job Applications

Sample Letters 10.11 through 10.24 are designed to be used in a variety of circumstances to respond to job applicants.

Sample Letter 10.11 is an example of a standard acknowledgment of a job application that was written to a recent applicant. The letter writer courteously acknowledges the reader's application and assures him that his application will be reviewed. She concludes by expressing her appreciation that the reader applied for the position. This letter may easily be used as a model letter for any applicant search in which acknowledgments must be sent out.

Sample Letter 10.12 is an example of an acknowledgment sent to an applicant qualified for a position. The letter writer thanks the applicant, informs him that there were many qualified applicants, and asks him to feel free to inquire about his status once a certain date has passed.

Sample Letter 10.13 may also be sent as an acknowledgment to a qualified applicant, but here the letter writer asks the applicant to call his office to arrange for a second interview. He expresses the fact that he was impressed with the applicant and that he would like to have him meet more members of the firm.

Sample Letter 10.14 was written to inform a qualified applicant about the status of a job search to fill a position for which the reader has applied. The letter writer clearly spells out the status of the job search to date and lets the reader know exactly what procedure the search committee will be taking to make its decision.

Sample Letter 10.11. Letter acknowledging application for position.

[date]

Mr. Maxwell L. Topor
988 Boston Avenue
Huntington, ME 04021

Subject: Writing Instructor Position

Dear Mr. Topor:

Thank you very much for applying for the writing instructor position at Boonton Community College. Please be assured that your application will be reviewed along with others that have been received. If your qualifications are considered appropriate for this position, you will be contacted again for the purpose of setting an appointment date for an interview.

In any event, please accept the appreciation of Boonton Community College for wishing to include us in your future professional plans.

Sincerely yours,

Elizabeth R. Jennifer
Director of Personnel

erj:jls

Sample Letter 10.12.   Letter responding to qualified applicant.

[date]

Mr. Brian Aberbroom
3 Forrester Place
Bethany, OH 43067

Dear Mr. Aberbroom:

Thank you for your application for the position of clerical supervisor.

We have had an overwhelming response to our ad for this position and expect to select a qualified applicant by June 5. Please feel free to get in touch with us after that date.

Thank you for your interest in the company. Best wishes for the future.

Cordially,

Blaise T. Rendeler
Personnel Director

btr/nls

Sample Letter 10.13. Letter inviting applicant in for second interview.

[date]

Mr. Peter Jensen
34 Eckerd Drive
Fontaine, NE 68053

Dear Peter:

Thank you very much for having taken the time to meet with me during my recruiting trip to Fontaine. I was most favorably impressed with you, and our recruiting committee has concurred in my recommendation that we invite you to meet more members of our company.

If you continue to be interested in our company, I would appreciate it if you would call our recruiting coordinator, Bill Cryer, at 803-555-1439, to arrange a mutually convenient time to visit us.

We look forward to hearing from you. Again, thank you for your interest in our organization and for having taken the time to talk with me.

Best regards,

Gary A. Tieszen

GAT:jls

Sample Letter 10.14. Letter giving applicant status report on search for employee.

[date]

Mr. Trevor L. Kemper
56 Longacre Road
Belvedere, WA 90056

Dear Trevor:

I wanted to send you a short note to tell you where we are in the search for an alumni director for Boonton Community College. As of August 1, we had received 34 applications. A selection committee composed of members of the alumni council, faculty, and staff has been appointed and will review résumés by mid-August. The committee will select four or five applicants who seem to be best prepared to do the job and will invite them to Boonton for an interview later in the month. Following those interviews, the committee will recommend to the president its first three choices in order of preference. The president will choose from among the three the person he thinks can best do the job. He will announce the appointment on or about September 1.

Please note that we will not be reporting on the progress of the search until an appointment is announced. Should you have any questions, however, please do not hesitate to telephone me.

Trevor, let me tell you again how much we appreciate your willingness to be considered for this important position. You are well qualified for the position, and I know that the committee will be very interested in your candidacy. It is going to be a difficult task for the selection committee.

Thank you for all you have done and will do for Boonton Community College.

Sincerely,

David R. Xenadnas
Chair, Search Committee

drx/ras

Sample Letter 10.15 was written to an applicant who did not qualify for a position. The letter writer thanks the applicant for his interest and regretfully informs him that he does not have the qualifications to fill the position. She then wishes him her best in his job search.

Sample Letter 10.15.   Letter to applicant who did not qualify for position.

[date]

Mr. Adam Beazle
67 Yorkway Plaza, Apt. 4
York, NJ 07032

Dear Mr. Beazle:

Thank you for your interest in the position of production manager for the Belmont Sheet Metal Company. I have carefully reviewed your application and regret to tell you that I do not feel you have the qualifications necessary to fulfill the responsibilities of this job.

Good luck in your job search. I feel certain that you will find a position where you can use your talents and experience to good advantage.

Sincerely,

Gwendolyn T. Quackenbush
Personnel Director

gtq:nls

Sample Letter 10.16 was written to respond to a qualified applicant to inform him that no position was open. The letter writer makes it clear that he thinks the applicant is well qualified but that there were simply more applicants than the company had positions to offer.

Sample Letter 10.16. Letter responding to qualified applicant informing him that no position is available.

[date]

Mr. Stanley R. Pixell
32 Roskanokov Drive, Apt. 3A
Endicott, WI 53056

Dear Mr. Pixell:

We want to thank you for interviewing with our company during our recruiting trip to Brighton. You have an outstanding academic background, and you made a very favorable impression.

We delayed making final determinations about employment offers until we were able to interview the majority of potential candidates, including those whose schedules did not permit them to interview until the Christmas holidays. It is unfortunate that we have fewer available spaces than we do qualified candidates. Accordingly, we regret that we will not be able to make an offer to you at this time.

Thank you again for your interest.

Cordially,

Craig D. Creyton III
FISKE, TRUSOME, SCADABOUT & YIELDS, P.C.

CDC: GAD

Sample Letter 10.17 was written to a qualified applicant whose qualifications did not match exactly the qualifications that were being sought for an open position. The letter writer thanks the applicant for his interest, then explains that because there were so many applicants from which to choose, they chose the applicant who was an exact fit. The writer then suggests that perhaps in the future there will be a more suitable position open. She closes by wishing the applicant well in his search.

Sample Letter 10.17. Letter to qualified candidate who did not match position exactly.

[date]

Mr. Martin L. Preston
43 Lorraine Terrace
Punxatawney, PA 15056

FACULTY POSITION AT PUNXATAWNEY COALITION COLLEGE

Mr. Preston, thank you for your interest in a faculty position at Punxatawney Coalition College. We received many responses from very highly qualified candidates like you.

With so many superbly qualified candidates, we looked finally for the one whose background and qualifications gave us just the right fit for our exact needs this semester. I'm sorry to have to say that the position is being offered to one of the other candidates.

This does not mean, however, that we were unimpressed with your credentials. Perhaps in the future we will have another opening that will better fit your qualifications. I wish you well in your pursuit of the right position.

DR. HELEN L. DAVIDS
CHAIR, HUMANITIES

jls

Sample Letter 10.18 is a variation of Sample Letter 10.15. It was written to inform an applicant that a different applicant who was deemed more appropriate was chosen to fill an open position. The letter writer clearly explains the situation and closes by thanking the applicant for his interest.

Sample Letter 10.18. Letter informing applicant that someone else got the job.

[date]

Mr. Harold M. Peeking
543 Houghton Place
New Britain, CT 06045

Dear Mr. Peeking:

Thank you for the time you took to come in and talk with us about the quality control engineer position. We cannot place you now because we have chosen another candidate whose background, we feel, is more closely suited to our current needs. We will keep your résumé in our active file, however, in case a more suitable position opens up.

Thank you again for your interest in Ainsworth Sheet Metal Company. Best wishes for success in your career endeavors.

Cordially,

Letitia T. Hall
Personnel Officer

LTH:mln

Sample Letter 10.19 was written to an applicant explaining that no positions were open that matched her training or experience. The letter writer acknowledges the employment inquiry, explains that the company has no positions open currently to match the reader's credentials, but asks to keep a record of the applicant's qualifications on file for future job openings.

Sample Letter 10.19. Letter informing applicant that there are no positions matching her training or experience.

[date]

Ms. Pauline R. Yeltar
34 Douglass Road
Far Hills, VT 05043

Dear Ms. Yeltar:

Thank you for inquiring about employment possibilities at Farmington & Gray. We appreciated the opportunity to review your qualifications in relation to our current job openings.

At this time, however, we do not have a position open that would properly use your training and experience. We would like to keep a record of your qualifications in our active file, however, so we may consider you for any appropriate future openings.

Although we are currently unable to offer you a position, we do wish you success in your career.

Cordially,

Linda B. Blaisdale
Personnel Officer

lbb/dls

Sample Letter 10.20 was written to reject an application that came as a result of an online advertisement. The letter writer thanks the applicant, informs him that he did not get the job, assures him that a record of his application will be kept on file, and closes by wishing the applicant well in his search for employment.

Sample Letter 10.20. Letter rejecting an online advertisement applicant.

[date]

Mr. Jacob L. McGuffie
5 Merrimac Trail
Trailblaze, ID 83245

Dear Mr. McGuffie:

Thank you for your letter responding to our online advertisement for an executive secretary. As you can guess, the response was overwhelming. Although your résumé was impressive, we had only one opening.

Even though we were unable to place you in this job, we will keep your résumé on file for future reference in the event that a suitable position becomes available.

Thank you for your interest in Vladmir, Tilling & Underquist. Best wishes in your search for employment.

Sincerely,

David Marshall
Personnel Officer

mn

Sample Letter 10.21 was written to reject a summer-job applicant. The letter writer keeps the letter short and to the point, thanking the applicant for her inquiry, but explaining that no summer jobs are open. He assures the applicant that her name will be kept on file and thanks her for her interest.

Sample Letter 10.21.   Letter rejecting applicant for summer job.

[date]

Ms. Tricia Levon
34 Rightone Road
Greenfreer, WV 26045

Dear Ms. Levon:

Thank you for your inquiry about the possibility of summer employment at our company. While we do not anticipate any summer openings currently, we will be glad to keep your name on file in the event that the situation should change.

Thank you again for your interest.

Sincerely,

Francis K. Cheff
Personnel Officer

fkc/jls

Sample Letter 10.22 was written to reject an applicant who was recommended for a job. The letter writer thanks the applicant and acknowledges the recommendation, but explains that the response to the opening was overwhelming and that he is unable to offer the applicant a job.

Sample Letter 10.23 was written to the person recommending a candidate who was not hired to fill a position. The letter writer thanks him for the recommendation, but explains that since the company is cutting back, few jobs are being offered. The writer offers to keep an eye out for other jobs in the field, but is not overly encouraging that anything will change at her company.

Sample Letter 10.22. Letter rejecting person recommended for job.

[date]

Mr. Wilson Davidson
P.O. Box 704
Sparta Community College
Sparta, WV 26032

Dear Mr. Davidson:

Thank you for applying for the position of editorial assistant at our organization. While you were recommended by Professor Gary E. Limes, and your education and experience appear to be exceptional, the response that we received from the few inquiries that we made was overwhelming. I regret to inform you that a candidate was chosen shortly before your letter of interest arrived.

Best wishes for success in your career search.

Best regards,

David Marshall
Personnel Director

DM:ll

cc: Gary E. Limes

Sample Letter 10.23.   Letter to person recommending a candidate who could not be hired.

[date]

Mr. Frederick T. Jones
Jones, Jones & Gary
43 Edgar Drive
Humanity, SC 29045

Dear Fred:

Thank you for sending me Eugene Balk's résumé.

Arlington Products, Inc., is in the midst of a severe staff reduction program, which, it appears, will continue throughout the summer. As a result, a hiring freeze is in effect.

There is some growth in the computer industry. I wonder whether Eugene has looked into the possibility of working with one of the city's many computer firms. He has impressive credentials in programming support.

I will keep my eyes open for other possible jobs available in artificial intelligence, both at our company and elsewhere. But in view of the current situation here, I would not want to get Mr. Balk's hopes up.

Cordially,

Hope T. McCormick
Personnel Director

HTM:lmn

Sample Letter 10.24 was sent as a letter of rejection to a person who had been asked to apply for the job. The letter writer thanks the applicant for applying, but explains that after reviewing the applicant's work samples and experience, she does not feel the job would be appropriate for the applicant.

Sample Letter 10.24. Letter rejecting solicited employment application.

[date]

Mr. Mark Perkins
95 Belltoll Road
Ketchum, ID 83205

Dear Mr. Perkins:

Thank you for sending your work samples and discussing your views about the editor's position we have open. I've reviewed your work and reflected at length on our last conversation, particularly your hesitancy to take on an assignment to demonstrate your editorial approach to analytical topics. Since we talked I've interviewed several other candidates with substantial editorial credentials and have become convinced that proven analytical skills or technical knowledge of the investments area is an important prerequisite for the job.

My conclusion is that your background is not appropriate for the position and, frankly, that you would not enjoy the job during a necessary period of training. If, however, you are interested in establishing a freelance relationship with our publication, I'd be happy to consider using you.

Thanks again, Mark, for your interest in the job.

Cordially,

Florence Hoagland
Publisher

FH/ec

Letters Thanking People Who Recommended Applicants

Sample Letters 10.25 and 10.26 were written to thank people who recommended applicants for jobs. Sample Letter 10.25 was written to thank a person who had recommended someone who was offered the job but decided to take a job elsewhere. The letter writer explains that she really would have liked to hire the applicant. She asks that the reader keep in mind other potential applicants.

Sample Letter 10.26 was written by an applicant to thank someone for recommending him for the job he got. The letter writer is direct and sincere in expressing his gratitude.

Sample Letter 10.25. Letter thanking someone for referral of prospective employee.

[date]

Dr. Lisa L. Ekorb
Brikton Management Services, Inc.
43 Clark Street
Bayonne, WV 26234

Dear Lisa:

Thank you so much for referring Carla Sorel and Donna Asconia. Your assessment of each was right on the mark. Both are superior candidates at their respective professional levels.

I offered the assistant's job to Carla. She, however, decided to take a position with another public relations firm in town, Vladmir & Associates. Donna and I were interested in each other, but we both agreed that someone with her credentials was overqualified for the position I was seeking to fill.

I am still looking for someone. It's very hard finding candidates as good as Carla and Donna. Carla was the person I wanted.

Please keep me in mind if you have any other suggestions. I would very much like to take you to breakfast or lunch at your convenience. It would give me a better chance to understand what Brikton Management Services does.

I look forward to hearing from you.

Cordially,

Maryanne L. Niltes

mln/mfr

Sample Letter 10.26.   Letter acknowledging reference.

[date]

Mr. Martin Heady
Raphel Design, Inc.
312 West Main Street
Boonton, NJ 07005

Dear Mr. Heady:

Graphcon Tittle, Inc., has offered me a position as a graphic designer beginning January 15, 20X4. I realize you are probably just finishing up with the holiday madness, but I'd like to stop by and see you before I start the new job.

Thanks so much for the kind words you had to say about me to Al Newport, the managing director at Graphcon Tittle. The designer's position promises to be grueling, but the internship I had at Raphel Design was good training for anything they plan to throw my way.

Thanks again. I look forward to seeing you soon.

Sincerely,

Brad T. Zeiber

Job-Offer Letters

Sample Letters 10.27 through 10.33 are job-offer–related letters.

Sample Letter 10.27 is an example of a straightforward job-offer letter. The letter writer expresses pleasure at offering the position, lists the various benefits the prospective employee will receive, specifies the date by which she hopes to receive acceptance, and offers to answer any questions.

Sample Letter 10.28 confirms an offer that had already been verbally accepted. The writer clearly confirms the offer by naming the position and salary offered. He then explains some of the benefits that will be offered and the regular hours of employment expected of employees. He closes by stating the date on which he expects the reader to report for duty.

Sample Letter 10.29 was written to offer an executive position to an applicant. The letter writer makes the offer, briefly recounting the responsibilities and compensation, then closes by asking for confirmation by a specific date.

Sample Letter 10.27.   Letter making a job offer.

[date]

Ms. Joan B. Delan
3045 Triston Road
Blarneysville, IL 60076

Dear Ms. Delan:

We at Hinsdale-Reed Construction Company are pleased to offer you the position of assistant controller at the annual salary of $117,000. In addition, you will be paid cash in lieu of profit sharing until you are eligible for the normal profit sharing plan, and you will receive two weeks' paid vacation in 20X3 if you start on or before May 31, 20X3. Hinsdale-Reed will also reimburse you for family medical insurance coverage until you are picked up on our plan. I hope this letter will assist you in making your decision.

Hinsdale-Reed hopes you will be able to join its family. We look forward to hearing from you on or before Monday, May 22, 20X3.

If you have any questions about Hinsdale-Reed, please call me.

Sincerely,

Tracey Hunt
Assistant Personnel Officer

TH/LG

enc.

cc: Jack Reed
     Personnel File

Sample Letter 10.28.   Letter confirming job offer.

[date]

Mr. Ambrose L. Mason
323 Alewife Brook Parkway
Hyde Park, NH 03045

Dear Mr. Mason:

It gives me great pleasure to confirm our verbal offer and your acceptance to join Parrisi Accounting as an auditor.

Your compensation will include your monthly salary of $4,083.34 (which is equivalent to $49,000.08 annually) plus the benefits outlined in the enclosed summary. After three months of employment, you will be eligible for nine days of vacation in the calendar year 20X6. According to the terms of our current policy, your salary and performance will be reviewed in October 20X6.

Our regular working hours are from 9 A.M. to 5 P.M., Monday through Friday. On your first day, please report directly to Carl Josephs in the Personnel Department to arrange orientation and to initiate the administrative procedures. We believe that you will make a significant contribution to Parrisi and, at the same time, will realize both the personal and professional growth you seek.

As soon as possible, please acknowledge your acceptance of this job offer by signing the enclosed copy of this letter and returning it to me. We very much look forward to your joining the company on Monday, January 27, 20X6.

Best regards,

Roy E. Early
Employment Supervisor

ree:jls
Enclosures

cc: John Taylor
        Personnel File

Sample Letter 10.29.   Letter offering executive position.

[date]

Mr. Kent L. Bernard
56 Savin Hill Avenue
Beacon, CO 80045

Dear Kent:

It was a pleasure to meet with you in Houston last week. I'm glad we had the time to have lunch and talk.

I was very impressed with your ideas about architectural design and your suggestions for growth for our company. After discussing you and your application with the Board of Directors for Gagnon Architectural Company, I am pleased to offer you the position of design director of our Commercial Design Division.

In this position, you would report directly to me. You would be responsible for strategic planning and budgeting for the Commercial Design Division.

We spoke briefly about benefits, but a brief rundown might be helpful for you. The salary is $134,000 a year. You will be eligible for 4 weeks' vacation, master medical coverage for you and your family, a daycare subsidy of $150 a week, a retirement plan, and stock options in the company. We can discuss these benefits in more detail if you are interested in accepting the position.

I hope you will give this offer your serious consideration. I would like to receive an acknowledgment by May 9. I hope it will be an enthusiastic yes.

Best regards,

Joanna Murray
Principal

jm/ns

Sample Letter 10.30 is a job-offer letter that includes the conditions of employment. Sample Letter 10.31 is a job-offer letter that explains the bonus structure to the recipient. Sample Letter 10.32 is a job-offer letter that lays out the basic details of a stock option plan being offered.

Sample Letter 10.30.   Letter offering job, with conditions of employment.

[date]

Ms. Priscilla Venture
45 Terrace Drive
Blacksburg, WY 82023

Dear Ms. Venture:

I am pleased to offer you the position of executive assistant to the chief operating officer of Global Enterprises, Inc. We'd like to hear from you in writing by October 8, about whether you plan to accept the offer. The specifics of the offer are outlined below:

The salary for the position is $65,000. We issue paychecks to employees twice a month. You will receive two weeks of paid vacation and be eligible for our employee health insurance benefits after a three-month waiting period. After six months, you'll also become eligible to participate in the company's 401(k) retirement plan.

If you accept the position, we ask that you agree not to hold any other jobs during the length of your employment at Global. Because you will have access to confidential trademark information and financial records of the company, we ask that you agree in writing to keep all proprietary information confidential. We also ask that you agree not to compete directly with the company for a year after you cease working for Global Enterprises. You will find a confidentiality and noncompete letter of agreement for you to sign enclosed with this letter.

The term of this job offer is for one year, at which time we will renegotiate. If the employer decides to terminate this agreement, he may do so as long as you are given 60 days' written notice.

Please call me if you have any questions or if I can assist you in any way. I look forward to receiving your response by October 8.

Sincerely,

Alan Karl
Personnel Director

Encs.

Sample Letter 10.31.   Letter offering job with bonus.

[date]

Mr. Bob Roberts
44 Forunet Drive
Biscayne, AL 35032

Dear Mr. Roberts:

We are pleased to offer you the position of manager of our retail showroom. The salary for the position is $57,000. You are also eligible for a bonus of 10% of all net profits at your location for those months in which you meet your target sales goals. The target sales goals are projections based on monthly sales at your location last year.

After you have worked for us for one year, we will renegotiate your compensation package. Either of us can terminate our relationship as long as two weeks' written notice is given.

Please call me if you have any questions, Bob. We are really looking forward to having you on board here.

Sincerely,

Alan Ellenson
Personnel Director

Sample Letter 10.32.   Letter offering job with stock options.

[date]

Ms. Alexis Bratelle
34 Riverway Boulevard
Houston, ID 83245

Dear Ms. Bratelle:

I am pleased to put in writing the offer we made to you to become marketing director for Rope Software, Inc. We agreed you would begin work on October 15, 20X2, and that your employment would run for two years.

Your salary will be $86,500, payable every other Friday. You will also be eligible for all employee benefits we offer, including health and life insurance and a generous 401(k) retirement plan into which Rope Software will match your contributions.

In addition to your salary and benefits we are also offering you the option to purchase up to 250 shares of our common stock at the end of each year. To exercise your stock options, sometime between January 15 and February 15 you must submit your request for the number of shares you wish to purchase, along with a check for $5 for each of those shares, to the secretary of the board of directors. These stock options are not transferable, and unexercised options expire after you've held them for one year.

We may terminate our agreement with you as long as you are given 60 days' written notice. In the case of termination you are entitled to one month's severance pay.

Please confirm your acceptance of this offer by signing this letter and returning it to us. I have enclosed an extra copy for your records.

Sincerely,

Dwight Lavine
Personnel Director

Accepted by,

Name: _____

Date: _____

Sample Letter 10.33 was written to inform a candidate of her acceptance to an internship program. The letter is factual and direct, opening with the most pertinent information: the candidate was accepted. The writer then relates other important facts about the position and the terms of the internship. Information about whether the internship is paid or unpaid would be considered highly pertinent, and should be included in the first paragraph, preferably at the conclusion for impact. The conclusion of the letter is more personal and reassuring.

Sample Letter 10.33. Letter offering summer intern position.

[date]

Ms. Rhashondra Askew
23 Crescent Trace Circle
Decatur, CT 06054

Dear Ms. Askew:

I am pleased to offer you a position as an unpaid summer intern at the Decatur City Schools' Central Office. The internship program begins June 28, 200X, and runs through September 4, 200X.

On June 28 at 8:30 A.M., please report to our Human Resources Department at the Piedmont Street Building. There you will be required to fill out temporary employment paperwork, and you will be photographed for your staff identification card, which must be worn at all times while in the Central Office environs. Please bring two forms of identification with you; one should be a picture ID. If you would like to enroll in the Central Office's cafeteria plan, which provides a variety of lunch specialties at reduced prices, you may do so at that time. Lunch is from 12:30 P.M. to 1:30 P.M.

Attire for the summer is casual but professional. Your day will be spent under the supervision of Ms. Darlene Nichols, who will escort you to your cubicle from Human Resources at 9:15 A.M. and then introduce you to her staff. The majority of your duties will be secretarial. Your work day will end at 5:00 P.M.

I am happy that you have chosen to participate in our summer intern program, and I am confident that this experience will be a rewarding one for both you and the Decatur City Schools' Central Office. Please call me at 404-373-2437 if you have any questions.

Sincerely,

Siah Ngo
Personnel Supervisor

Letters Accepting or Rejecting Job Offers

Sample Letter 10.34 was written as an acceptance of a job offer. The letter writer confirms when he will start and to whom he will report.

Sample Letter 10.35 was written to turn down a job offer. The applicant expresses appreciation for the offer but explains that he thinks it is best for him to stay at his current job.

Sample Letter 10.36 was written to an applicant who has accepted a job offer. The letter writer expresses pleasure at the applicant's decision, confirms his starting salary, and states the date on which she'd like the applicant to begin work.

Sample Letter 10.34. Letter accepting job offer.

[date]

Mr. Mark L. Weyton
Dynoplast Plastics, Inc.
123 East Manning Street
Brigton, NJ 07005

Dear Mr. Weyton:

I was delighted to receive your job offer. I am pleased to accept your offer of the position of associate quality control director at Dynoplast Plastics, Inc.

On Tuesday, December 1, 20X4, I will report to the personnel office to fill out the necessary forms and to arrange for an orientation session.

After meeting you and the others at Dynoplast, I knew it would be a place where I would enjoy working. Thank you for giving me this opportunity.

Sincerely,

Alan R. Rabsen

Sample Letter 10.35. Letter turning down job offer.

[date]

Ms. Mary Matin
Blast Management Consulting
312 Main Street
Alenton, NJ 07005

Dear Ms. Matin:

Thank you for offering me the associate's position at Blast Management Consulting.

I am sorry that I will have to decline your generous offer. The prospect of working at Blast is an exciting one. But right now, I think there is much I can learn at my current position at Houston & Fretter. That, coupled with the big move from Denver to Alenton that the job would entail, convinces me that it's just not the right time for me to accept your offer.

Thanks again for the kind offer. I enjoyed meeting you and all the people at Blast Management and wish you well.

Best regards,

Simon T. Blasder

Sample Letter 10.36.   Letter to applicant who has accepted offer.

[date]

Mr. Edward J. Cole
301 Morlan Street
Bethany, NC 27015

Dear Edward:

We are very pleased that you have accepted the position of assistant communications director at the annual salary of $62,500, with one week's paid vacation in 20X2. We hope that this will be a mutually rewarding and long-lasting relationship.

I hope that you can start work on August 1, 20X2, at 8:30 A.M., at which time you can sign up for our benefits plan and I can orient you to our company. Once again, it is a pleasure to have you in the Petuchnik Brothers family.

If you have any questions, please call me.

Best regards,

Joanne L. Berrigan
Personnel Director

JLB:KAT

cc: John Crimen
     Personnel File

Letter Welcoming New Employee

Sample Letter 10.37 was written to welcome a new employee. The letter writer expresses her enthusiasm for the new employee's arrival and offers help in making his transition easy.

Sample Letter 10.37. Letter welcoming new employee.

[date]

Mr. Alan Drake
15 River Road
Bagdad, VT 05055

Dear Mr. Drake:

We are looking forward to having you as part of the Allagash Cane Company. We were very pleased when you accepted our offer of employment and are sure that you will be a valuable employee.

As you know, the company has plans for growth in many areas. In your new position as controller, your experience and knowledge will help fuel that growth.

Please let me know if there is anything I can do to make your move easier. We are looking forward to having you in the office on June 15, 20X3.

Sincerely,

Martha Granaloff
Personnel Director

MG:ns

Recommendation Letters

Sample Letters 10.38 through 10.43 are examples of letters related to recommendations.

Sample Letter 10.38 is an example of an unqualified letter of recommendation. The letter writer explains that he has been privileged to know the applicant and that he found her to be an invaluable employee. He goes on to enthusiastically support the applicant.

Sample Letter 10.39 was written on behalf of a prospective job applicant. The writer uses a format similar to the recommendation, in which she explains her relationship with the applicant before launching into a description of the candidate's qualifications for a particular job. By the conclusion, the writer has listed not only the candidate's ability, but factual information to enable the recipient to contact this person. The tone throughout is confident, complimentary, and professional. A letter such as this written on behalf of a candidate can also be sent as an email. The text of the letter can easily be used as the text of an email message.

Sample Letter 10.38.   Letter of recommendation.

[date]

Mr. Thomas Stout
Personnel Officer
Riderim Manufacturing Company
12 Western Street
Bont, NJ 07017

Subject: Allison K. Sullivan

Dear Mr. Stout:

I have been privileged to know Ms. Sullivan for three years in my role as managing supervisor at Perceval, McKormick Manufacturing. I am currently director of business products.

While Ms. Sullivan reported to me at Perceval, McKormick, I found her management abilities to be invaluable in helping me to establish our firm as a leader in the office products market. Her conscientious effort and cooperation in doing professional, high-quality work were appreciated.

As a group supervisor, Allison was efficient, innovative, and responsive. She motivates her people with challenge and the opportunity for personal growth.

If you find that Allison's career objectives match your position description, I know of no reason you would be disappointed by her employment performance. Please let me know if you require further information.

Sincerely,

Edward R. Erante

ere/mjm

Sample Letter 10.39.   Letter recommending an outside person.

[date]

Ms. Pamela Lundgren
Queen Bee Renovation
2000 Avenue Maria, Suite 300
North Dorchester, MA 02143

Dear Ms. Lundgren:

The woman I mentioned to you last Thursday on the phone as a potential carpenter with Queen Bee is Elizabeth Tudor. She worked independently as a subcontractor in the Natchez area from 20X3 to 20X7, before joining us at Architects, Inc. in the winter of 20X7. Sadly, she is relocating, but our loss is your gain: she will be moving to the Dorchester area in three weeks.

Elizabeth has extensive experience in carpentry, and worked on the Natchez Trail Memorial project, which is the feather in the cap of our building firm. She served as project manager of the Carpentry Division on the Memorial, and brought her team in under budget and on time. I know that she has many contacts in the construction industry in Mississippi, many of which she used to our benefit on the Memorial and other projects. She seems to know everyone, and I can say that she herself is a good person to know.

I spoke with her about our conversation and your company, and when she heard there was a carpentry position opening up, she expressed an interest in meeting with you to discuss it. If you would like to go over the details of the job with her, you can give her a call at 378-908-1369; youcan reach her by mail at 818 Clairmont Lane, Natchez, Mississippi 64460 or by email at elizabeth_t818@yahoo.com. I'm sure she would love to hear from you. I think you'll find her an enthusiastic and knowledgeable craftswoman. Please let me know how your conversation goes; I would like to know that she has found work with a quality organization like yours.

Sincerely,

Joan Ark

Sample Letter 10.40 is an example of a qualified letter of recommendation. Here the letter writer explains that she is not in a position to comment on the applicant's ability for the type of job for which he is applying. She does comment that the applicant was an average employee who seemed enthusiastic. Such an underwhelming recommendation is severely limited without being out-and-out negative.

Sample Letter 10.40.   Qualified letter of recommendation.

[date]

Ms. Stacey R. Zeno
Personnel Director
Elevated Buildings, Inc.
66 High Street
Directed, TX 75076

RECOMMENDATION FOR WILLIAM B. TROMBOND

Ms. Zeno, I am writing to you in response to your request for a recommendation of Mr. William B. Trombond, who worked for me in the bookkeeping department of Big Buildings Corp. He was not a clerk when he worked for me, however, but rather a bookkeeper. I am not qualified to comment on his capabilities as a clerk.

Bill was an average bookkeeper. He is a pleasant person who got along well with his fellow employees.

He also seemed enthusiastic about his job in the bookkeeping department. His attitude toward his work and his cooperation were above average.

If you need any further information from me, please let me know.

JENNIFER R. TRUDESCAH
CONTROLLER

JRT:mrm

Sample Letters 10.41 and 10.42 were both written as recommendations for employees who had been terminated by the letter writer's company. In Sample Letter 10.41, the employee being recommended was let go because of company cutbacks. The tone of the letter is positive. In Sample Letter 10.42, the employee was let go because of incompetence. The writer is careful to lay out the facts without misleading the recipient in one direction or another about the qualifications of the employee. Instead, he sticks to the basic truths he can say about the employee and leaves it at that.

Sample Letter 10.41. Good recommendation for employee you've terminated.

[date]

Mr. Joe P. Terno
Personnel Director
Abel & Dexter Public Relations
45 Tyrone Avenue
Touchstone, AZ 85089

Dear Mr. Terno:

You've asked that I give you an assessment of James Time, who worked here at Preston & Sturges Advertising up until a couple of months ago. I am glad to oblige.

We've organized our company into autonomous teams with each handling its own client acquisition and servicing as well as profit-and-loss responsibility. Jim has always contributed professionally and been a reliable and positive presence in our company.

As you know all too well, the economy has hit the advertising business pretty hard and we've had to reexamine every aspect of our business to ensure we were operating as efficiently as possible. Unfortunately, Jim's team was not profitable, and we made the decision to shut down the operations of all unprofitable teams in an effort to improve our overall bottom line. Neither Jim nor his fellow team members were absorbed into other teams.

As a result, Jim left Preston & Sturges to search for other employment opportunities. Please call on me if I can be of more assistance.

Sincerely,

John DeLuca
Personnel Director

Sample Letter 10.42. Letter of reference for employee terminated because of incompetence.

[date]

Mr. Pat Fitzgerald
Personnel Director
Big Longhorn Steaks, Inc.
P.O. Box 3542
Alantown, DE 19734

Dear Mr. Fitzgerald:

You recently requested a reference for Ben Shoulder, who worked here at Boonton Bagels from September 24, 20X4, through August 25, 20X5. Mr. Shoulder was an energetic employee, who got along well with his colleagues. He added to the collegial atmosphere and approached his work with a positive attitude.

Sincerely,

Paul Window
Personnel Associate

Sample Letter 10.43 was written to request a recommendation from a reference who was listed on an applicant's résumé. The letter writer clearly explains the position for which the applicant is applying and asks that the reader send a verification of the applicant's employment and his performance record.

Sample Letter 10.43. Letter asking for reference from former employer.

[date]

Ms. Alison T. Lewis
Personnel Manager
Andoris Products Company
476 North Main Street
Pontoon, NJ 07025

Dear Ms. Lewis:

Zed Phlange has applied for the position of marketing supervisor at our company. On his résumé, Mr. Phlange has listed your company as a former employer.

Could you please send us verification of Mr. Phlange's employment, including his job description, dates of employment, performance rating, and the reason for his departure? We will, of course, consider this information to be confidential.

Thank you for your assistance.

Sincerely,

Farley T. Zummerzalt
Personnel Manager

ftz/jls

Commendation Letters

Sample Letters 10.44 through 10.50 are examples of commendation letters. All of these letters are positive greetings to employees who have done well on the job.

Sample Letter 10.44 was written to commend an employee for her job performance over the year. The letter writer mentions some specific accomplishments and asks that the reader join her for dinner at an awards banquet.

Sample Letter 10.44.   Letter commending employee on job well done.

[date]

Ms. Katherine T. Hardsdale
Sales Representative
Better Copier Than Yours, Inc.
43 Hemingway Drive
Bullard, WI 53456

Dear Katherine:

Congratulations on your outstanding performance during 20X4. Adding 10 new clients with an average gross profit of $150,000 each is truly commendable.

Please plan to join my husband and me at the annual awards dinner slated for January 29, 20X5. I hope that Jeffrey will be able to accompany you.

Please accept my sincerest congratulations on a job well done.

Very truly yours,

Kate McGuffie
President

KM/js

cc: KTH Personnel file

Sample Letter 10.45 was written to congratulate an employee on an outstanding report. The letter writer acknowledges the good work the employee has done and expresses pride that the employee is on his staff. Sample Letter 10.46 was written to commend an employee for a large sale she had made.

Sample Letter 10.45. Letter congratulating employee on outstanding report.

[date]

Ms. Dorothy R. Levine
67 Granscome Road
Clifton, PA 15045

Dear Dorothy:

I wanted to let you know how much I appreciate the efforts you made to prepare the monthly report for the meeting of the division heads. The report was comprehensive and well organized. It was simply an outstanding job.

I am certainly proud to have you on my staff, and to have the benefit of your careful, conscientious approach to any project you are assigned. Congratulations on a job well done.

Best regards,

John Kerrigan
Group Manager

jk/ns

cc: DL Personnel File

Sample Letter 10.46. Letter congratulating employee on large sale.

[date]

Ms. Susan Shmansky
56 Yourite Road
Tripoli, PA 15045

Dear Susan:

Congratulations on your sale of 130 cases of Zinnia Styling Mousse to Jovan Salons in Philadelphia. Yours was the largest sale of Zinnia Mousse since the product was developed in 20X1.

I know that Jovan Salons has been a difficult franchise to sell to. Yet, with its international distribution network, it has proved worth all the extra hours you put in.

Your willingness to learn your market and your creative ideas will take you far in the Zinnia Corporation.

Again, thank you and congratulations.

Sincerely,

Zweno Shalk
Sales Manager

ZS:LG

Sample Letter 10.47 was sent to congratulate an employee on community recognition. The letter writer commends the employee for the recognition and offers support for the group in which the employee has become involved.

Sample Letter 10.47. Letter congratulating employee for community recognition.

[date]

Ms. Joan R. Linster
56 Yorkaway Terrace
Resnick, ND 58245

Dear Joan:

I learned last week that you had been elected to the board of directors of the Spruce Shelter. Their work to protect and support battered women and children is well known and admired throughout the state. Your election is the well-deserved outcome of your work with this worthy organization over the years. You bring credit to our firm.

Endeavor Apprise Company has supported the shelter movement over the years. I will make sure we provide particular financial and volunteer support to the Spruce Shelter because of your initiative and good work.

Sincerely,

Donald T. Barter
Executive Vice President

dtb:ltg

Sample Letter 10.48 was written to congratulate an employee on a new idea. The letter writer goes on to explain how others have commented on her good work, and extends an offer of help should it be needed.

Sample Letter 10.48. Letter congratulating employee on new idea.

[date]

Ms. Sally Devine, LICSW
Westland Community Services, Inc.
176 North Pine Street
Detroit, MI 48021

Dear Sally:

It was a pleasure to join you and your staff for your workshop at the regional meeting last week.

Your outreach and education program in the Detroit public schools focusing on adolescents and sex is truly exemplary. I was most impressed by your education program and the openness and availability of your staff.

The handbook you have developed, including topics from contraception to AIDS, was clear, with examples the teens could understand. Since your staff has its own experiences as inner-city adolescents it is particularly empathic and sensitive to the population. The staff seemed so open that I felt that almost anyone could talk with them.

Your work is being recognized throughout the agency. I talked with Andrew Brown in San Francisco, who will be calling you to talk about starting a similar program out there.

Call me any time. Meeting with your staff was invigorating and informative. Keep up the good work.

Sincerely,

Wil Denehy, LICSW
Director

wd/lg

Sample Letter 10.49 was written to commend and congratulate an entire department for its successful performance. It is general only because of its audience; the letter contains specific references to improvements in market share and to products that the department has helped promote. In closing, the writer accentuates the importance of the department's contributions to the company's success as a whole.

Sample Letter 10.49. Commendations for entire department.

[date]

To All Marketing Personnel:

First-quarter results are in, and I want to take this opportunity to tell you that our market share of the magnetic poetry field is up 22%, largely thanks to your efforts to promote our latest products. Your team has been instrumental in getting the word out on "Magnetic Love Poems," "Magnetic Modernist Poetry," and "Magnetic Renaissance Literature." These highly specific literary categories have met with enthusiastic response in college English departments throughout the country, and your group's "College Tour 200X" on-the-road campaign was extraordinarily successful.

Thanks to all of you and your creative and ingenious marketing strategies. Your department is one of the main reasons I feel Mag-Neato will be the number one magnetic specialty business in the country! Keep up the good work—you've raised the bar for the rest of us.

Sincerely,
Jean Summers
CFO

Sample Letter 10.50 was written to commend two employees on a job well done. The writer addresses her praise to the employees' supervisor and gives detailed specifics about the performance of these two individuals in what was a critical situation for her. The letter is positive throughout, with enthusiastic diction and the judicious use of the exclamation mark. In closing, the writer commends not only the two employees who helped her, but their boss as well, leaving the letter's recipient with a sense of satisfaction.

Sample Letter 10.50.   Commendations to outside staff.

[date]

Ms. Susan Griffith
R & I Networking Group
600 Industrial Boulevard
Buford, AL 35051

Dear Ms. Griffith:

I'm very happy to tell you that I'm thrilled with the help I've received from your company! Your two technical support staffers, Werner Shaw and Laura Palmear, provided me with top-notch assistance in the resolution of my local area network difficulties last week, saving my company hundreds of hours in potential downtime and thousands of dollars in lost business.

Last Wednesday, I arrived at the office with a voicemail box full of hysterical messages: our network had crashed hours after I went home Tuesday night, and the third shift didn't know how to bring it back up online, since our Shift Manager was on vacation. Immediately, I called R & I, and was patched through quickly to the dedicated technical support representatives for my region, Mr. Shaw and Ms. Palmear. They identified our domain server, accessed our system history, and sent us the required software patches. While doing so, they demonstrated a calm attitude and a professional demeanor that reflect well on your company. Our network was up and running before the first shift came in for the day, and a crisis was averted.

I'm glad to know that R & I has employees like Werner Shaw and Laura Palmear to guide your customers through the sometimes troubled shoals of the LAN-WAN sea. Kudos to you for hiring these two fine professionals!

Sincerely,

Rachel N. Whisenhunt
Purchasing Coordinator

Letters About Job Promotions

Sample Letter 10.51 is a short and clearly written letter to a candidate who has been granted a job promotion.

Sample Letter 10.52 was written to a valued employee who didn't get a job promotion he anticipated. The letter writer writes a personal letter to the employee (using the official-style format) telling him who got the position and what this means for the employee's future role in the company.

Sample Letter 10.51. Letter offering a promotion.

[date]

Mr. Michael Keeler
45 Torrance Drive
Fall River, ME 04045

Dear Michael:

After extensively interviewing almost two dozen applicants, we have decided to offer you the position of chief purchaser for our retail showrooms. You were by far the most qualified candidate for the position. That plus your many years of dedicated service to the company convinced us that you were the ideal person to fill this position.

Congratulations on the promotion. We are all thrilled to be able to give you the opportunity to continue the valuable contribution you make to the company.

Sincerely,

Ross Whiting
Personnel Director

Sample Letter 10.52. Letter to employee who didn't get an anticipated promotion. [sent to home]

[date]

Dear Jesse:

We have decided to hire Larry Stacy, the chief operating officer over at Sensible Hard-goods, Inc., to fill the COO position you applied for. I'm sorry to be the deliverer of what is likely to be disappointing news for you, but we felt that your role as chief information officer has become indispensable for us in our current rapid growth stage.

Rest assured that we consider your role as CIO as important to the future of the company as Larry's will be as COO. As we continue to grow, there will be other opportunities that arise that we hope you'll consider.

As an indication of your value to us, we have reviewed your salary relative to your contribution to the company and have made a salary increase, which Betty Walker in personnel will go over with you in a separate letter and a face-to-face meeting.

Please give my regards to your family.

Sincerely,

Dennis Duben
President

Mr. Jesse Howlty
75 Boume Street
Las Vegas, OH 89889

New-Employee Announcement Letter

In Sample Letter 10.53, the letter writer expresses his pleasure at announcing the arrival of two new employees. He goes on to give a brief background on both of the newcomers, and closes by adding what he thinks the two new employees will bring to the company.

Sample Letter 10.53.   Letter announcing new people added to the business.

[date]

David R. Slater
Financial Products Marketing, Inc.
312 Silver Place
Running Woods, MO 63045

Dear Mr. Slater:

The Review is pleased to officially announce the appointment of Larry T. Letz as southwest sales manager and Sally Phenon as managing editor.

Larry has worked for the past two years with financial advertisers to our publication in the southwest. He brings a keen understanding of the financial services industry and is anxious to work with each of you to define and meet your marketing objectives.

Sally comes to *The Review* from *The Journal of Financial Services Marketing* where she covered the financial industry as a news editor. Sally has also been a staff writer for both United Press International and Associated Press.

These new appointments bring additional strength to *The Review*. I encourage you to call Larry at 232-555-4432 for your advertising needs or Sally at 322-555-6543 for editorial assistance.

Sincerely,

Martin L. Noten
Publisher

jls

Letters Requesting and Refusing Raises

Sample Letter 10.54 was written by an employee to request a pay raise. The letter is short and to the point. After requesting the raise in the introductory paragraph, the writer reasonably states her case and her contributions in the second paragraph, and then closes by asking for a personal audience with her supervisor to discuss the merits of her request.

Sample Letter 10.54. Letter requesting a raise.

[date]

Mr. John Teason
Personnel Supervisor
Icee Thermos Company
214 Ponce de Leon Avenue
Maryville, MD 20632

Dear Mr. Teason:

This February marks my third anniversary with Icee Thermos Company, and my second as Senior Chemical Analyst for the Research and Development Division. I would like you to consider raising my salary by $2,000 a year. I believe that this amount, which is 3% of my current annual salary, is appropriate in light of my contributions to the company.

In my two years as a Senior Analyst, I have not received a pay raise, despite my discovery last year of a chemical process that resulted in improved thermal retention for the Icee Supreme model. The new process also cut overhead costs by 15%, as our company no longer needed to order multiple carbonate cylinders for inclusion in the synthetic refrigeration compound we use in the Supreme model.

I would like very much to schedule a meeting with you to review both my performance and my request. Please notify me in writing or call me at X5415 to indicate when you are available to meet with me. Thank you for your consideration.

Sincerely,

Ann Marie Ellis

Sample Letter 10.55 was written to inform an employee that he would not be receiving a raise. The writer has a positive relationship with the employee and indicates from the beginning how valuable the employee is to the company but then moves swiftly and directly into an explanation of company policy. The letter closes with a reassuring restatement of the employee's worth to the company.

Sample Letter 10.55. Letter refusing a request for a raise.

[date]

Mr. Denzel E. Whitemyer
301 Crescentwood Drive
East Lake, GA 30333

Dear Mr. Whitemyer:

I want you to know how valuable you are to Norcross Plumbing. In the six months that you have been an employee here, the entire Drainage Department has demonstrated marked improvement in both billing and accounts receivable, largely because of your enthusiasm and administrative support.

However, it is our policy at Norcross to assess employee performance and award raises annually. Since you have not yet reached your first anniversary as an employee with us, I cannot grant your request for a raise. In December of this year, I will be happy to meet with you and review your salary. At that time, it will be appropriate for me to consider raising your current salary.

Thank you again for your excellent service to the company and know that your performance is both monitored and valued.

Sincerely,

Jacob Gary
Supervisor

There are numerous reasons why an employee may not receive a raise. Sample Letter 10.56 refused a raise because the employee's performance did not warrant it.

Sample Letter 10.56. Letter refusing a request for a raise because performance does not warrant it.

[date]

Ms. Jiu Xiu Wang
115 Pleasantdale Lane
Bethany, KS 66013

Dear Ms. Wang:

I recently received your request for a raise. However, your current performance level does not merit a raise at this time. There are several specific reasons why I tell you this.

Your attendance at mandatory departmental meetings has been less than satisfactory. Of the three Budget Review meetings this quarter, you were an hour late to the April meeting and missed both the May and June meetings. Your absence was notable, since as economic adviser in the Marketing Department your input was critical. While you gave advanced notice of your absence in May, you were expected at the June assembly. Your absence forced all members of the entire management team to reschedule their agendas.

Several of your recent budget analysis reports have had incomplete or inconsistent data projections. For an administrator at your level, this is unacceptable. In the past, your work has been characterized by an attention to detail and a thoroughness that were superior to those of our competitors, but the quality of your analyses has slipped as of late.

Additionally, I have received several complaints from your subordinates about your delegation of administrative tasks. I would like to address these concerns with you in a formal, face-to-face review at the end of this month, as I am still in the process of investigating the merit of these claims.

It appears that there is a discrepancy between our assessments of your performance. I would like to schedule a review meeting with you for Tuesday, March 29, 20X5. At that time, I will address your specific salary concerns, and I will report to you on my findings about your subordinates' complaints. Please respond to this letter in writing with a time for our meeting that would be convenient for you.

Sincerely,

Roscoe Guerra
Staffing Coordinator

cc: Gabriel Fremian
    Personnel File

No-Longer-With-Us Letters

Sample Letters 10.57 and 10.58 are examples of letters that were written to inform people that specific employees were no longer with the company. Sample Letter 10.57 simply states that a particular employee is no longer with the firm and that all information formerly directed to her should be directed to a different, specified, employee.

Sample Letter 10.58 was written to inform someone that the employee in question had left the company years ago. The letter writer asks that the reader remove her name from any future correspondence to the company. He then gives a forwarding address for the former employee.

Sample Letter 10.57. Letter informing that employee is no longer with the company.

[date]

Mr. Quinn T. Renege, Vice President
Renege and Company, Inc.
23 Franklin Drive
Liberty Corner, CA 90056

Dear Mr. Renege:

Ms. Lesley W. Hamilton is no longer with our company. All future correspondence about service and sales should be directed to Larry R. Wireblade, who is the sales representative for your area.

Thank you for noting this change.

Sincerely,

Fred Williamson
Personnel Director

fw/ap

Sample Letter 10.58. Letter giving forwarding address for former employee.

[date]

Mr. John S. Tucker
Tucker Systems Corporation
13 April Street
Gary, IL 60045

Dear Mr. Tucker:

Jane L. Berrigan, vice president of personnel, left Andore Products Company five years ago. Please remove her name from any correspondence you direct to Andore Products.

Ms. Berrigan can be reached at Bixley Products, Ltd., 62 Recognition Road, Porzio, Utah 19614.

Sincerely,

Ralph E. Jersey
Vice President

rej/jls

Letter of Resignation

Sample Letter 10.59 is a brief letter of resignation. The employee clearly states his intention to retire, gives a reason why, thanks his employer for a rewarding business relationship, and then closes. This formal letter will probably be followed by a face-to-face conversation; the letter is official and for record-keeping purposes.

Sample Letter 10.59. Letter offering resignation.

[date]

Mr. Dow Jones
2100 Jump Street
Tempe, AZ 85065

Dear Mr. Jones:

I write to inform you of my decision to retire from my position as a creative director for Handi-Snacker Industries.

I have very much enjoyed my tenure with Handi-Snacker, first as a product tester and then as creative director for the New England Region. In keeping a promise to my wife, I must step down from the company at the age of 60 and join her in her charitable work with the Easter Seals Foundation.

My time with Handi-Snacker has allowed me to develop professionally and personally, for which I am extremely appreciative. It is my hope that I have served the company well. I wish you and all my colleagues the best of fortune in all future endeavors.

Sincerely,

Proctor N. Gamble

Letters to Retiring Employees

Sample Letters 10.60 and 10.61 are examples of letters written to an employee upon retirement.

Sample Letter 10.60 is a joyful letter written to congratulate an employee on his retirement. The letter writer reminisces about the employee and wishes him well in retirement plans.

Sample Letter 10.61 was written to an employee retiring for health reasons. The writer expresses regret over losing the employee but wishes her the best on her retirement plans. The letter is sympathetic without being maudlin.

Sample Letter 10.60. Letter congratulating employee on retirement.

[date]

Mr. Robert E. Lang
345 West Hartford Street
Trumball, VT 05034

Dear Bob:

After I gave that small talk at your retirement dinner, I was struck with how quickly the 15 years have passed since you first came to Andoris Publishing Company. It seems like only yesterday when you heeded my call for a well-seasoned chief financial officer to come in and put financial controls in place at a haphazardly growing publishing company.

Looking back on the 15 years, it's safe to say that you've surpassed my wildest dreams in helping Andoris to grow to where it is today—a $10 million company. No small feat considering we barely broke a million when you first arrived.

You'll be missed here, Bob. But our loss is somewhat tempered by the fact that you and Gwen will be chasing another dream out in Kokomo. I'm not sure that buying into that Triple-A baseball team was what I would consider a relaxing retirement, but for someone who is determined to live out a baseball dream, it seems perfect.

Zoe and I wish you the best in your retirement and in your new adventures. We hope you will still find time to visit us up in the Northeast whenever you're in town.

Sincerely,

Martin L. Nathan
President

MLN:jls

Sample Letter 10.61. Letter to employee retiring for health reasons.

[date]

Mrs. Jeanette Long
45 Twinscomb Place
Transit, CA 90056

Dear Jeanette:

When we met last week, I told you how distressed I am at the prospect of your leaving Los Angeles and Pet World. It is our loss, and we all regret the development of your allergies to the Los Angeles smog.

Your work has been outstanding, particularly in your supervision of staff. I also appreciate your loving attention to our pets.

I wish you the best as you move to the Sierras. Any time you need a letter of recommendation, please let me know.

Sincerely,

Barbara Cole

bc/lg

Letters Regarding Leaves of Absence

Notifications of extended leaves of absence are often handled personally or over the telephone with Human Resources personnel, but it is a good idea to confirm the particulars of leaves of absence in writing. The employee in Sample Letter 10.62 confirms a previous phone call informing her employer of her need for maternity leave.

Sample Letter 10.62. Letter notifying an employer of maternity leave.

[date]

Ms. Megan Doss
Human Resources Director
MSD Lawrence Township
1801 West 68th Street
Carmel, IN 46066

Dear Ms. Doss:

In our phone conversation of February 23, 20X5, I informed you of my pregnancy, which will necessitate a leave of absence from my current position as a classroom teacher during the fall semester, 20X5. My delivery date is August 4, 20X5; the academic year begins two weeks after that on Monday, August 18. After taking the six weeks' leave the District generously affords me, which will end on October 1, 20X5, I plan to use my accumulated personal illness leave of thirty-five days to supplement this official leave. This seven-week period will end on November 13, 20X5.

In order to spend more time with my newborn, I will extend my absence through to the end of the semester in December. I recognize that the time from November through December 18, 20X5 will be counted as unpaid leave. My official return to teaching duties will be at the start of the spring semester, on January 3, 20X6.

Thank you for your assistance, and thank you for your kind words of congratulation and support. I appreciate your flexibility in this matter. Please call me on my cell phone at (317) 555-9285 if you have any further questions.

Warmest regards,

Ayanna Plass

cc: CE Quandt, Principal
    Ed Armstrong, English Department Chair

Sample Letter 10.63 was written to grant an employee a leave of absence and to tell him some of the conditions of the leave. The letter writer clearly states that the employer can't hold the employee's position. She then tells the employee to call with any questions on specifics of the leave.

Sample Letter 10.63. Letter granting an employee a leave of absence.

[date]

Mr. Barry Krowbath
65 Lorraine Terrace
Boston, ME 04022

Dear Barry:

The personnel committee has decided to grant you the unpaid leave of absence you requested to begin November 1, 20X5. During your leave, some of your benefits will continue and some will not. I suggest you meet with Donna Relita in the personnel department to go over your health insurance, 401(k) plan, and other benefits that could be affected by your leave.

While we can't guarantee that we will hold your position for you while you are on leave, you should know that you have been a valued employee in our department and we would enjoy having you back with us if there is an appropriate position available when you're ready to return.

Should you have any questions about the conditions of your leave, please don't hesitate to call on me or Donna. I wish you the best.

Sincerely,

Phyllis Sanctions
Personnel Director

Letter Offering Employee a Lesser Position

Sample Letter 10.64 was written to inform an employee that because of economic conditions his position at the company is being done away with. The company has offered him a lower position within the company should he decide to stay.

Sample Letter 10.64. Letter offering lower position because of economic conditions.

[date]

Mr. Kyle Redder
43 Lorraine Terrace
Mountainville, NM 87034

Dear Kyle:

Yesterday, you and I discussed that because of economic conditions, Big Empire Furniture Company has decided to eliminate the position of regional sales director effective November 1.

You already know how tough a year it's been for the company to stay profitable. As much as we tried to meet profit goals by cutting costs other than the payroll, we were forced to eliminate many positions to stay on track. The duties of the regional sales directors will now be assumed by Brad Ellen, our national sales manager.

We do value the contribution you've made to the company and would like to offer you the position of Southwest retail sales director at a base salary of $40,000, plus commissions. While the base salary is shy of the $55,000 you made as regional sales director, we're hopeful that the commissions on your sales will make up the difference. Rob Fahey, our current Southwest retail sales director, has accepted our offer to move north to take over the Northwest retail sales director position.

Kyle, I really hope you'll accept the new position. It will allow you to maintain your ties in the Southwest and allow us to keep a valued member of the sales team. If you decide not to accept the position and to look elsewhere, you should know that you can always use me as a reference to attest to the wonderful job you've done at Big Empire Furniture.

Please respond to the offer by October 1. Regardless of your decision, I wish you the best.

Sincerely,

Tom Paine
Personnel Director

Reprimand

Sample Letter 10.65 was written to an employee as a reprimand for inappropriate use of company materials, in this case the email system that the company used. Reprimands should be clear and controlled, remaining professional without degenerating into insult. This writer explains the situation initially and then proceeds to inform the recipient why his actions were inappropriate. The conclusion is both complimentary and cautionary, letting the chastised employee know his value to the company but firmly restating company policy. The "cc: Personnel" is as threatening as the writer needs to be, and emphasizes the message.

Sample Letter 10.65.   Letter of reprimand for inappropriate behavior.

[date]

Manfred Marx
Systems Analyst
400 Peachtree Parkway
Alpharetta, AL 35002

Dear Mr. Marx:

It has come to my attention that you were responsible for this past weekend's "Halloween Scare" email that was circulated through our corporation's intranet mail system. The rather large graphic file you created and mass-mailed to all departments and all personnel was not only thematically and visually inappropriate, but it clogged up our servers and crashed key hubs in Charlotte, Biloxi, and Mobile, temporarily crippling business in the Southern Region.

You must know that this kind of behavior cannot be condoned at The Dogwood Firm. Your expertise as a systems analyst is vital to us, but your outstanding ability does not justify your singular poor judgment. In the future, please limit your use of The Dogwood Firm's technology to work-specific business. Thank you in advance for your compliance.

Sincerely,

Bhendra Patel
Chief Technology Officer

cc: Personnel

Termination Letters

Termination letters are one type of correspondence that is almost invariably difficult to write. Few people want to sit down to write a letter firing an employee. Unfortunately, it is a task that must be handled from time to time. When termination must be faced, it is best to be well equipped to deal with the situation.

A standard dismissal letter does not exist. Since every job termination has particular circumstances, each termination letter must be written to fit the situation at hand. Each termination letter is a very personal matter. Each employee has a different relationship with a company. As a result, the employee will have to be informed about the procedures to take upon termination, on everything from severance pay to collecting accumulating pension benefits.

As such, the sample termination letters included here are meant to serve as a starting point upon which to build. Using these letters as basic samples, you can develop your own termination letters to fit the particular circumstances you face.

When a termination is for cause, however, before writing a termination letter most companies follow a procedure that is known as "progressive discipline." Some also refer to this process as "building a case" against an employee. The process involves an oral warning, followed by a written warning that clearly spells out the consequences of an employee's further actions, followed by some sort of disciplinary action such as a suspension, and ultimately termination. Each step of the process, including the oral warning, should be noted in the employee's personnel file.

The need for disciplinary action will often show up during employee performance evaluations. Rather than write a separate warning letter, managers doing the evaluation will indicate on a performance appraisal form where job performance has been unsatisfactory. These evaluations serve as warnings to employees about poor job performance. They also serve as a good record of the employee's performance in the corresponding personnel file.

As far as following a set procedure for terminating an employee, one personnel director of a major business recommends that you should:
- Send termination letters by registered or certified mail, return receipt requested. Such action gives the employer proof of sending a letter and puts a damper on claims that a letter was never received.
- Clearly state the reason for the termination.
- Write termination letters in a brief but understanding tone.

Sample Letters 10.66 through 10.69 are examples of termination letters. Sample Letter 10.66 was sent as a warning to an employee. The letter writer clearly states the violation the employee has made and warns that if he does not hear from the employee by a specific date he will face possible termination. Please note that none of the letters in this section are appropriate to be sent as an email.

Sample Letter 10.66. Letter warning employee of possible termination.

[date]

Mr. Eliot R. Davids
28 Laurel Avenue, Apt. 3
Somerville, NY 10045

Dear Mr. Davids:

We have not heard from you about your absence since Wednesday, March 22, 20X3. At that time I informed you of the problems we have been having with your performance as a sales representative for our organization. Before you left the office, I reminded you that your performance—documented in your biannual performance appraisals—simply was not acceptable by company standards. I tried to present you with possible solutions to the problems you are facing.

Now, in light of the fact that you have broken company policy by not reporting to work for the last 8 days without notifying anyone here, I am concerned that you have compounded your problems.

Please get in touch with me before April 8, 20X3, or you will face the possibility of termination from Pandora Engineering. Our company policy states that employees who are unable to report to work must notify their supervisor within the first half hour of the working day. An absence is considered excused only when an employee has notified his or her supervisor and has obtained approval.

We would like to work with you to solve this problem, Eliot, but you must comply with company policy and work with us to successfully find a solution.

Cordially,

David Penny
Personnel Director

DP/jh

Sample Letter 10.67 was sent to an employee who broke company policy and refused to respond to a warning letter. The letter is brief but clearly points out why the employee is being terminated.

Sample Letter 10.67.   Letter terminating employee. Follow-up to no response to Sample Letter 10.66.

[date]

Mr. Eliot R. Davids
28 Laurel Avenue, Apt. 3
Somerville, NY 10045

Dear Mr. Davids:

Your employment with Pandora Engineering has been terminated effective April 8, 20X3, because of your failure to comply with Personnel Policy #34-Z, and your failure to respond to my letter of April 1, 20X3.

Please contact Muriel Wilson in the personnel department to discuss severance pay and pension plan disbursements.

Cordially,

David Penny
Personnel Director

dp/js

Sample Letter 10.68 was written to an employee who is being laid off because of a corporate downsizing. It is clear from the tone of the letter that the employee already knows he is being laid off. The letter tells him when he'll receive his last paycheck.

Sample Letter 10.68. Letter to employee being laid off because of corporate downsizing.

[date]

Mr. Timothy Wagner
54 Golden Place
Triathlon, NV 89045

Dear Tim:

On November 1, you will receive your last paycheck from Big Empire Furniture, Inc. I know that you're already aware of what a tough year it's been for the company. Regardless of how we tried to trim costs, we still found ourselves unable to turn a profit without shrinking our payroll. These economic conditions resulted in the decision to dismiss you and many other employees in your division.

George Noble, your immediate supervisor, speaks very highly of your work over the five years you've been with the company. I am hopeful that you'll be able to find fulfilling work elsewhere. Please do not hesitate to list me as a reference. I will be glad to share with prospective employers how dedicated and diligent an employee you have been.

It is always difficult to be the bearer of such bad news. It is especially difficult when the recipient has been as great an asset to the company as you have been.

Thank you for your work at Big Empire Furniture. I wish you the best.

Sincerely,

Tom Paine
Personnel Director

Letting an employee go can be one of the toughest jobs an employer has to do, especially when the dismissal is not due to the employee's ineptitude or lack of professionalism. Like the writer of Sample Letter 10.68, the writer of Sample Letter 10.69 gently but firmly informs the employee that he is being laid off due to corporate downsizing. The salutation is personal, rather than formal, to soften the blow; the closing emphasizes the close connection between writer and reader. Clearly, the writer has high regard for the employee he is dismissing. In the first paragraph, the writer both explains the current economic environment and delivers the news of the employee's dismissal. Next are the formal details of the layoff, including the effective date and the benefits for which the employee is eligible. The offer of the company's resources in the second paragraph cushions the impact of the news, and the final paragraph is brief: there is nothing more to say at that point.

Sample Letter 10.69. Letter informing employee of layoff.

[date]

Mr. Robert McAllister
123 Coventry Avenue
Wichita, KS 66034

Dear Bob:

As I'm sure you're aware, unusually low revenues from our Merchandising Division combined with a general sluggishness in the national and international markets have necessitated a restructuring of our entire production staff in the Southeast Region. One of the effects of this reorganization is that your position as one of the six quality control supervisors is being eliminated, effective six weeks from the date of this letter. As an employee dismissed in good standing, you will be receiving full benefits for which you are eligible.

I recognize that this news, although not unexpected, will still come as a shock. I want you to know how much I've appreciated your contributions to Mateo, Inc. The Human Resources department will be contacting you within the next week to set up an exit interview, and I've instructed that group to throw the resources of its entire professional support staff behind you in your efforts to find a new job. I would also like to personally offer my assistance in your job search and will be happy to write a letter of professional recommendation for you. Please let me know how I can help you during what must be a difficult time for you.

I regret that we must make this decision. I hope that your efforts, combined with those of the Mateo, Inc. support staff, will enable you to find a job that suits both your interests and your talents.

Sincerely,

Beall Slade
Division Manager

Letter Acknowledging Anniversary Date

Sample Letter 10.70 was written to inform an employee that there will be a commemorative luncheon in her honor for all her years of service to the firm. The writer begins with the announcement of the luncheon, giving the why, when, and where information that the reader needs to know. The next paragraph acknowledges the employee's service in detail, and then the writer moves into a paragraph requesting a reply and gently giving a deadline at the same time before closing.

Sample Letter 10.70.   Letter acknowledging anniversary date of service to firm.

[date]

Ms. Cynthia Hicks-Jacobus
111 Abernathy Court, Apt. 2A
Mapleton, NY 10003

Dear Cynthia:

We are pleased to commemorate your twenty-fifth year of service at Diamonex Jewelers with a special company-wide luncheon on Friday, July 15, at the Mapleton Hyatt. Lunch will be at 12:00 noon in the Pollock Room. I hope you will be able to attend.

There are only a handful of us who have been with the company as long as you have, and you have seen us grow from a tiny mom-and-pop jewelry store to a transnational corporation with private mines in South Africa. As we grew, we knew we could count on you to represent us professionally and ethically on the African continent, and your focus on human rights has been instrumental in the development of our Ethics Code at Diamonex.

You have also proved that, sometimes, doing good is good for business, and your work has garnered Diamonex human rights accolades and an increased market share. Thanks are in order, and July's luncheon is a small way of giving you the attention you deserve. You will be the guest of honor, and we hope you will say a few words at the meal. Please let me know by June 10 if you are planning to give a few remarks, so that I can pass that information on to the program printers.

I look forward to seeing you on July 15. Thanks again for all the years of service you've given Diamonex.

Sincerely yours,

Berteil de Kooning
President

Letter Announcing Staff Changes

Sample Letter 10.71 was written to announce to a company the internal promotion of a staff member. The author begins with the most important information, follows with a cordial mention of her pleasure at the promotion, and then substantiates the decision to promote by describing the staff member's qualifications for the job and long history with the company. Promotions can occasionally be touchy issues within a company; this writer proactively presents the staff member as a thoroughly qualified and deserving recipient of the promotion. The writer closes by asking for all employees to congratulate the newly promoted staff member, encouraging positive responses to her decision.

Sample Letter 10.71.   Letter announcing promotion to staff.

[date]

To All Employees:

Effective December 1, 200X, Jean-Marie Sartre will be promoted to Vice President of Sales for Western Europe, reporting directly to Frederick Nietz. We are both proud and pleased that Jean-Marie will be moving up to this position.

Jean-Marie has been with Norton Enterprises since its founding in 19X1 and has served in the Sales department in almost every capacity. She started with us as a sales representative, selling up and down the East Coast, and moved up quickly to regional manager. Her groups were consistently among the top-sellers in the company, and her dedication to detail and quantitative analysis of sales efficiency revolutionized the way we at Norton interpreted our sales data. She was promoted in 19X8 to Special Chair,

Sales, where she supervised our North American representatives and instituted our Systematic Sales Support (3S) program, which has made us an industry leader.

In her role as Vice President for Sales for Western Europe, Jean-Marie will be called upon to represent Norton in our European Union negotiations. Her fluency in French, Spanish, and German will come in handy, and she will attempt to customize the 3S program for a European market. In Western Europe, Norton Enterprises has 850 sales representatives in 12 countries, and Jean-Marie will be responsible for standardizing commercial processes, finances, and training procedures among these many different nations, each with its own set of business practices.

Please join me in congratulating Jean-Marie Sarte on her accomplishment. We wish her a hearty "good luck" as she represents Norton Enterprises in this bold new venture.

Sincerely,

Commerce York
President

Letter Requesting Mentorship

Sample Letter 10.72 is a letter requesting mentorship from a seasoned veteran in the letter writer's industry. The writer is clear, straightforward, and respectful. The letter closes with a clear indication of how the writer will follow up with the recipient. This letter could easily be written as an email without significant changes being made to the text of the letter.

Sample Letter 10.72.   Request for a mentor relationship.

[date]

Mr. Sam Stiles
Fort Worth Butchers
1532 Abalone Way
Forth Worth, TX 75065

Dear Mr. Stiles,

Paul Sturges, with whom I studied butchery at Emerson Meat Studies Institute, suggested I write to you. He told me that when he worked with you at Abercrumb Meat

House you were instrumental in guiding him to become the butcher he is today.

Now that I am beginning my career as a butcher at Alamo Meat Packing, I was hoping that you might be willing to serve as a mentor to me as I continue to learn the ropes of our trade.

If you are willing to consider serving as a mentor to me, I would appreciate it very much. If possible, I am hopeful you will be able to meet with me to talk about how we might get started in this relationship.

I will call you by the end of the month to set up a time for us to meet.

Sincerely,

Priscilla Knifeskills

Farewell Letter to Employee

Sample Letter 10.73 was written as a farewell to an employee who has decided to leave the company. Its tone is understanding, touched with regret. The writer leaves the door open for the employee to return, if he desires. The employee is obviously valued, and this writer indicates his respect for the employee's decision to depart.

Sample Letter 10.73. Letter bidding farewell to employee who has decided to leave.

[date]

Tony Gosurvace
Home Products, Inc.
334 Keetchan Lane
Halfway, KY 40005

Dear Tony:

Home Products, Inc. has certainly benefited from the last two years of your devoted service. We can't begin to count the letters we've received from happy customers whom you've assisted. Not only has your enthusiasm helped to sell more kitchen cabinets, it has served to energize the entire design department. You've been a good a mentor to other members of the staff.

We were very sorry to hear about your grandmother in Uruguay. And we understand that you must leave our company to tend to serious personal business. There will always be a place for you on our team when and if you return.

Again, thank you very much for all of your hard work and devotion. We will always consider you to be part of the family. Please let us know if there is anything that we can do for you. I would be happy to write a positive recommendation. Good luck in your future endeavors.

Cordially,

David James
Human Resources Manager

CHAPTER 11

Transmittal letters

Letters that accompany enclosed material are frequently referred to as transmittal letters. Their chief function is to identify the material that is enclosed. This chapter features many of the more common forms of transmittal letters that you may have to write.

Many of the letters in this chapter can be sent as emails or as attachments to emails. For those letters that can be adapted to emails, it's simple enough to copy the text of the sample letter into the text of your email. If written as an email, you'd refer to "attachments" rather than "enclosures," but the text of the message would remain fundamentally the same.

Letters Transmitting Payment

Sample Letters 11.1 through 11.6 are examples of transmittal letters that were written to accompany payment.

Sample Letter 11.1 is a standard transmittal of payment on account letter. The letter writer clearly identifies the amount enclosed and the purpose of the payment. He closes by thanking the reader for her services.

Sample Letter 11.1.   Transmittal of payment on account.

[date]

Ms. Alice D. Edwards
Tisk-a-Disk Office Supplies
76 Tuscon Drive
Lake Forest, KY 40034

Dear Ms. Edwards:

My check for $75.42 is enclosed. This is my final payment on my order number 73A2 for office supplies for Kearney Public Relations, Inc., placed on March 30, 20X8.

Thank you for extending us the credit. We appreciate the service you provided us.

Sincerely,

Allen T. Quagmire
Office Manager

atq/fwd

enc.

Sample Letter 11.2 was sent to transmit a payment that was different from the total on an invoice. Here the letter writer indicates the amount he is transmitting, explains the discrepancy, and asks the reader to call if there's any confusion about the account.

Sample Letter 11.2. Letter transmitting payment in a different amount from invoice.

[date]

Mr. Brandt Henry
Quimby Office Supplies, Inc.
312 Respite Way
Santiago, ID 83256

Dear Mr. Henry:

Enclosed is my check for $27.22 to cover payment of stationery supplies I purchased from your company. You'll notice that the amount does not match the amount stated on the invoice dated April 30, 20X1. This is undoubtedly because my check of May 5, 20X1, in the amount $67.25, was not credited to my account.

Please call me if there is any problem with my account. If I do not hear from you I will assume that my account has been paid in full.

Sincerely,

Zachary T. LeBoeuf

ztl/pcd

enc.

Sample Letter 11.3 was sent to transmit payment to a speaker whom the letter writer found to be outstanding. The writer announces in the first paragraph that the payment is enclosed, but goes on to praise the speaker for playing such an integral role in the success of the convention at which he spoke. The writer clearly is pleased with the speaker's performance.

Sample Letter 11.4 was written to a speaker who was not particularly outstanding. The letter writer indicates that she is transmitting payment and thanks the speaker for his participation. Nowhere does she complain about the speaker's performance. She simply does not lay on as much praise as the writer did in Sample Letter 11.3. Sample Letter 11.4 is a courteous letter used to transmit payment.

Sample Letter 11.3. Letter transmitting payment to outstanding speaker.

[date]

Mr. James Lewis
Funny for Money, Inc.
228 West 78th Street
Manhattan, KS 66056

Dear Mr. Lewis:

Enclosed is a check covering your speaking fee for the luncheon speech you delivered at our group's annual convention.

Once again, the annual convention of the Association of Internal Auditors (AIA) met with the resounding approval of its membership. On their evaluation forms, our members rated your talk as one of the top speeches given during the four-day convention.

Thank you for helping to make our convention a success. We hope to call on you again to enlighten our group.

Sincerely,

Oscar D. Terradect
Convention Director

ODT:jls

enc.

Sample Letter 11.4. Letter transmitting payment to not-so-great speaker.

[date]

Mr. Martin Laramy
Modifier Parries Company
312 West Main Street
Boonton, NJ 07005

Dear Mr. Laramy:

Enclosed is a check for your appearance as a speaker at our weekend retreat in Chatham. Thank you for agreeing to speak to our group of brokers.

Once again, our brokers found the retreat to be a useful time to gather and share knowledge with fellow professionals.

Thank you again.

Sincerely,

Sheila T. Picksups

stp/fwd

enc.

Sample Letter 11.5 was written to transmit payment to a reviewer of a manuscript. The letter is brief but clear. The letter writer states the amount enclosed and thanks the reader for his services.

Sample Letter 11.5. Letter transmitting payment to reviewer.

[date]

Professor Adam R. Ecuamen
Holiday University
67 Right Venere Hall
Holiday, NM 87045

Dear Professor Ecuamen:

Enclosed please find your check for $250 for the recent review you did for me. I appreciate the time and effort you put into it.

I hope to be able to call on you again.

Sincerely,

Edward Colen
Program Director

EC/jh

enc.

Sample Letter 11.6 was written to accompany the final payment of an account.

Sample Letter 11.6. Letter transmitting final payment of an account.

[date]

Mr. David Palay
Sales Director
Grand Forks Parts, Inc.
55 Lincoln Drive
Boonton, NY 10008

Dear Mr. Palay:

Enclosed is my check for $543.95, which is the final payment on the two heavy-duty retractors I ordered on July 30 from Grand Forks Parts. We are very pleased with the parts we purchased and thank you for the generous payment schedule you set up for us.

Sincerely,

Alan Jacobs
President

Enc.

Letter Transmitting Contracts

Sample Letter 11.7 is an example of a letter that was written to transmit contracts. It was sent to transmit a representation agreement. The letter writer indicates in the first paragraph what she is enclosing and what the reader must do. The writer offers to furnish any explanation if it is needed, and closes by expressing delight over the prospect of working with her new client.

Sample Letter 11.7. Transmittal of representation agreement.

[date]

Ms. Adrienne D. Storm
54 Cadillac Road
Water Hills, CA 90023

Dear Adrienne:

Enclosed are two copies of a representation agreement. Please countersign one copy and return it to me. Of course, if you have any questions, feel free to call.

I'm delighted that we'll be working together, Adrienne. I look forward to a long and productive relationship.

Best regards,

Vanessa J. Jewett

vjj/jjm

Enclosures

Letters Transmitting Requested Materials

Sample Letters 11.8 and 11.9 were written to accompany material that had been requested. Both letters are short and serve only to confirm what is being transmitted.

Sample Letter 11.8.   Transmittal of requested materials.

[date]

Robert E. Black
51 Trevor Avenue
Dorfleck, NJ 07010

Dear Bob:

Enclosed are printouts of the results of the calculations you requested for the insurance rate of return if you were to buy term insurance instead of whole life and invest the difference in cost. I used our new five-year renewable and convertible term rates, which include a $40 policy fee.

Please feel free to call me if you have any questions.

Best regards,

Mary T. Amock

mta/mld

encl.

Sample Letter 11.9.   Transmittal of supplies.

[date]

Mr. Lawrence R. Effredge
Effredge and St. Paul, Inc.
186-A Savin Road
Rontclen, NH 03068

TRANSMITTAL OF STATIONERY

Larry, enclosed are approximately 500 sheets of stationery and 500 envelopes for your project. We hope you like them, and that they will be useful for your project.

Please call me if you need any further assistance.

LEONARD D. DELB
ADMINISTRATIVE ASSISTANT

LDD:pt

ENC.

ransmitting Manuscript

etter 11.10 was written by an editor to an author to accompany the copy-edited
ript of an article the reader had written. The editor instructs the author what he is to
n the copyedited manuscript. This letter could easily be written as an email without
sig. icant changes being made to the text of the letter. Remember, however, to substitute
"the attached…" for "the enclosed…" as needed.

Sample Letter 11.10.   Transmittal of edited copy.

[date]

Mr. Allen T. Price
Price & Price Company, Inc.
17 Metro Drive
Horticulture, AK 99556

Dear Allen:

Enclosed for your review is an edited copy of your article, which will appear in an
upcoming issue of *Guam City Magazine*. Please look it over and telephone me in the
copyediting department within 72 hours. Alert us to any factual inaccuracies. We will
not be able to accept substantive editorial changes at this time, owing to the time
constraints of our production schedule.

Your immediate attention to this matter will expedite our production process. You
need not mail back the enclosed copy.

Thank you for your cooperation.

Sincerely,

Lauren J. Palay
Copyediting Supervisor

ljp/kka

enc.

Letter Transmitting Manuscript to Reviewer

Sample Letter 11.11 is an example of a letter written to accompany a manuscript that was being transmitted to a reviewer. This transmittal letter is an excellent model to use when sending out a manuscript for review to a first-time reviewer. This letter could easily be written as an email without significant changes being made to the text of the letter. Remember, however, to substitute "the attached…" for "the enclosed…" as needed.

Sample Letter 11.11. Transmittal of instructions to reviewer.

[date]

Mr. Jeffrey L. Jacobs
Rice & Hall, Inc.
4567 Yourow Place
Falstaff, NJ 07045

SIX POINTS TO COVER IN A REVIEW

Mr. Jacobs, thank you for agreeing to review *Electronmagnetics Today*. You will find the manuscript enclosed. In looking over the manuscript, would you comment on the following:

1.   Is the material well organized, up-to-date, and accurate? If not, please include a sample of specific criticisms.

2.   Has the author placed too much emphasis upon certain topics? Should any be excluded? Added? Transposed? Please feel free to suggest changes.

3.   Are the vocabulary and information suited to the intended target market?

4.   What are the current trends in this area? Does this manuscript reflect them?

5.   If this text were now available in published form, would you use it, or recommend its use?

6.   Please make any suggestions you have for improving the manuscript.

We do not identify the reviewer to the author, so please do not let your name appear anywhere on your review.

If possible, we would like to have two copies of your review within three weeks. If you cannot complete it by then, please let me know. We will be happy to send you an honorarium of $225 for your assistance with this project.

Thank you for your efforts. If you should have any questions, please call me at 343-555-6754.

MAXWELL L. NICHOLAS
EXECUTIVE EDITOR

mln/jls

enc.

Letter Transmitting Final Invoice

Sample Letter 11.12 was written to accompany a final invoice that was being transmitted to a customer. The letter writer expresses pleasure at having been able to serve the customer. He then indicates that a final invoice is enclosed.

Sample Letter 11.12.   Transmittal of final invoice.

[date]

Ms. Annmarie L. Long
186 Grampian Street
Alexander, WI 53021

Dear Annmarie:

It was a great pleasure having your reception/luncheon/dance in the London Room. We do hope that you and your guests were pleased with all of the services provided.

Enclosed you will find the completed invoice for your function. If you have any questions about it, please do not hesitate to call us.

We look forward to the opportunity to be of service to you again in the near future.

Sincerely,

R. David Lawrence
Director of Marketing

RDL/jls

encl.

CHAPTER 12

Confirmation letters

When you receive information or material from someone, most often the courteous thing to do is to write a confirmation letter. The letters in this chapter are examples of some basic confirmation letters that you might have to write.

Many of the letters in this chapter can be sent as emails or as attachments to emails. For those letters that can be adapted to emails, it's simple enough to copy the text of the sample letter into the text of your email.

Letter Confirming Supplier's Oral Instructions

Sample Letter 12.1 was written as a follow-up to a supplier's oral instructions. By writing this type of confirmation letter, the letter writer makes sure that she has understood the supplier's instructions correctly. The writer clearly reiterates the discussion she had with the supplier, asks that the reader call to discuss the instructions, and expresses interest in her feedback.

Sample Letter 12.1.   Letter confirming a supplier's oral instructions.

[date]

Ms. Joan Whitener
Bright & Shining Shirt Service
150 Western Street
New York, NJ 07045

Dear Joan:

As we discussed at the area meeting last week, I am revising the schedule of shirt deliveries for New York. The deliveries should take place between 6:30 A.M. and 3:30 P.M., Monday through Friday. Those loyal customers with a long-standing relationship with Bright & Shining should be surveyed and given priority for day and time of delivery each week.

Please call me in the next week to discuss this plan. I would appreciate your thoughts on the feasibility of reworking the schedule.

Again, it was good to talk with you last week and hear of your high volume. Your feedback on this new plan is appreciated.

Sincerely,

Eliza Rodriquez

er/lg

Letter Confirming Prices and Quantity Discounts

Sample Letter 12.2 was written to confirm prices and quantity discounts that were quoted to the letter reader by the letter writer. The writer clearly recounts the price discount and lists the prices he quoted. As a result, he reduces the risk of a misunderstanding.

Sample Letter 12.2. Letter confirming prices and quantity discounts.

[date]

Mr. Mario Dumas, Owner
Mercado Mexicano
114 West Webster Street
Chicago, KS 66056

Dear Mario:

As we discussed on the telephone on October 15, Enrico's Enchiladas is planning a special enchilada festival to begin on December 1. From December 1 through December 31, all of our enchiladas will be available at a 25% discount. All online, email, phone, and mail orders placed during this period will receive the discount. Special freezer displays and complimentary aprons will be sent with each order.

The discount applies to those enchiladas listed on our spring order sheets, page 3, in boxes of 12. These include:

Order #	Type	Regular Price	Discount Price
#1062	Cheese Enchiladas	$24	$18
#1063	Bean Enchiladas	$20	$15
#1064	Beef Enchiladas	$28	$21
#1065	Chicken Enchiladas	$32	$24

We will ship your order within 24 hours of receipt.

I look forward to our December Enchilada Festival and to hearing from you soon. I will be glad to handle your shipment with special care.

Sincerely,

Enrico Sanchez

es/js

Letter Confirming Arrangements for Speaker

Sample Letter 12.3 was written to a person who had committed to speak at a conference. The letter writer confirms the agreement and gives the speaker information on the luncheon he will be attending.

Sample Letter 12.3. Letter confirming arrangements for a speaker.

[date]

Mr. Mario L. Rodriguez
312 West Main Street
Boonton, NJ 07005

Dear Mr. Rodriguez:

Thank you for agreeing to speak at the IAFPAA Conference luncheon on Friday, November 7. Here are the final details of the event.

The luncheon will start at noon at the City Club, 12 State Street, Morriston (see the enclosed map for directions). If you wish a vegetarian menu, please call me at 632-555-8706 before Wednesday, November 5.

The luncheon should last about one hour, after which you will address the attendees. We have arranged for a microphone and lectern for your speech. If you need other equipment or have any questions about the luncheon, please call me.

We look forward to your talk.

Sincerely,

Samuel D. Nead
Program Coordinator

sdn/mls

enc.

Letter Confirming Appointment

Sample Letter 12.4 was written to confirm an appointment. The letter writer briefly confirms the date and time when she is to meet the reader. She mentions that she will be bringing two people to the meeting.

Sample Letter 12.4.   Letter confirming an appointment.

[date]

Mr. John Egnald
Managing Director
Association Widgets, Inc.
5775 Peachtree Road
Quantico, AK 99556

Dear Mr. Egnald:

I look forward to meeting you on Monday, September 21, to further discuss the North Widget Project, which Legyern Associates will be designing. I will plan to arrive at your offices around noon.

I will be bringing my colleagues Mack MacIntyre and Bethany Cole with me. We are all extremely excited about this project and the prospect of your participation.

Cordially,

Martha Long

ml/kw

cc: Mack MacIntyre
     Bethany Cole

Letter Confirming Travel Plans

Sample Letter 12.5 was written to a prospective customer to confirm his travel plans to the letter writer's company. The letter writer lays out the specifics, telling the customer where she will meet him and giving him a brief itinerary for the visit.

Sample Letter 12.5.   Letter confirming travel plans.

[date]

Mr. Jeffrey Leigh, President
Fortuitous Ceramic Supplies, Inc.
67 Lathrop Avenue
High Point, NC 27054

Dear Mr. Leigh:

It was so good to meet you at your studio in North Carolina last month. I am glad you're going to be paying us a visit here in Minneapolis to consider offering our kilns to your customers in your catalog of ceramics supplies.

I have enclosed an itinerary and tickets for your visit here. Your North Air flight 1226 leaves Raleigh Airport on October 4 at 10 A.M. You're scheduled to arrive in Minneapolis at 3 P.M. I'll pick you up at the airport and take you to Quartermaster Inn, a lovely old inn and restaurant just outside of downtown Minneapolis. Georgia Long, our sales representative for the Southeast, and I will meet you for dinner at the inn at 7:30 P.M.

Please call if you have any questions about your visit. I'm looking forward to showing you the latest in our state-of-the-art kilns.

Sincerely,

Lauren Palay
President

enc.

Letter Confirming Telephone Conversation

Sample Letter 12.6 was written to confirm the facts discussed in a telephone conversation. The letter writer briefly confirms the information she had given the letter reader over the phone and asks that he call if he has further questions.

Sample Letter 12.6   Letter confirming a telephone conversation.

[date]

Mr. Mack MacIntyre
Mandate and Associates
45 Winck Road
Pechee, AZ 85054

Dear Mr. MacIntyre:

As we discussed in our phone conversation earlier this week, I have sent a letter to each of the 15 project advisory board members for the North Widget Project. As you can see from the enclosed copy, the letter welcomes each member to the board and asks him or her to enclose a biographical profile.

A file has been set up for each advisory board member.

If you need further information or assistance, feel free to call on me.

Cordially,

Ellen Short
Assistant Coordinator

es/kw

enc.

cc: Bethany Cole

Letters Confirming Receipt of Materials

Sample Letters 12.7 and 12.8 were sent to confirm receipt of materials. Sample Letter 12.7 confirms that the material has been received and that the letter writer will send it out for review. Sample Letter 12.8 also confirms receipt of the material, but here the writer explains that the person to whom it was sent is away and that he will turn his attention to it when he returns.

Sample Letter 12.7.   Letter confirming receipt of material.

[date]

Dr. Alice T. Cooperburg
Department of Mathematics
Fortified College
P.O. Box 3542
Westernite, CT 06056

Dear Dr. Cooperburg:

This letter will acknowledge receipt of the outline and 12 chapters of your manuscript on mathematical modeling. We are very pleased to receive your material and welcome the opportunity to review it.

Your material has been referred to several critics for their comments. I should have their recommendations within three to four weeks and will be glad to send you their reactions at that time.

Thank you for sending this material to me. I will be in touch with you soon.

Cordially,

Maxwell L. Nicholas
Executive Editor

mln/jls

Sample Letter 12.8.   Letter confirming receipt of material.

[date]

Dr. Lionel T. Aramet
Department of Economics
Transit University
43 Alban Hall West
Transit, NY 10055

Dear Dr. Aramet:

I'm writing this letter to acknowledge receipt of the outline and five chapters of your manuscript on econometrics.

Mr. Nicholas is currently away on business. I will bring your material to his attention immediately upon his return. He will be in touch with you as soon as your material has been reviewed.

Sincerely,

Chauncy D. Tortoise
Secretary to Maxwell Nicholas

cdt

CHAPTER 13

Request letters

The letters in this chapter fall into the broad category of request letters. These are commonly written to request everything from information and assistance to reprints of articles.

Many of the letters in this chapter can be sent as emails or as attachments to emails. For those letters in this chapter that can be adapted to emails, it's simple enough to copy the text of the sample letter into the text of your email.

Letter Requesting Information About Accommodations

Sample Letter 13.1 was written to request information about accommodations that were to be provided to a speaker. The speaker writes to request information about the room he will be speaking in and the equipment he has requested. He opens by saying that he is looking forward to the meeting, then asks a series of questions about the accommodations that will be provided. The letter is clear and to the point, and should get the letter writer the results he needs.

Sample Letter 13.1.   Letter requesting information about accommodations.

[date]

Mr. James B. Dreyfus
Assistant Seminar Director
Business Writers Association
23 Floriador Street
Ausley, NY 10095

Dear Mr. Dreyfus:

I am looking forward to speaking at your upcoming seminar. I've completed and enclosed the form you sent me. I've also checked off the audiovisual services I will need for my talk.

At your earliest convenience, please let me know how many people will attend my two seminar sessions, "Public Relations Primer." There are a few other questions I hope you can answer for me as soon as possible:

1. Will I be able to see the room where I'll be speaking before my first session on Tuesday at 9:00 A.M.?
2. Will I be able to check the handouts to ensure they are all there?
3. Will I be able to check the audiovisual equipment I requested?
4. Should I plan to meet you (or someone else) on Monday or should I just show up for my sessions?

Can you also correct the name of my company to Napier Public Relations, Inc., not Napier Communications, as you refer to it in your outline? I would also appreciate the initials APR (Accredited Public Relations) being used after my name. I've enclosed a business card for your reference. Thanks very much.

I look forward to speaking with you.

Best regards,

Max Napier, APR

mn/pb

Enclosures

Letter Requesting Information About Seminars

Sample Letter 13.2 was written to request information about seminars available in the letter writer's area of interest. The writer wastes no time; he gets right to the point in the first paragraph, thanks the recipient in the second, and closes the letter.

Sample Letter 13.2. Letter requesting information on seminars offered.

[date]

Ms. Carla Moore
Wholesale Carpeters Association
One Park Avenue
Westport, NE 68032

Dear Ms. Moore:

Please advise me of any seminars you might have that focus on training wholesale carpet distributors on effective management skills.

Thanks for your assistance.

Best regards,

Lin O. Leehum

lol/jls

Letter Requesting Assistance

Sample Letter 13.3 was written to request the assistance of a former life insurance policy holder by asking him to fill out a questionnaire about the company's services. The letter writer clearly states why she is asking the reader for the information, is cordial, and does not attempt to sell anything in the process. For companies asking customers to fill out online surveys, this letter could be easily adapted to serve that purpose and then could be sent as a letter or an email.

Sample Letter 13.3.   Letter requesting assistance by filling out questionnaire.

[date]

Mr. Timothy Marshall
Dean, Haskell, Marshall & Quiksilber
65 Basil Place
Attic, MT 59035

Dear Mr. Marshall:

New Day Life Insurance Company is committed to providing the small employer with the best service and group insurance products. Although your group health insurance policy is no longer in effect, it is important to us that we obtain your feedback about the quality of our service and products.

By completing the enclosed questionnaire you will provide us with the ideas and suggestions necessary to better serve small employers like you. Your opinions and comments are especially important to us.

Please take a few minutes to complete the questionnaire as accurately and honestly as possible. It is important that the person in your company who has the most influence and decision-making authority over group insurance coverage fill out the survey, so if that is not you, please pass this letter and form to the appropriate party. All responses are for planning purposes and will be used only in combination with other responses.

We would appreciate your response by December 28, 20X7. Simply fold this questionnaire and place it in the postage-paid envelope provided. If you have any questions, please call Mr. Alan Suez, market research and product development administrator, at 534-555-0987.

Thanks for your consideration in this important matter.

Very truly yours,

Joanne Tufts
President

jt/mn

Enc.

Letters Requesting Return of Material

Sample Letters 13.4 and 13.5 request the return of materials of one sort or another.

Sample Letter 13.4 requests the reader to fill out a form that the writer needs to have on file. The writer makes the request, briefly explains why she needs the form, and closes.

Sample Letter 13.5 is a short letter written to request that materials be returned. The writer is courteous and explains why she has to have the materials.

Sample Letter 13.4. Letter requesting completion of required form.

[date]

Mrs. Roberta Cupelman
Cupelman Contractors
139 Station Place
Rutineo, IL 60056

Dear Mrs. Cupelman:

The purpose of this letter is to request your organization to assist Coleridge Ship, Inc., in fulfilling its obligation to the Department of Defense by completing the enclosed Representation and Certification Form.

As prime contractor for the U. S. government, Coleridge Ship, Inc., requires that this information be obtained on an annual basis. Failure to respond may be detrimental to the future business between our companies.

Please forward the completed form to the above address. If you have any questions or desire additional information, please feel free to call me.

Sincerely,

COLERIDGE SHIP, INC.

Roxane Trustman
Manager of Contracts

rt/mn

enc.

Sample Letter 13.5. Letter requesting that materials be returned since too much time has passed.

[date]

Mr. John Blank
Fortified Developers
45 Rineland Drive
Hasquath, NM 87056

Dear Mr. Blank:

Thank you for consenting to review the architectural plans for our downtown shopping mall project. Since there was a time element involved in having these plans reviewed, we have had to make other arrangements concerning the project.

Please return the material to us at your earliest convenience.

We appreciate your willingness to review this plan, Mr. Blank, and hope that we may call upon you for future critical reviews.

Sincerely,

Fran Lison
President

ls

Letter Requesting Material from Speaker

Sample Letter 13.6 was written to request material from a speaker. The letter writer explains that he needs the material, offers to help the speaker if he needs assistance filling out the forms requested, and stresses the importance of the reader sending in the information.

Sample Letter 13.6.   Letter requesting that speaker supply material.

[date]

Mr. Larry C. Rebekkah
Emline Products, Inc.
34 Richardson Drive
Farnsworth, KY 40056

Dear Mr. Rebekkah:

I have been looking daily for the speaker's suggestion form that was mailed to you on December 1, 20X3.

If you are having difficulty or if you have any questions about what information we want, please write to me or call me at the Boonton office. I will be glad to answer any questions that you might have.

It is important that we have this information. I would appreciate it if you would return the forms at your earliest convenience.

Sincerely,

Mack Leges
Program Coordinator

ml/ms

Letter Requesting Correction on Charge Account

Sample Letter 13.7 was sent to a credit service asking that a correction be made on an account. The letter writer clearly states her case in the opening paragraph, mentioning that she is enclosing copies of documents to verify her claim. Rather than go off on a tirade, she clearly states her problem and asks for a solution.

Sample Letter 13.7.   Letter requesting that correction be made on charge account.

[date]

Mr. Lawrence Brians
Customer Service Representative
Cabot Credit Company
56 Frithy Drive
Lanscome, ID 83256

Dear Mr. Brians:

Enclosed is a copy of my cancelled check #161 for $20.95. This amount was not credited to my account, and this month's statement shows a past-due balance. I neglected to write my account number on the check. Whoever at Cabot Credit wrote the number on the check put the incorrect number on the face of the check.

I am enclosing a check for $44.93, which takes into account all new charges through November 1. I hope that this will settle the account balance.

Please let me know that this matter has been resolved.

Sincerely,

Lisa L. Long

encs.

Letter Requesting Reprint of Article

Sample Letter 13.8 was written to request a reprint of an article that was published in a magazine. The letter writer clearly states his request, leaving little doubt what he is after.

Sample Letter 13.8.   Letter requesting reprint of article.

[date]

Mr. Marl Simons, Editor
Options Trading Review
312 West Main Street
Boonton, NJ 07005

Dear Mr. Simons:

I would like to purchase a reprint of the article you published on options trading on pages 23 through 30 in your March 20X6 issue. Please send the reprint and any invoice to me at: 456 Frunton Street, Denville, Pennsylvania 15021.

Thank you for your assistance.

Sincerely,

Giles K. Julian
Vice President

gkj/jls

Letter Requesting Subscription Cancellation

Sample Letter 13.9 was written to restate the desire to cancel a subscription. The letter is short, direct, and clear. The letter writer is precise in what he asks the letter reader to do.

Sample Letter 13.9.   Letter sent to cancel a subscription.

[date]

Ms. Deborah Klein
Subscription Manager
Incorporated Magazine
44 Advertising Way
New Rochelle, CA 90009

Subject: Subscription Cancellation

Dear Ms. Klein:

I wrote you back in June and asked that you cancel my subscription to *Incorporated Magazine* and refund whatever was left on the subscription. It is now September and I am still receiving the magazine. The October issue just arrived in today's mail.

I am sending you the mailing label from this issue in hopes that it will help you expedite the cancellation of my subscription. I also trust that you will refund my money for the four months of issues that I've received since my initial cancellation request.

Thank you very much for your attention to this matter.

Sincerely,

Simon MacIntyre

enc.

Letter Requesting Free Products

Sample Letter 13.10 was written to a contact who had been able to get the letter writer free samples in past years for a conference he planned every year. The writer lays out the specifics and graciously asks the contact if he might be able to provide goods for the conference.

Sample Letter 13.10.   Letter requesting free products.

[date]

Mr. Forrest Kirk
Marketing Director
Fritter Potato Chip Company, Inc.
345 Avenue Road
Bristol, CA 90990

Dear Mr. Kirk:

Every year *Incorporated Magazine* stages a conference for owners and founders of companies that have recently gone public. This year the conference is to be held in Bristol County. In addition to the wonderful program we have planned for attendees, the conference is also a perfect opportunity for the host community to attract business to its area by showcasing the products manufactured by area businesses.

Traditionally we have contacted area companies, asking them to contribute products that will be placed in the hotel rooms of conference attendees as part of a welcome basket. Would you consider providing us with 900 bags of Fritter Potato Chips that we can include in the welcome basket? Of course, we will also include literature on your business and your line of products.

The conference will be held at the Bristol Hotel and Convention Center starting November 5. The product samples can be sent to me at the convention center, where we will assemble the welcome baskets. Or, if it is easier for you, we will send a pickup van to get the samples just before the conference.

I will give your office a call sometime over the next couple of weeks to follow up on this letter. Please feel free to call me at 888-456-7890 if you have any questions. Thank you in advance for participating in the conference.

Sincerely,

Alan Satin
Conference Coordinator

Letter Requesting Information About a New Product

Sample Letter 13.11 was written by a retail store owner to a company that makes a product her customers had requested. She also takes the opportunity to ask the recipient to send any other relevant material.

Sample Letter 13.11.   Letter requesting information about a new product.

[date]

Ms. Jane Coleman
Regional Sales Director
Amherst School Products
34 School Street
Lesley, MA 02334

Dear Ms. Coleman:

We have been receiving a handful of requests for the sock puppet assembly kit that your company manufactures. While we are primarily a bookstore catering to children, we have begun to expand our offerings to include products that are complementary to our books.

Please send me some information on your product as well as any additional material that will help us decide if it's the type of product that will interest children who generally range in age from pre-school to 12 years old. Thank you very much.

Sincerely,

Jeri Corridor

Letter Requesting Pricing Information

The writer of Sample Letter 13.12 has written to a company to see if he could get bulk price discounts on a product he wanted to buy a lot of. The letter writer clearly states his needs and asks the recipient for prices on specific products and for specific-size orders.

Sample Letter 13.12.   Letter requesting pricing information.

[date]

Mr. Edward Coleson
Special Sales Director
Prestige Clipboards and Folders, Inc.
P.O. Box 3542
Jonesboro, NJ 07007

Dear Mr. Coleson:

Every summer we run a series of soccer clinics at our college for coaches of high school soccer teams. When they arrive we like to give each attendee a clipboard or folder that contains the week's agenda and a pad on which to take notes and provides pockets in which to store handouts they receive during the week.

A colleague showed me a catalog featuring your Abundant Series of folders that also act as clipboards. The catalog price was $12 for each clipboard. We would be ordering at least 75 of these at once. Do you offer a volume discount for bulk orders? I'd also be interested in how much the unit price would be on additional orders of 10 or more clipboards.

Please send me the pricing information and any other relevant material.

Sincerely,

Paul Caldor
Program Director

CHAPTER 14

Replies

The letters included in this chapter serve as models that you can use in a variety of common situations. Whenever you are writing a response to a letter, it's good practice to make sure that you read the letter to which you are replying a second time to make sure you are addressing that letter writer's issues.

Many of the letters in this chapter can be sent as emails or as attachments to emails. For those letters that can be adapted to emails, it's simple enough to copy the text of the sample letter into the text of your email.

Letter Acknowledging Order

Sample Letter 14.1 was written to acknowledge an order for a product. The letter writer explains that more information is needed before shipment can be made, and clearly explains what the reader must do to ensure timely delivery of his order.

Sample Letter 14.1.   Letter acknowledging order.

[date]

Mr. Blake Brinne
Hanley Hascomb & Doyle
327 Merrimac Trail, Suite 4B
Williamstown, MO 63045

Dear Mr. Brinne:

Thank you for your order for 250 customized executive desk calendars. We will ship your calendars as soon as they are printed.

Before we ship, however, we need to know how you would like us to ship the calendars. You failed to indicate on your order whether you wanted overnight delivery, first-class mail, or parcel post. If you will check off your preference on the enclosed postage-paid card and return it to us, or call us toll-free at 800-555-6563, we will ship you your calendars immediately.

Thanks again for your order. We look forward to filling it as soon as we receive your instructions.

Sincerely,

Jeffrey L. Oscar

jlo/jls

Letter Acknowledging Registration for Conference

Sample Letter 14.2 was written to a person who had registered for a conference. In the first paragraph, the letter writer politely thanks the reader for his registration and lets it be known right off that his letter confirms the registration. The writer continues by explaining some specifics about the conference and closes by offering any help the reader might need.

Sample Letter 14.2. Letter following up on registration for conference.

[date]

Mr. Mark Holden
Pover Products, Inc.
45 Savin Avenue
Boonton, NJ 07005

Dear Mr. Holden:

Thank you for your recent registration to the Independent Wholesalers Trade Exposition at the Elmira Inn. This letter will confirm our receipt of your registration form and fee.

The Wholesalers Trade Society registration desk will open at 10:00 A.M. on Thursday, April 28, 20X5, followed by the opening general session. The national exposition will conclude at 5:30 P.M. on Saturday, April 30. Please note the enclosed pamphlet, which provides general information about the conference.

We look forward to welcoming you to Elmira and to this innovative national conference. Should you have any questions, please call me.

Cordially,

Simon Lexington
Education Coordinator

sl/pp

encl.

Remittance Letter

Sample Letter 14.3 is a remittance letter that was written to accompany payment for a product. It is brief and clearly states what is included with it. By writing such a letter, the writer minimizes the chances of a mistake on the part of the recipient. Sample Letter 14.3 could also be used as a guide for transmittal letters (see Chapter 11).

Sample Letter 14.3. Remittance letter.

[date]

Mr. Oscar T. Rodman
Rodman and Sons Stationery, Inc.
5432 Red Bank Drive
Chelmsford, MA 02145

Dear Mr. Rodman:

I have enclosed a check for $119 for the stationery and envelopes I ordered from you for our business. Also enclosed is a copy of your invoice number 3352217. Please credit the $119 to my account number 12-26-5631.

Sincerely,

Loudon P. Schlenger

lps/kpc

encs.

Response to Request for Clarification

Sample Letter 14.4 was written as a reply to a request for clarification on an account. The letter writer clearly explains what he is enclosing with the letter and offers an explanation for the discrepancy in the account. He closes by apologizing for the discrepancy.

Sample Letter 14.4.   Letter responding to a request for clarification.

[date]

Mr. Alan Lahsram
The Lahsram Literary Agency, Inc.
55 Nosidam Street
Los Angeles, CA 90023

Dear Mr. Lahsram:

Enclosed is a copy of the original royalty statement for the period January–June 20X3, and corrected copies for July–December 20X2. An error in our computations caused the problems you cited in your letter to me.

The prepublication sales that you refer to in your letter were not as great as we originally thought. Those are also reflected in the corrected royalty statements.

I'm sorry for the delay and the error in royalty statements.

Sincerely,

Phlange R. Lunk
Controller

prl/ajh

encls.

Response to Request for Information About Member of Organization

Sample Letter 14.5 was written to respond to a request for information about a member of a professional organization. The letter writer indicates in her opening paragraph that the professional in question is no longer a member of the organization, but provides the letter reader with what information she can about the former member. She closes by thanking the letter reader for his letter.

Sample Letter 14.5.   Letter responding to request for information about member of a society.

[date]

Mr. Jacob L. Irons
Investigative Management Magazine
25 Huntington Avenue, Suite 408
Boonton, NJ 07005

Subject: Membership of Bill Senyl

Dear Mr. Irons:

As we feared, Mr. Senyl is no longer a member of the Investment Managers Society of America. He was a member for just one year from May 20X2 through May 20X3, at which point he allowed his membership to lapse.

In his application, he indicated licenses and registrations in accounting, life insurance, law, real estate, and securities. He also indicated he was a registered investment adviser with the Securities and Exchange Commission. He indicated his highest level of education was a Ph.D., not a Masters degree as you mention he suggested to you. He also stated that he had memberships in the American Bar Association, American Society of Certified Life Underwriters, and the Million Dollar Round Table.

We certainly appreciate your interest and assistance. Your information will be lodged with the membership department of the Investment Managers Society of America.

Sincerely,

Lisa Antolini
General Counsel

la/js

Letters Responding to Requests for Materials

Sample Letter 14.6 responds to a request for an article to be submitted for a publication. The letter writer expresses an interest, but first wants to know more about the publication. She clearly spells out her questions in a numbered list in the letter.

Sample Letter 14.7 responds to the recipient's request for materials. The letter writer briefly explains what he has enclosed with the letter and mentions that some of the material may change as a result of the gathering of more information. If this letter is adapted to be sent as an email, the press kit may be sent as an attachment.

Sample Letter 14.6. Letter responding to request for material and asking for more information.

[date]

Mr. Marvin Hopping
The Armchair Reader's Review
350 Bixley Hall Drive
Boonton, NJ 07005

Dear Mr. Hopping:

Thank you for inquiring about my interest in submitting an article for *The Armchair Reader's Review*. I am interested in this opportunity to put my ideas about deposit insurance reform before an audience of financial services marketing professionals. Before committing myself, however, I would like to know more about the *Review* and its editorial policies:

1. Is this a new publication or have you published one or more issues? A recent copy of the publication would be appreciated, if it exists.
2. Will the published article be subject to peer review, in-house editorial review, or both?
3. What is your objective for my article in terms of style and technical complexity? An example of a "typical" article would be a good response to this inquiry.
4. Do you offer an honorarium for solicited articles?

Again, many thanks for thinking of me. I hope we can find a way to work together.

Yours truly,

Eleanor Elypdiva

ee/dp

Sample Letter 14.7. Letter sending materials requested.

[date]

Mr. Evan Efferen, Editor
The Reader's Review
25 Huntington Avenue, Suite 408
Boonton, NJ 07005

Dear Evan:

Enclosed is the media kit you requested. As I told you this morning, we will be updating this kit with more specific information about ratings and demographics. We are currently gathering the information from WLEE-TV, channel 37 in Bayonne.

I hope all is going well for you and that you might find our show an interesting story for your publication. If I can be of further assistance, please call.

Sincerely,

Lee Iname
Sales Coordinator

LI/mn

enc.

Letter Replying to a Sales Letter

The letter writer in Sample Letter 14.8 is writing in response to sales materials sent him. He clarifies what he is interested in and expresses interest in the recipient's product line if it can meet his needs.

Sample Letter 14.8.   Reply to a sales letter.

[date]

Mr. Compton P. Davidson
Balliwick Planning Guides, Inc.
76 Lathrop Avenue
Boonton, MO 63090

Dear Mr. Davidson:

Thank you for the information you sent me about your company's planning guides. While I believe such guides could be very useful to any professional organization, the guides you sent information about were targeted at engineers and architects. I'm not sure that these are easily applied in a professional school setting in which I operate.

If there is a Balliwick Planning Guide specifically targeted at professional schools like ours (we cater to training hotel management personnel), I'd like to look it over. Please send me a sample. Once I've evaluated it, I'll give you a call if it seems like something that will benefit our students.

Thanks for your interest in our school. I look forward to hearing from you.

Sincerely,

Denzel Dress
Curriculum Director

Letter Responding to a Request for Free Products

The letter writer in Sample Letter 14.9 is responding to a request for free products. The letter writer clearly states that he can accommodate the request and lays out the specifics of what he'll send, how much, when, and where.

Sample Letter 14.9. Letter responding to request for free products.

[date]

Mr. Alan Satin
Conference Coordinator
Incorporated Magazine
45 Rooster Place
Wootton, NJ 07890

Dear Mr. Satin:

We've arranged to ship 900 bags of Fritter's Gourmet Potato Chips to your attention at the Bristol Hotel and Convention Center. These should arrive early on the morning of November 3.

Thank you for giving us the opportunity to showcase our products. We are pleased to be able to participate in your conference and trust that it will introduce the business owners among your attendees to all that Bristol County has to offer.

Please call on me should you need anything else from Fritter Potato Chip Company.

Sincerely,

Mr. Forrest Kirk
Marketing Director

Letter Responding to Request for Information About a New Product

The letter writer of Sample Letter 14.10 is responding to a request for information about a new product. She quickly and clearly tells the customer what's included with the letter and offers any other help the customer might need.

Sample Letter 14.10. Letter responding to request for information about a new product.

[date]

Ms. Jeri Corridor
Owner
The Children's Corridor Bookstore
56 Tystimond Way
Raleigh, MA 02133

Dear Ms. Corridor:

Thank you for your inquiry about Amherst's Sock Puppet Assembly Kits. I am enclosing some literature on this product as well as information about the complete line of educational craft kits we manufacture. I have also enclosed a sample kit for you to review.

Please call me if I can be of further assistance. I look forward to doing business with you.

Sincerely,

Jane Coleman

encs.

Letters Responding to Requests to Be a Speaker

Both letter writers in Sample Letters 14.11 and 14.12 are responding to requests for them to speak at an event. In Sample Letter 14.11, the writer accepts the offer and states which of the dates presented to him works best for him. In Sample Letter 14.12, the writer regretfully announces that he must turn down the invitation because of a schedule conflict, but offers to speak at another time should the opportunity arise.

Sample Letter 14.11.   Reply accepting a request to speak.

[date]

Mr. David R. Friedman
Program Director
Automated Carriage Suppliers of America
756 Corporate Boulevard
Fishbein, WI 53065

Dear Mr. Friedman:

Thank you for your invitation to speak at your annual convention of the Automated Carriage Suppliers of America. I welcome the opportunity.

You mentioned that you were interested in having me deliver a keynote speech at either the breakfast session on Saturday, February 3, 20X2, or at the luncheon session on Monday, February 5. The session on Monday, February 5, works better for my schedule. Please let me know if this works for you.

I'm looking forward to the event and appreciate the opportunity to speak. I look forward to word from you on the confirmation of the date.

Sincerely,

Wess Daniels

Sample Letter 14.12.   Reply declining a request to speak.

[date]

Mr. David R. Friedman
Program Director
Automated Carriage Suppliers of America
756 Corporate Boulevard
Fishbein, WI 53065

Dear Mr. Friedman:

I am flattered by the invitation to speak at your annual convention in February. Unfortunately, I have a conflict in my schedule that makes it impossible for me to accept the offer.

You mentioned in your letter that you also have regional meetings throughout the spring and summer. My schedule is more flexible for the months of March through May than it is for the month of February. I would be glad to try to find a date that works for both of us for me to speak at one of your regional meetings. Please give me a call to explore possible speaking dates.

Thank you for your interest in me. I look forward to talking with you.

Sincerely,

Jerry Collins

CHAPTER 15

Permissions letters

The letters in this chapter were written to seek permission of one sort or another. In most cases the letters seek permission to reprint or use copyrighted material. When you use part of an article or book it is crucial that you receive the permission of the owner of the copyright on the material, not only to protect yourself, but also to appropriately acknowledge the person whose work is being used.

Many of the letters in this chapter can be sent as emails or as attachments to emails. For those letters in this chapter that can be adapted to emails, it's simple enough to copy the text of the sample letter into the text of your email. In that case, remember to change "the enclosed" to "the attached" as appropriate.

Letters Seeking Permission to Reprint

Sample Letters 15.1 through 15.4 were all written to seek permission to reprint material. Sample Letter 15.1 was written by an editor to an author to seek permission. Sample Letter 15.2 was written by an author to a publishing company seeking permission to reprint. Sample Letter 15.3 was written by the permissions editor of a publication seeking permission to reprint material. And Sample Letter 15.4 was written by an editor to a reviewer seeking permission to use part of his review in the advertising copy for a book.

Sample Letter 15.1. Letter from editor requesting permission to reprint material.

[date]

Mr. Mark Nies
45 Productive Row
Northcross, WI 53045

Dear Mr. Nies:

I am editing a book tentatively titled *Basic Market Research* and wish to include a reprint of your article entitled "Everything You Ever Wanted to Know About Market Research." The material intended for use will extend from November 20X8 through November 20X3. I have already acquired permission to use the material from *The Reader's Review* with the understanding that I will meet the regular requirements governing such use.

Any comments you wish to make would be most welcome. I am enclosing a postage-paid card, which I ask you to return to me to grant your permission.

Cordially,

Christina Dinah
Editor

cd/js

enc.

Sample Letter 15.2.   Letter from author requesting permission to include material in book.

[date]

Ms. Zoe Long, Permissions Editor
Best Books Publishing Company
86 Grampian Way
Plattsburgh, NY 12901

Dear Ms. Long:

In my book on marketing, which is designed for use as a hardcover textbook priced at approximately $50, and is scheduled for publication by Business Textbook Publishing Company, Inc., in June 20XX, I would like to include material found in the first two paragraphs of Chapter 3 (page 45) in *Basic Marketing* by John Struddelson, published by your company in 20XX.

May I have your permission to include this material in my forthcoming book and in all future editions and revisions, covering nonexclusive world rights in all languages? These rights will in no way restrict republication of your material in any other form by you or others authorized by you. If you don't control these rights in their entirety, would you tell me who does?

A release form is provided below and a copy of this letter is enclosed for your files. Your prompt consideration of this request will be appreciated.

Sincerely,

Jeffrey Palay

mp

enc.

I grant the permission on the terms stated in this letter.

CREDIT LINE TO BE USED: _____

Date: _____

By: _____

Sample Letter 15.3. Letter from publication's permissions editor seeking permission from author to reprint material.

[date]

Mr. Max Kemper
45 Troublesome Road
Boston, NJ 07076

Dear Mr. Kemper:

We are considering the enclosed item for possible use in *Home Life*.

May we have your permission to use this material in every edition of *Home Life* worldwide? Such use will be limited to one-time publication in each edition. Should this item be used in a foreign edition, it may be translated and the wording may vary to conform to local idiom.

Payment of $120 will be issued upon first publication of your item in an edition of *Home Life*.

You warrant that you have the authority to grant the above rights. We have already received permission from *Boonton* magazine, where your work first appeared.

If you are in agreement with these terms, we would appreciate your signing and returning one copy of this letter at your earliest convenience.

Sincerely,

Jacob L. Alan
Permissions Editor

PERMISSION GRANTED

BY: _____

If additional permission is required, name and address: _____

Date: _____

Sample Letter 15.4.   Letter requesting permission to quote from critic's review.

[date]

Professor Larry E. Duerr
Campbell College
13 Bethany Hall
Campbell, WV 26056

Dear Professor Duerr:

I would like to take this opportunity to thank you again for reviewing the *Business Communications* manuscript for us.

We are now working on the advertising copy for the book and would very much appreciate it if we might have your permission to quote you in our advertisements. The quotation we'd like to use from your review is enclosed with the letter.

If we may have your permission to quote you, would you kindly sign both copies of this letter, return the original to us, and retain the other for your personal files? I have enclosed a stamped, self-addressed envelope for your convenience.

Sincerely yours,

Marvin Norts

mn/br

encls.

_____

Signature of Professor Larry E. Duerr

Letters Indicating More Information Needed for Permission

Sample Letters 15.5 and 15.6 both instruct people on the appropriate procedure to take for getting permission to reprint. Sample Letter 15.5 informs the letter reader that he must get in touch with the author of the material to secure permission and gives him his address.

Sample Letter 15.5.   Letter referring permission request to author.

[date]

Professor Carlton Long
Sathceko University
45 Kit Clark Lane
Dorchester, MA 02145

Dear Professor Long:

We have your letter of October 25, 20XX, requesting permission to reproduce material on pages 134 and 135 from *Labor Negotiations Handbook* in your forthcoming publication by Important Management Books Corp.

I am sorry but I am unable to grant you this permission since the copyright has been assigned to the author and it is to him you must direct your request. The latest address we have for him in our files is: Professor Simon Nemplar, University of the Upper Midwest, 56 Cochran Hall, Grand Forks, North Dakota 58201.

I am sorry I could not be of more help.

Sincerely,

Serge Bukoski
Permissions Editor

mn

Sample Letter 15.6 acknowledges receipt of a request for permission to reprint but asks for more information before permission can be granted.

Sample Letter 15.6.   Letter asking for more information before permission to reprint can be granted.

[date]

Mrs. Rita Margolis
23 Point Breeze Drive
Allentown, MI 48045

Dear Mrs. Margolis:

We have your letter of October 20, 20XX, requesting permission to reprint from page 435 of *Introduction to Management*.

I am sorry, but I cannot consider your request until I know exactly what material from that page you wish to reproduce, and in what context the material will appear. Would you kindly resubmit this request, quoting the beginning and ending words of the passage? I will then be happy to consider your request.

I would also like to know the approximate size of the printing of your book, the tentative publication price and date, and the name of your publisher.

I look forward to hearing from you.

Cordially,

Serge Bukoski
Permissions Editor

sb/mn

Letters Granting Permission

Sample Letters 15.7 and 15.8 grant permission to reprint material. Sample Letter 15.7 grants permission to reprint from a specified page and indicates how the permission line should read in the book holding the reproduced material. Sample Letter 15.8 is a letter from a publisher to an author granting him permission to republish specific portions of a book he had published with the publisher's company.

Sample Letter 15.7. Letter granting permission to reproduce material from a book still in print.

[date]

Ms. Joan W. Sherman
45 Heritage Drive
Dictionary, PA 15034

Dear Ms. Sherman:

We have your letter of May 29, 20X9, requesting permission to reproduce material from page 345 of Professor Janice McNurty's *Basic Marketing*.

We are pleased to be able to grant you permission for use of this material. The fee is $50 and is payable upon publication of the reprints. We ask that a credit line appear on the first page or on an acknowledgments page of every copy as follows:

> from *Basic Marketing* by Janice McNurty, Copyright 20X8 by Andoris Publishing Company, Boonton, New Jersey. Reprinted with permission.

Thank you again for your interest in this title.

Best regards,

Serge Bukoski
Permissions Editor

sb/mn

Sample Letter 15.8. Letter from publisher to author granting rights.

[date]

Mr. John L. Neorn
34 South Street
Massasoit, NJ 07045

Dear John:

You have our permission to use any and all information that appears in sections one and three of your book, *Business Writing Handbook*, in any and all books that you write on any subject so long as the book(s) that you write does (do) not compete with the sale of the above-mentioned book. We would consider a book to be competitive if it were sold to the same audience and written on the same subject.

I wish you the best of luck with your future writing efforts.

Sincerely,

Adam R. Quartermain, Jr.
Executive Editor

ARQ:jls

Letters Denying Permission

Sample Letters 15.9 and 15.10 were written to deny permission to reprint material. Both letters clearly state reasons why the permission is being denied. Sample Letter 15.9 explains that allowing the requested material to be used might hurt sales of the existing book. Sample Letter 15.10 explains that the volume of material requested is too large for permission to be granted.

Sample Letter 15.9. Letter denying permission to reprint because of potential to hurt sales.

[date]

Mr. Webster Berrigan
24 Watershed Drive
Maui, HI 96790

Dear Mr. Berrigan:

We have your letter of July 15, 20XX, requesting permission to reprint from pages 345 to 365 of *America's Entrepreneurs* by Alice Gompers.

After careful consideration, our editorial board has advised me that, although permitting sections of *America's Entrepreneurs* to be reprinted freely in magazines throughout the country might publicize the book to some extent, it could seriously curtail its sale.

We are extremely sorry not to be able to give you permission to use this material. We are compelled to take this position because we have had previous requests of a similar nature and are likely to have many more.

Cordially,

Serge Bukoski
Permissions Editor

sb/mn

Sample Letter 15.10. Letter denying permission to reprint because of volume of material asked to be reproduced.

[date]

Ms. Patrice Rhodese
56 Trainway Parkway
Montclair, PA 15056

Dear Ms. Rhodese:

We have your letter of March 1, 20XX, requesting permission to reproduce material on pages 233 to 253 of *Acting Techniques* by Dr. Edmond Jonson for use by you in a book you are writing for Best Books Publishing Company.

After careful consideration, our editorial board has advised me that they do not feel justified in allowing this material to be reproduced. While it has been our policy to be as accommodating as we possibly can be in the matter of granting permission to use material from our books, we feel that, in all fairness to our authors and to ourselves, we should not give permission for such an amount of material to be reproduced or reprinted.

I am very sorry not to be able to grant your request.

Sincerely,

Serge Bukoski
Permissions Editor

mn

Cover Letter for Contract

Sample Letter 15.11 was sent as the cover letter to accompany a contract being offered an author. The letter writer cordially welcomes the author, explains that the company will support the author, introduces the author's in-house editor, and requests that the author fill out enclosed material.

Sample Letter 15.11.   Letter used as cover letter for contract.

[date]

Mrs. Venita Applebaum
34 Lucrese Drive
Winchester, PA 15055

Dear Mrs. Applebaum:

Our entire staff joins with me in extending our best wishes to you as a future Andoris Publishing Company author. Your decision to work with Andoris is appreciated. I am confident that your textbook on macroeconomics will make a unique contribution to the field of economics. A copy of our agreement is enclosed for your personal records.

Andoris is ready to assist you in every way possible. Our editorial facilities are at your disposal, and we want you to call upon us for any guidance or help that we can give.

We look forward to working with you for many years to come. With this in mind, let me take this opportunity to remind you of the importance of timely revisions of successful textbooks. Your editor, Nan Long, will remain in close contact with you throughout your association with Andoris, and she will work with you on plans for future editions.

Please complete and return the enclosed contract. Again, welcome to Andoris.

Sincerely,

Kate Allen
Executive Editor

ka/mn

encls.

Letter Requesting Reversion of Rights

Sample Letter 15.12 was sent by an agent to a publisher requesting the reversion of rights on a book his client has written. Such a letter would be written when a book has had slow sales or a publisher has decided to take the book out of print. The letter writer introduces himself, makes his request, and closes.

Sample Letter 15.12.   Letter requesting reversion of rights.

[date]

Mr. Mark More
Andoris Publishing Company
23 Lathrop Avenue
Boonton, NJ 07005

Dear Mr. More:

As the agent for Loren Gray, I am writing to request reversion of rights to two of his books, *Fun on a Shoestring* and *Fun with More Shoestring*, which he wrote for Andoris under the pseudonym Bud Genry. I believe that these two titles are both out of print.

Please include the original certificate of copyright for both of these titles when you acknowledge reversion.

Thanks for attending to this matter.

Cordially,

Ephrain Noldercan

mj

CHAPTER 16

Social, personal, and miscellaneous letters

We all know that some occasions that call for a letter have little to do with specific business matters like closing a big sale or acquiring a small company. The rules of effective letter writing apply as much to social and personal letters as they do to more business-related letters.

The sample letters in this chapter consist of various letters you may find yourself needing to write. The letters here were written by professionals for a diverse range of social and personal occasions, and can serve as ideal models on which to base your own social and personal letters.

Many of the letters in this chapter can be sent as emails or as attachments to emails. For those letters that can be adapted to emails, it's simple enough to copy the text of the sample letter into the text of your email.

There are also occasions when writing personal letters that a handwritten note or card is appropriate. Again, while the samples here are in letter format, they can easily be adapted to a handwritten note or card.

Thank-You Letters

Sample Letters 16.1 through 16.21 are all examples of thank-you letters that were written for a variety of reasons. Thanking someone for something is not only courteous, it also builds goodwill with the person you are thanking.

Sample Letter 16.1 was written to thank someone for a personal favor. The letter writer clearly expresses gratitude to the reader without getting schmaltzy. She thanks him, wishes him well, and closes.

Sample Letter 16.2 was written to thank someone for her hospitality. Here too the letter writer expresses gratitude, specifically mentioning what he is thanking the reader for.

Sample Letter 16.3 was written to thank a contributor for a charitable contribution. The letter writer thanks the reader for the gift, briefly recaps what it was for, mentions how the donation will help, and closes.

Sample Letter 16.4 thanks someone for a public service. Here the letter writer expresses his appreciation and gratitude to the reader. He closes by reiterating his thanks.

Sample Letter 16.5 was written to thank someone who had appeared on a television panel show. The letter writer thanks the reader, expresses appreciation, lets him know that he was a good guest, and closes.

Sample Letter 16.1. Letter thanking someone for a personal favor.

[date]

Dr. Ralph Junot
Key Vineyards
43 Rensit Chateau
Tours, OR 97045

Dear Dr. Junot:

I can't tell you how much Ward and I appreciate the loan of your automobile when we were in Tours. The rental car was completely demolished; fortunately it was insured!

I hope the new wine wins critical acclaim in the contest next month. We've already placed our personal order for a case.

Best regards,

Jacqueline Shopenhauer

JS:lh

Sample Letter 16.2.   Letter thanking someone for hospitality.

[date]

Ms. Eileen Durga
Seminole College of Engineering
32 Rajpoor Drive
Jaipur, India 48113

Dear Eileen:

Once again you've treated us to an enjoyable annual meeting. India was breathtaking. We've just uploaded our photographs to our computer and they look amazing. We'll send you any photos that feature you and Prakash.

Anna and I have decided to return to India in December. It looks like we'll be touring Rajasthan. We'd love to meet you and Prakash in Jaipur and take you to dinner.

Let us know when you are planning a trip back to the States. We're eager to show you some of *our* favorite places.

Sincerely,

Nils Loflin

Sample Letter 16.3.   Letter thanking contributor for contribution.

[date]

Mr. Loren Terrece
56 Yorkway Place
Eufala, AR 71621

Dear Mr. Terrece:

Thank you for your generous gift to the Ellen Y. Timmons Scholarship Fund. The award is intended to provide an annual full-tuition scholarship to a deserving journalism senior or master's candidate at Highlands University.

Your gift will help future generations of students receive an outstanding education. Thank you for this tribute to the memory of Ellen Timmons.

Sincerely,

John T. Dalnor
Development Officer

JTD/JLS

Sample Letter 16.4.   Letter thanking someone for public service.

[date]

Mr. Maxwell Y. Samson
Andover Company
217 West Street
Boonton, NJ 07005

Dear Max:

I appreciate your service to your alma mater, Max, and the variety of forms it takes. Your most recent contribution, as part of the professionals' seminar, was quite valuable to our students.

With alumni like you who are willing to pitch in and lend their help when we need it, it is truly a joy to be in my position as alumni director.

Thanks again.

Sincerely,

Sam C. Leigh
Alumni Director

SCL:fcl

Sample Letter 16.5. Letter thanking panelist on talk show.

[date]

Mr. Jacob Trust
Byers Public Relations
478 North Street
Astoria, NJ 07005

Dear Mr. Trust:

Thank you so much for joining us on *Cyclorama*. We appreciate your taking time from your busy schedule to be with us. Your discussion with our host, Jimmy Lewis, was both interesting and informative.

It was a pleasure having you on the show. We wish you continued success and happiness.

Sincerely,

Claire B. Janeway
Executive Producer

CBJ:eel

The writer of Sample Letter 16.6 thanks a journalist for mentioning her in her magazine column and tells her that she admires her work.

Sample Letter 16.7 was written to thank a book reviewer for her comments. The writer thanks the columnist for reviewing his book positively and expresses his gratitude.

Sample Letter 16.6. Letter thanking writer for mentioning person in article.

[date]

Ms. Etsuko Chin
The Armchair Reader's Review
34 Eliot Boulevard
Piscataway, TX 75003

Dear Etsuko:

I didn't want to let 20X7 slip away without extending my thanks for including *Women's Issues* magazine and me in your marketing column last month. The article was terrific. It pulled together all the pertinent statistics and showed why women need and want to plan, without making us look like weak-kneed ninnies. A delicate balance indeed!

Here's hoping that 20X8 brings you much health and prosperity.

Sincerely,

Ellen T. Cincinnati

etc/jls

Sample Letter 16.7. Letter thanking reviewer for comments.

[date]

Ms. Alice Longworth
Professional's Magazine
287 Merrimac Trail
Boonton, NJ 07005

Dear Ms. Longworth:

Thank you very much for your insightful and kind review of my book *How to Manage Your Way to the Top* in the May issue of *Professional's Magazine*.

When the book was published, I told the publisher that there were two publications whose review would be critical to its success: *Global Management*, for the international manager, and *Professional's Magazine*. I really had my heart in my mouth when I picked up the May issue. It was a terrific kick for me to read your review.

I wish that there were a way for me to return the favor. Suffice it to say that I am grateful to you and the magazine for the kind words you have to say about my book.

Sincerely,

Arnold T. Yarrum
President

aty:caf

cc: RTS, Publisher

Sample Letter 16.8 was written to thank the reader for an outing that the letter writer had attended. The writer thanks the reader, follows up by mentioning he is enclosing an article that the two had discussed at the outing, and closes by offering assistance to the reader if he should need it in the future.

Sample Letter 16.8. Thank-you letter for outing.

[date]

Mr. Alan Marshal
Tillinghurst & Partners
423 West Watchung Road
Ordeal City, IL 60345

Dear Alan:

It was good seeing you and meeting your wife at the Tillinghurst annual bash. Maggie and I had a great time. It's always nice to see familiar faces and to catch up on our hectic lives.

As promised, I'm enclosing an article on public relations activities relating to the law profession that appeared in a recent issue of *Lawyers and Professional Practice*.

Again, it was great to see you at the outing. If I can ever be of service to you, please call on me.

Best regards,

Julius Norton

jn/js

Enc.

Sample Letter 16.9 was written to thank the recipient for dinner. The letter writer briefly expresses his thanks, mentions that he is enclosing an article he thought the letter reader might find interesting, and closes by suggesting they meet soon.

Sample Letter 16.9. Thank-you letter for dinner.

[date]

Mrs. Minerva T. Uronim
Executive Director
The Brain Trust of New Jersey
54 General Road, Suite 600
Circle City, VT 05434

Dear Minerva:

Sarah and I want to thank you for the lovely dinner we had at your home last week. We enjoyed both the cuisine and the company of the other invited guests.

Enclosed is an article from one of the publications to which I contribute. I thought you'd find this article of particular interest.

I'll call your assistant next week to check your schedule for lunch.

Best regards,

Ambrose Kinton

ak:js

enc.

Sample Letter 16.10 was written to thank the recipient for the kind words he had to say about the letter writer's newspaper column. The writer expresses her thanks, suggests that the reader stop by if he is ever in the area, and closes by expressing her best wishes.

Sample Letter 16.10. Thank-you letter for compliments on article.

[date]

Mr. Jacob L. Prentice
Prentice Public Relations, Inc.
312 West Main Street
Boonton, NJ 07005

Dear Mr. Prentice:

Thank you for your kind words about my newspaper column and for the thoughtful gift of *Marketing Financial Advisory Services*. It is always a pleasure for me to hear that my column is read, and even more that it is appreciated. I have found it to be a great outlet for creativity with many of the matters that I deal with in my insurance business.

If you are ever in the Denville area, please stop by my office, which is located at the Morris County Village Center, across the street from the Powerville Inn. It would be my pleasure to meet you and thank you in person for making my day.

My best wishes to you during this holiday season.

Sincerely,

Anne L. Krauss, C.L.U.

ALK:JLS

Sample Letter 16.11 was written to thank someone for his professional services. While the letter writer had hired the recipient to do a job, she took the time to write a letter expressing her thanks for such a good job.

Sample Letter 16.11. Letter thanking professional for help with services rendered.

[date]

Mr. Jacob L. Prentice
Prentice Public Relations, Inc.
312 West Main Street
Boonton, NJ 07005

Dear Jacob:

Thank you for your assistance in making the visit of our national director to the Boonton area a highly successful one. Your hard work on publicity and press arrangements was most appreciated.

I feel that Dr. Helen Louise McGuffie's tour went quite well. By traveling to such historic sites as Jockey Hollow and touring New Hope she was able to experience firsthand a bit of New Jersey and Pennsylvania history. The weather for the weekend was not ideal, of course, but it certainly could have been worse. Both days we were fortunate enough to miss the worst of it, with rain coming before or after, but never actually during any of the events. We must have been doing something right to be blessed with cooperative weather.

Again, my sincere thanks to you and your staff. I look forward to seeing you again.

Very truly yours,

Minerva T. Uronim
Executive Director

MTU:mln

Sample Letter 16.12 was sent to thank someone who had nominated a professional for recognition. The letter writer thanks the recipient, acknowledges that the nominee will be considered, and closes by thanking the reader again.

Sample Letter 16.12.   Letter acknowledging nomination.

[date]

Ms. Anne L. Krauss, C.L.U.
Morris County Village Center,
P.O. Box 3542
Denville, NJ 07076

Dear Ms. Krauss:

Thank you for your nomination of Dr. Roscoe T. Miller, LIA, CLU, ChFC, for the 20X5 Rebecca A. Grimes Award for Excellence in the Industry. We will be glad to include his name in the book of biographies we will consider at our meeting on May 25.

Thank you again.

Cordially,

Geoffrey Spaulding
Director of Awards

GS/wb

Sample Letter 16.13 was written to thank someone for his advice. The letter writer of Sample Letter 16.14 goes a step further to tell the recipient the results of taking his advice.

Sample Letter 16.13. Letter thanking someone for advice.

[date]

Mr. Christopher Online
Hilary Works, Inc.
45 Commercial Wharf
Key Biscayne, NY 10009

Dear Chris:

Thank you so much for your note suggesting we consider hiring an outside vendor to help us develop our webpage. I had been wrestling with whether we should hire in-house staff or hire seasoned professionals on an independent contractor basis. Your point about waiting until we have a home page designed and have evaluated its effectiveness before we commit a lot of salary and overhead to new employees is well taken and one, I fear, that I hadn't thought hard enough about until you raised it.

I've decided to definitely go with an independent contractor. Thanks for your guidance.

Sincerely,

Jeffrey Freedman
New Business Manager

Sample Letter 16.14.   Letter thanking someone for the results of taking his advice.

[date]

Mr. Christopher Online
Hillary Works, Inc.
45 Commercial Wharf
Key Biscayne, NY 10009

Dear Chris:

Once again, you've come to the rescue with advice that has had great results for us here at Barnicle Bedsprings. I figured you'd like to know that we followed your advice in hiring the outside contractors to develop our website and the results have been wonderful.

I'd like to take you to lunch to fill you in on the specifics and to thank you in person. I'll give you a call later this week to set something up. Thanks again.

Sincerely,

Jeffrey Freedman
New Business Manager

Sample Letter 16.15 was written as a social follow-up to a luncheon. The conversation at the luncheon apparently turned to business, and the writer expresses his optimism for the recipient's business success. The letter contains particulars of the lunch, the conversation, and the reader's business and closes with an offer of future business help.

Sample Letter 16.15.   Thank-you letter for social luncheon.

[date]

Ms. Nancy Egland
112 Oxfordshire Drive
New London, CA 98110

Dear Nancy:

Thank you for the delicious meal and excellent conversation at the Pleasant Pheasant on September 21. I have already given your regards to Bill and Beverly Witherspoon, and they were glad to hear that you and I finally met.

Congratulations on the promising beginning of your independent pharmacy, Montague Apothecary. In this day of mega-corporations and big business, you have a daunting task ahead of you, but with your enthusiasm and knowledge of both pharmaceuticals and modern business practices, I have no doubt you'll be a success.

I look forward to our continued communication and the possibility that you may come to East Verona for a visit to our expanded facility. I would be happy to share with you any professional knowledge that might improve your understanding of the way we do business at Benevolent Pharmaceuticals.

I wish you the best for your new enterprise, and please let me know if there is any way I can help Montague Apothecary make it in the New London community.

Sincerely yours,

Marc Usshio

Sample Letter 16.16 was written to commend a speaker for a lecture he gave. It is clear from the writer's tone and specifics that he benefited greatly from attending the lecture. The use of specific details shows the writer's knowledge of the subject matter and reminds the reader of the particulars of his lecture. In closing, the writer offers to meet with the recipient at some future date, if at all possible.

Sample Letter 16.16. Thank-you letter to a speaker.

[date]

Mr. Ellmann Tatum
2500 Mouton Avenue
Memphis, TN 38155

Dear Mr. Tatum:

I want to tell you how much I enjoyed your informative lecture at this past weekend's special event. Before hearing you address the members of the Chattanooga Aquarium on the topic of "Freshwater Predators," I frankly had no idea how diverse our rivers and lakes were. I may never look at fishing the same way.

When I lived in Boston, I was a member of the New England Aquarium, and I must admit that I had a particular bias toward saltwater species. Freshwater aquariums? Boring. However, when I moved down to the Chattanooga area last fall, I became a member of the Chattanooga Aquarium. Old habits die hard, I guess. Your speech taught this old dog a new trick, though; you opened my eyes to the possibilities inherent in freshwater hydrobiology, and I plan on taking my two children to the Aquarium regularly to explore the myriad life forms in the waters around us here in Tennessee.

Thank you for making my weekend an educational and enjoyable one. If you are ever in Chattanooga again, I would welcome the opportunity to discuss your theories on predatory evolution in closed ecosystems—I found them particularly intriguing.

Sincerely yours,

Jonah W. Hale

Sample Letter 16.17 was written to compliment a chairperson on her fine job in coordinating an academic program. The author uses specific references to elements of the program that she enjoyed, indicating a real connection to the event. The close is congratulatory and erudite.

Sample Letter 16.17. Thank-you letter to a program chairperson.

[date]

Ms. Rachel Richards, Department Chair
Bright Lights School of Acting
2340 Clarendon Parkway
Boston, MA 02125

Dear Ms. Richards:

I was greatly impressed by the professional and informative program you recently coordinated, "Tragedy: A Funny Business." The title alone intrigued me, but when I saw the cast of actors and theorists you had assembled, I knew I had to attend.

Your day of seminars and discussion groups lived up to its public relations. I hope that you will consider offering these mini-courses again, although I know how much work you must have put into arranging such an edifying and well-run series of events. I was only able to attend Mr. Adolphus Finn's workshop on the dramatic monologue and Ms. Jacobine Picard's lecture on the theater of the absurd, but I heard from my colleagues who also attended that those two classes were a fair representation of the program as a whole.

Your hard work resulted in a significant contribution to the arts and entertainment industry in Boston, and considering our city's reputation as a cultural mecca, that's no small task. Congratulations on pulling off such a coup. You deserve a standing ovation.

Sincerely,

Jean Tseng

Sample Letter 16.18 was written to thank a service provider for a job well done. The writer includes specific references to the excellent work that her reader performed. The letter is glowing and would be suitable for the recipient to display in his office.

Sample Letter 16.18. Thank-you letter to a service provider.

[date]

Mr. Roscoe Albertson
Green Day Lawn Care
343 Lily Street
Topeka, KS 62210

Dear Mr. Albertson:

Thank you so much for your hard work and professionalism in getting Jayhawk University's campus looking its best for the Commencement Weekend activities. As you know, Commencement is one of the two major weekends in our academic calendar, and next to Alumni/ae Weekend/Homecoming, it is the most important time of year for us to show off our facilities. When parents and alumni/ae come back to South Shell or stroll down Dawson's Boulevard, we want them to see that they've left the University in good hands.

Your team of landscape architects and floral planners made Jayhawk U. look like a million dollars and may have helped us earn many times that much in charitable pledges! On several occasions, parents stopped to thank me for the education their children received and told me that they would have come to campus more often if they had known how beautiful it was. That beauty was the result of Green Day Lawn Care. You can bet that we'll be contacting you in the future for our landscaping treatment.

Sincerely,

Johnetta Rafia, Ph.D.
President

Sample Letter 16.19 was written to thank someone for his participation in a discussion panel. The letter is complimentary and specific, indicating that the author is familiar with the details of the recipient's work. The close is cordial and allows for further partnership between writer and reader.

Sample Letter 16.19. Thank-you letter for participation in a project.

[date]

Dr. Lester Redfeather
681 Sedgewick Avenue
Rochester, IN 52150

Dear Dr. Redfeather:

I want to thank you for coming to the Indiana University program "Conversations in Education: Using Multicultural Literature to Teach Critical Thinking" this year. I hope that you found the experience both interesting and fun.

The small group panels are truly the heart of the program. Your participation on the panel that covered Louise Erdrich's *Love Medicine* was especially helpful, as your work on Erdrich's fiction is highly respected in the field and accessible to our undergraduate population. I know that Erskine Mankiller appreciated the chance to work with a college professor, and he told me after the seminar that your reading of Erdrich's novel has inspired him to include the book in his Advanced Placement Literature class for the 20X3–20X4 school year at Cross Keys High School.

I'm very glad that you were a part of the "Conversations" program, and I hope you'll consider returning for our fall seminar series entitled "Midwestern Literature and the Origins of a Regional Canon." All of us at the University wish you well for the end of your academic year.

Sincerely,

Homer Bard
Director of Interdisciplinary Studies

Sample Letter 16.20 is a letter thanking someone for leading a seminar. The details of what the seminar leader did are laid out and the appreciation for the effort is clear. Such letters are often useful for a person's personnel file to indicate work that was done to assist with a not-for-profit effort. They are also useful as testimonials that might lead to other such tasks in the future.

Sample Letter 16.20. Letter thanking recipient for leading seminar.

[date]

Professor Gerald Jeffries
Harson College
Department of Journalism
210 Notyslob Street
San Diego, CA 90022

Dear Professor Jeffries:

On behalf of the Romanian Institute at Briarcliff College, thank you for recently leading a seminar for our delegation from Romania.

As you know, our program offered participants the opportunity to examine the direction of journalism in the 21st century. The participants' time with you was short, but the insight you offered allowed them to reflect on important issues in their field. We are confident that this newfound perspective will enrich their work at home.

Your seminar on ethics was engaging and meaningful. Thank you for your thorough preparation and for making the session one of the highlights of the program.

We hope that you will be able to keep in touch with the participants you met. We find that the relationships developed through the program help to break down cross-community divides and create collegiality among all participants.

Thank you again for a wonderful seminar. We greatly appreciate it.

Sincerely,

Aoife Czlad
Director

It's wise to make thank-you letters short. Sample Letter 16.21 also includes specific detail to indicate familiarity with the speaker's service.

Sample Letter 16.21.   Letter thanking a speaker.

[date]

Ms. Ellen Arkin Poe
45 Divinity Lane
Francis, MA 02118

Dear Ms. Poe:

Thank you so much for your recent address to our marketing cohort group. Our new hires stated that your panel entitled "SNAP! Social Networking And Promotion" was far and away the most engaging and informative breakout session of the weekend. Clearly, your expertise in the field combined with your enthusiasm for the topic has made you a valued and desirable speaker.

Enclosed is a check for our agreed-upon speaking fee of $2,000.00. I hope that you will consider speaking to next year's new employees, as well.

Sincerely yours,

Emerson Thorow

ET/hm

encl.

Invitations

Sample Letters 16.22 through 16.29 are examples of invitations. Sample Letter 16.22 was written in official-style format to invite the reader to a company-sponsored dinner. The letter writer clearly explains who is making the invitation and spells out the details. She closes by asking the reader to call her office to confirm her attendance.

Sample Letter 16.22.   Letter making invitation for dinner.

[date]

Dear Lois:

Mark Nilton, the president of Andoris Products, Inc., joins with me in inviting you and Jacob to cocktails and dinner at 6 P.M. on Wednesday, June 30, 20X6, at the House of Fine Foods Inn, 23 Berkely Street, Boston, Massachusetts.

While the evening will be principally social, I do expect that Mark will have some informal remarks to make after dinner on a topic of interest to the gathering. We anticipate about 30 good friends of the company joining us for the evening.

I hope you will be able to attend. Please call my office to indicate if you plan to join us. I look forward to seeing you that evening.

Yours truly,

Lisa T. Gray
Editor

Ms. Lois T. Kemper
Kemper Lifestyles, Inc.
232 Scituate Road
Brookline, NH 03034

LTG:WLG

Sample Letter 16.23 was written to invite the reader to an open house. The writer makes a brief invitation by clearly spelling out the date and the event. She closes with a personal note to the reader.

Sample Letter 16.23. Letter inviting someone to an open house.

[date]

Max G. Growne
5A Stomping Hill Lane
Tretorne, NE 69044

Dear Max:

Oz and I are having an open house to celebrate our move to Westwood. The date is June 6 starting at 6 P.M. We're hoping that it will be warm enough for people to use the swimming pool. Do bring your suit.

Please feel free to bring your new friend; we'd love to meet him.

Best regards,

Tenia Lapadoor

Sample Letter 16.24 was written to invite the reader to a special event. The writer describes the seminar, then asks that the reader call to confirm whether or not he can attend.

Sample Letter 16.25 was written to invite a speaker to speak at an event. The letter writer invites the speaker, gives the dates, and asks that the reader respond by a specific date.

Sample Letter 16.24. Letter inviting someone to special event.

[date]

Mr. Jeffrey R. Kemper, Editor
Weekly Business Chronicle
8 Lorraine Terrace
Santiago, PA 15054

Dear Jeff:

I thought you might be interested in a tax seminar we are putting on next Thursday, October 30. It will be the first seminar available after the new tax bill gets passed. I've enclosed a brochure on the topics that will be covered at the seminar.

Let me know if you or one of your reporters would like to attend. I look forward to hearing from you.

Sincerely,

R. Kyle Yennik

jls

enc.

Sample Letter 16.25.   Letter inviting someone to speak at an annual meeting.

[date]

Mr. Terrence Derand
Derand Management Systems, Inc.
65 Follansbee Road
Wellsburg, OH 43060

Dear Mr. Derand:

During the May meeting of our products division, we voted unanimously to invite you to be our speaker at next year's annual meeting in Brasilia. We would enjoy hearing about your new research on distribution improvements in Lithuania.

The dates set for the meeting are July 2–5, 20X3. Travel arrangements are being handled by the company agency.

Because we are trying to finalize our arrangements in time for our regional meeting, I hope you will be able to respond to this invitation by August 1.

Sincerely,

Roxanna Hughes
Program Coordinator

rh/lh

Sample Letter 16.26 is a general invitation to attend a book reading. Since the audience is broad, the letter is impersonal but detailed. The writer gets to the point immediately, explaining who the author is and stating the date of her appearance. The entire letter remains focused on the author and her qualifications, while giving enough detail to make the reading appear interesting. The writer closes with directions to the bookstore and the hopes that the reader will attend the event.

Sample Letter 16.26.   General invitation to a reading.

[date]

Dear Friend:

Williette Bacard, author of *My Way or the Highway: Drawing the Line in Abusive Relationships*, is coming to Bluestocking Bookstore for a reading of her most recent publication, *Meet You at the Corner*, and I don't want you to miss this rare opportunity to hear such a celebrated author and activist as she comes to our neighborhood on Thursday, December 8, at 8:00 P.M.

Ms. Bacard's books have been touted as inspirational and life-changing, and they have given sisters everywhere the wherewithal to stand up for themselves and, in some cases, save their own lives. She herself is a survivor of an abusive relationship, and she has written extensively about the terrors of physical and emotional violence. I know that you will benefit from hearing her read. There is also a question and answer session afterward. The reading and Q & A program will last approximately one and one-half hours, and refreshments will be served at a reception in Ms. Bacard's honor at the end of the program. I hope you will be able to attend.

Bluestocking Bookstore is located at 333 Janus Street, next to the Emperor's New Clothes Apparel Shop. We expect that the event will be well attended, so please arrive early, since seating is limited. There is a parking garage on Walden Avenue, a short walk from the bookstore. I hope to see you December 8.

Sincerely,

Circe Jones
Owner

Sample Letter 16.27 was written to formally notify the reader of a company's quarterly meeting. It is a direct, succinct letter that relates the facts of the meeting in a no-nonsense format. The writer concludes by requesting that the reader indicate her intention to attend the meeting.

Sample Letter 16.27.   Invitation to quarterly business meeting.

[date]

Ms. Neve Blanc
561 Sasparilla Drive
Juniper, AK 99576

Dear Ms. Blanc:

The quarterly meeting of Structural Innovations, Inc. will be held on October 1, 20X2, in the Wycliffe Room at the Windham Estates Meeting Complex in Bradford, Washington. The meeting will begin promptly at 8:00 A.M. and will end by 6:00 P.M. Breakfast and lunch will be served.

Our keynote speaker, Jacques de Boeuf, will discuss the topic "Modernizing Antique Facades." As you are well aware, the modernization of existing structures is a key aspect of our business plan for the 20X3–20X4 fiscal year. I have included a meeting program to familiarize you with important issues facing Structural Innovations. I hope you will be able to attend the meeting and Mr. de Boeuf's presentation.

Please notify me whether you will attend by returning the enclosed card no later than September 10.

Sincerely,

Anna Oppenheimer
Head of Public Relations

AO/gcc

2 encs.

The writer of Sample Letter 16.28 extends an invitation to a charitable event. She is appreciative of the recipient's potential participation and makes clear the purpose of the charity for which the event is being run. The writer makes reference to an enclosure with more information about the event and the charity and highlights a website to make participation in the event and donating to the charity as simple as possible.

Sample Letter 16.28. Letter inviting recipient to charitable event.

[date]

Mr. Jeffrey Edwards
11 Bay Crops Road
East Yarmouth, IL 60044

Dear Mr. Edwards:

Once again, it is golf outing time for the Paul Red Memorial Fund! We hope you can join us in making this year's golf outing a success.

The Paul Red Memorial Fund Golf Outing is scheduled for Sunday, August 8, 20X9, at Green Dove Country Club, Biggsville, IL. Green Dove is ranked as one of our state's most difficult courses and is less than an hour drive from East Yarmouth. The enclosed brochure provides all of the details.

The Paul Red Memorial Fund awards college scholarships each year in Paul's name to graduates of East Yarmouth High School. It celebrates the life of a good young man who lost his life in a car accident when he was only 17 years old. Paul's donated organs helped four people to continue life.

I hope you can join us at the golf outing this year. The $95 fee includes a round of golf, both lunch and dinner, and a lot of fun!

If you are unable to make the golf outing, please consider making a donation to the memorial fund. A contribution of any amount is appreciated. You can register online or make donations at www.paulredjr.org.

Thank you in advance for your generous donation. We hope to see you at the golf outing.

Sincerely,

Betty Green, Chair
Paul Red Memorial Fund Golf Outing

Enc.

Sample Letter 16.29 is an invitation to someone to serve on a not-for-profit board. Since such letters are generally written after a meeting with the prospective board member occurred, reference to that meeting is appropriate in the letter as well as enthusiastic support of the offer of the position.

Sample Letter 16.29. Letter inviting someone to sit on a not-for-profit board.

[date]

Mr. Edward Dendrinos
18 Latin Road
Decatur, GA 30044

Dear Mr. Dendrinos:

On behalf of the board of trustees of the Flinty Private Trust, we would like to extend an invitation to you to sit on our board of trustees. Our board selection committee members enjoyed meeting you last week and believe that you bring a level of experience and character that we are looking for in board members as we continue to try to build the Flinty Private Trust.

The next trustees meeting will take place on October 18 at 6 P.M. in the Flinty Room of the Flinty Private Trust Building on 4345 Roanoke Drive in Decatur. Please call Rosie Cheeks at 404-555-2323 to confirm your ability to attend the meeting.

We look forward to your joining us on the board trustees and are confident you will help guide us in all of our efforts in the future.

Sincerely,

Mary Delano, Chair
Flinty Private Trust Board of Trustees.

Letters Accepting Invitations

Sample Letters 16.30 through 16.34 are examples of responses to invitations. Sample Letter 16.30 was written to accept an informal invitation. The letter writer accepts, confirms the date, and closes.

Sample Letter 16.30.   Letter accepting informal invitation.

[date]

Dr. Marston P. Farqhuad
65 Runabout Road
New London, GA 30056

Dear Marston:

Wilma and I are delighted to accept your invitation to accompany you and Sylvia to an Atlanta Braves game and to come to your benefit buffet dinner afterward.

It's been a long time since we've seen you. The twins must be so grown up by now.

We'll see you on June 16.

Best regards,

Claude Sylvia

Sample Letter 16.31 was written to accept an invitation to speak at workshops. The letter writer encloses the material and information the letter reader had requested, and closes by asking that the letter reader inform him if there is any other information she needs.

Sample Letter 16.31.   Letter accepting invitation to speak at workshops.

[date]

Mrs. Katherine R. Kicker
Wonderful Writers of the South Club
432 South Beauty Drive
Eufala, AL 34321

Dear Kate:

Thanks very much for your note of May 28. I would be delighted to attend your convention and take part in the workshops. As you requested, I'm attaching two photographs.

As for the biographical sketch: I am the president of the Lawrence R. Lamatin Agency, which represents authors of general adult and young-adult fiction and nonfiction. Previously, I was an agent with Global Agents of America. Before becoming an agent, I was a senior book editor with Andoris Publishing Company, Fun Books, and Wonderful Reader, Inc. I'm the author of a nonfiction book, *How to Read Your Way to Fortune*, as well as a number of articles on writing and publishing for various magazines. I live in Wisconsin with my wife, Coral Phlange, an actress, and our daughter, Penelope.

I have attached a brief summary of my workshop speeches.

Please let me know if there's anything else I can provide. I very much look forward to meeting you and to attending the conference.

Sincerely,

Lawrence R. Lamatin

lrl/gmf

encs.

Sample Letter 16.32 was written to accept an invitation to contribute an article to a publication. The letter writer clearly states that the invitation has been accepted, gives the reader a number where he can be reached, and closes by thanking the reader for his interest.

Sample Letter 16.32.   Letter accepting invitation to contribute article.

[date]

Mr. Martin L. Armont
The Reader's Journal
327 Merrimac Trail
Boonton, NJ 07005

Dear Mr. Armont:

Mr. Revonock has asked me to respond to your letter of September 28 asking him to submit an article on the benefits of deregulation to bank customers. The article would be used in your quarterly *Journal of Financial Services Marketing*.

Mr. Revonock would be pleased to submit such an article. Please call me directly about your deadlines and any other information he will need to prepare the article. I can be reached at 434-706-6050.

Thank you for your interest in the views of the Deregulation Regulatory Agency's Office. I look forward to hearing from you.

Sincerely,

Aaron S. Sorce
Communications Director

ASS:jls

cc: TR

In Sample Letter 16.33, the writer accepts the invitation to address a group at a convention. After expressing his thanks for the invitation, the writer requests information on lodgings. He compliments the reader on her commitment to his particular field of work, and closes by reiterating his expectation of logistical particulars pertaining to the convention.

Sample Letter 16.33. Letter accepting an invitation to address a convention.

[date]

Dr. Raphaela Donatrice
60 Bourbon Street
New Orleans, LA 70113

Dear Dr. Donatrice:

Thank you so much for your kind invitation to address the first-year medical students at The Bayou College of Medicine Convention, February 3–5. I would be delighted to attend and am prepared to speak at the seminar entitled, "Andrology: A Brave New World." I understand that I should arrive at your campus by 1:30 P.M. on February 3. Will you send me information on lodging opportunities in the area?

I am sure that the young men and women in your medical program appreciate your efforts to have practicing doctors speak to them about the practice of medicine, just as I appreciate your choice of me as speaker for this seminar. The field of andrology is an important one and deserves publicity, and I am glad that you have included it at length in your program.

Again, thank you for your invitation. I look forward to hearing from you with the specifics of the weekend.

Sincerely,

Napthali Benjamin, M.D.

The letter in Sample Letter 16.34 was written to accept the offer of a civic position. It is the type of letter that might be written in response to Sample Letter 16.29 offering a position on a not-for-profit board.

Sample Letter 16.34.   Letter accepting civic position.

[date]

Mary Delano, Chair
Flinty Private Trust Board of Trustees
4345 Roanoke Drive
Decatur, GA 30044

Dear Ms. Delano:

Thank you very much for the invitation you extended on behalf of the Flinty Private Trust board of trustees for me to sit on the board. I am both honored and pleased to accept your invitation.

As you know from my meeting with you and other board members, the mission of the Flinty Private Trust is one that is close to my heart. I envision that we will be embarking on years of fruitful collaboration.

I will give Ms. Cheeks a call to confirm my attendance at your next meeting.

Thank you again for the invitation to serve. I appreciate the confidence and trust that you and other board members have placed in me.

Sincerely,

Edward Dendrinos

Letters Declining Invitations

Sample Letters 16.35 through 16.40 were written to decline various invitations, invitations to everything from a weekend getaway, to writing an article, to serving on a board, to speaking at a convention. Sample Letter 16.35 was written to express regrets that the letter writer could not accept a social invitation. The writer makes it clear that he cannot accept, explaining he will be out of town, and closes by saying he will get in touch with the reader when he returns.

Sample Letter 16.35. Letter expressing regrets about turning down invitation.

[date]

Ms. Sue Ellen Nojjen
6789 Puscadora Drive
Trogladite, UT 56543

Dear Sue Ellen:

I am so sorry to tell you that Sierra and I will be out of town during the dates of your weekend getaway bash. How we wish we could come.

I'll phone when we get back and press you for a full report on the weekend's parties, which will no doubt be the hit of the season.

Sincerely,

Georgio Costovez

Sample Letter 16.36 declines an invitation to contribute an article to a publication. The letter writer states that he will be unable to contribute, expresses his appreciation, and closes.

Sample Letter 16.37 was written to decline an invitation to serve on an editorial board. The letter writer expresses his appreciation for the invitation but declines the offer because of a conflict.

Sample Letter 16.36. Letter declining invitation to contribute article.

[date]

Mr. Martin L. Armont
The Reader's Journal
327 Merrimac Trail
Boonton, NJ 07005

Dear Mr. Armont:

You flatter me by asking my participation as an author in your forthcoming journal. I regret, however, that I will be unable to accept.

I wish you well with the venture.

Yours very truly,

A. T. Redmont
Senior Vice President—Marketing

ATR:nwp

Sample Letter 16.37. Letter declining invitation to serve on editorial board because of conflict.

[date]

Mr. Martin L. Armont
The Reader's Journal
327 Merrimac Trail
Boonton, NJ 07005

Dear Mr. Armont:

Pardon the delay in responding to your letter of September 21, but I have been in the process of negotiating the sale of our *Financial Services Marketing Review* to Hunga-dunga Publications of Beloit, England. A copy of the most recent issue is enclosed.

I appreciate your invitation to serve as a member of the editorial advisory board for your forthcoming journal, but I believe it would be in conflict with our role with the *Financial Services Marketing Review*.

Best regards,

Alan C. Idomeck
Executive Director

aci/jls

encl.

Sample Letter 16.38 through 16.40 were each written to decline an invitation to address a group. Each writer handles the letter differently. In Sample Letter 16.38 the reason is common and unavoidable: a schedule conflict. The writer's tone is appreciative and conciliatory. He is grateful to have been considered but will not be able to change his schedule. In closing, he expresses his hope that his reader will find a substitute, and that the program will be successful without him.

There are other reasons to decline invitations to speak beside a schedule conflict, such as a conflict of interest, or even simple lack of interest (we wouldn't put this in the letter, however). Customize this type of letter as your needs dictate, but the letter does not need to be long in any case. The writer of Sample Letter 16.39 has the interest but not the time, and the writer of Sample Letter 16.40 has clearly mastered the art of brevity.

Sample Letter 16.38. Long letter declining an invitation to speak.

[date]

Dr. Raphaela Donatrice
60 Bourbon Street
New Orleans, LA 70113

Dear Dr. Donatrice:

Thank you so much for your kind invitation to address the first-year medical students at The Bayou College of Medicine, February 3–5. I am sure that these young men and women appreciate your efforts to have practicing doctors speak to them about the practice of medicine, just as I appreciate your choice of me for keynote speaker at the seminar entitled "Andrology: A Brave New World."

Unfortunately, however, I am slated to attend a urology convention in Miami that weekend. If circumstances had been otherwise, I would have welcomed the opportunity to come to New Orleans to your fine institution. I hope that you will find a suitable substitute for the seminar, as the field of andrology is an important one and deserves publicity.

Again, thank you for your invitation. I hope your program goes smoothly.

Sincerely,

Napthali Benjamin, M.D.

Sample Letter 16.39.   Short letter declining an invitation to speak.

[date]

Dr. Dani-Elle Frylin
Rutherford State University
123 Greymalkin Lane
Eastwood, NJ 07076

Dear Dr. Frylin:

Thank you very much for your kind invitation to speak to your exchange students about my experiences researching the history of the Jewish cemetery in Prague.

Unfortunately, my current work requires that I will be out of the country during the dates of your symposium, and so I will be unable to address Rutherford's students. Best of luck finding a speaker for this group. Please keep me in mind for future engagements.

Sincerely,

Michaela Chaviva, Ph.D.

Sample Letter 16.40.   Extremely brief note declining an invitation to speak.

[date]

Ms. Deborah C. Acesa, Director
AGIE Conferences
54 Westwood Terrace
North Blixi, MI 48034

Dear Ms. Acesa:

Many thanks for your letter of September 20 and your kind invitation to participate in your conference in February. Unfortunately, I will be unable to attend.

428 ■ THE LETTERS

I do appreciate your having thought of me. I hope the conference is a great success.

Sincerely,

O. C. Dillock

ocd/jls

Letter Expressing Interest in Speaking

Sample Letter 16.41 was written to express an interest in speaking. The letter writer follows up a conversation he had with the reader by sending her background information on him and spelling out the different topics he can speak on. He closes by expressing his enthusiasm at the prospect of speaking.

Sample Letter 16.41.   Letter expressing interest in speaking.

[date]

Professor Christine Franklin
Georgian Hotel School
Edwardus Jacobus University
543 South Michigan Drive
Holstice, KY 34321

Dear Christine:

It was good to hear from you. Your new job certainly sounds exciting and challenging. I wish you the best of luck.

I've enclosed my press kit. It will give the university an idea of my credentials to qualify for a guest lecture appearance. I was recently asked to speak at the January 20X5 Hotels and Motels Association of America Annual Meeting in Key West, Florida. I will be delivering a speech entitled "How to Make Your Money in an Independent Inn."

As you know, I can discuss myriad aspects of marketing, including advertising, direct mail, publicity, promotions, and special events. Just let me know what would be the most interesting for your students and I'll focus my presentation in that direction.

I am very excited about the possibility of speaking at the Georgian Hotel School of Edwardus Jacobus University. I look forward to hearing from you.

Best regards,

Maxwell R. Levine

jls

encl.

Letter Reserving Meeting Facility

Sample Letter 16.42 was written for the sole purpose of reserving a facility. The letter is factual, with a clear expression of the writer's needs. The writer closes with a request for confirmation of the reservation.

Sample Letter 16.42.   Letter reserving a meeting facility.

[date]

Brusstar Reynolds, Facilities Coordinator
Wyeth Hotels America
6900 Midway Boulevard
Kissimmee, FL 34747

Dear Mr. Reynolds:

My organization wishes to reserve the use of a large conference room in your Fort Lauderdale Wyeth Hotel. We will be holding our annual shareholders' summit on January 8, 20X2, from 3:00 P.M. until 9:00 P.M., and will need a room capable of holding 450 people.

Additionally, we would like to reserve a three-course chicken dinner ($18.95) for each shareholder. As per our earlier telephone conversation, a cash bar should accompany this meal.

Please confirm this written reservation by telephone (506-900-7683) or fax (506-900-7777). Thank you for your help in this matter.

Sincerely,

Jeannette D'Arby
Director of Events

Letter Requesting Membership in a Club

Sample Letter 16.43 was written to request membership in a club. The letter opens with a reference to the author's connection to the club, before smoothly making a transition to the writer's qualifications for membership in the club. The author's interest is evident: he supports his application with an extensive list of his related activities and then closes with his contact information in an attempt to establish a personal connection with the reader.

Sample Letter 16.43. Letter requesting membership in a club.

[date]

Mr. Rudolph P. Garnet
The Rosewood Club
1 Central Place
Charleston, SC 39909

Dear Mr. Garnet:

I would like you to consider me for membership in The Rosewood Club. I believe that my associate at Darlington, Rice, and Weathers, LLC, Marjorie Clements, mentioned my interest in your organization. I think you will find that The Rosewood Club's civic focus neatly parallels my own.

For the last twelve years, I have been concerned with preserving Charleston's historic housing, concentrating specifically on the restoration of hardwood flooring in our fine city's many antebellum homes. In the summer of 200X, I formally opened a restoration company, Hardhead Hardwoods, so that I could dedicate more time to the preservation of National Register homes, and I now manage that company in addition to my legal responsibilities at Darlington, Rice, and Weathers. I have long been an admirer of your club's balance between political activism and historic sensibility, and I would count it an honor to be a member of such a prestigious organization.

I hope that you will seriously consider my proposal. If you would like to speak with me further about the contributions I might make to The Rosewood Club, please call me at 678-876-3411. I have enclosed a résumé for your convenience. I look forward to hearing from you.

Sincerely,

Aiden Calhoun

Encl.

Follow-Up Letter to Speech Attendees

Sample Letter 16.44 was written by someone who had given a speech to a group that had included the reader. The letter writer expresses the pleasure he had in addressing the group and follows up by reiterating some of the thoughts he had expressed in his speech. He closes by offering to answer any questions the reader might have.

Sample Letter 16.44. Letter writen as follow-up to attendees of a speech.

[date]

Dr. Anne T. Laos
Whirling Computer Corporation
34 Reindollar Road
Statehood, NJ 07034

Dear Dr. Laos:

I was very pleased to have the opportunity recently to make a presentation on behalf of the Statehood Foundation to your Breakfast Group. Maxwell Nil has kindly given me a list of the attendees and I will see to it that you are all added to our mailing list. In the meantime, I thought you would find the enclosed case statement for the Statehood Foundation of some interest.

As the Statehood community's foundation and the largest grant issuer in New Jersey, the Statehood Foundation is in the position to have a major role in supporting programs that serve a broad sector of the Statehood community. As a public charity, we are also charged with increasing our permanent endowment (currently at $125 million) so that our efforts can continue to benefit the citizens of Statehood. For many individuals and corporations, the Statehood Foundation is a unique vehicle for carrying out charitable activities.

Please know that I would be happy to answer any questions that you might have about opportunities for giving through the Statehood Foundation.

Yours truly,

Oscar R. Atner
Donor Relations Officer

ORA:jls

enc.

Letter Expressing Compliments on an Article

Sample Letter 16.45 was written to compliment an author on an article he had written. The letter writer offers his commendation of the author's work and closes by offering his services should the author need them in the future.

Sample Letter 16.45.   Letter complimenting author on article.

[date]

Mr. Ambrose T. Kemper
The Armchair Reader's Review
34 Eliot Boulevard
Piscataway, TX 75003

Dear Mr. Kemper:

As a certfied financial planner with more than 20 years of experience, I would like to commend you on your fine article on financial planning in the January issue of *The Armchair Reader's Review*. Your article hit on the fundamentals of prudent money management in a forthright and easy to understand manner. Should your research in the future require my assistance, I would be more than happy to discuss my thoughts with you.

I would also like to suggest that *The Armchair Reader's Review* consider a monthly column that addresses money management concerns. It is evident that the publication is targeted to individuals who have achieved a certain level of financial success, and who would be interested in securing future financial security.

Congratulations again on a job well done. Please feel free to call on me in the future should the need arise.

Sincerely,

Manny N. Depocet, CFP

mnd/jls

cc: MLN, editor

Birthday Greetings Letter

Sample Letter 16.46 was written as a brief note to wish a business acquaintance well on his birthday.

Sample Letter 16.46.   Letter wishing someone a happy birthday.

[date]

Mr. Poindexter T. Spaulding
Lockridge and Lockridge
7654 Roundabout Plaza
Osaka, MT 59034

Dear Poindexter:

Happy birthday! Everyone here at the Piscataqua office sends their best and hopes for a wonderful year for you.

We hear you are enjoying your new position in the Osaka branch. Come visit us when you're in our area.

Yours truly,

Marvin Samantha

ms/lh

Public Service and Fund-Raising Letters

From time to time you may be called on to perform some public service, such as raising funds for an organization you are part of and believe in.

Sample Letter 16.47 was written to solicit a donation from the letter recipient. The letter writer comes right out and says what she is requesting, leaving no doubt to the recipient about why he is receiving this letter. Follow-up information is clear. This letter is a strong example of a request for donation.

Sample Letter 16.47.   Letter making donation request.

[date]

Mr. Harry Whittlewood
President
Pocket Knife Fabricators
43 Lorraine Terrace
Fairfield, MN 55088

Dear Mr. Whittlewood:

You have been a wonderful supporter of the arts in Fairfield in past years and we're hoping to encourage you to continue your valuable support.

On Sunday, March 3, Fortified Art Center will be holding its annual charity auction to raise funds for Fairfield Arts Week. We are hoping that you will be able to donate six or seven pocket knives that can be auctioned off. Last year, your knives were among the most popular items in the charity auction.

Your donation will be tax deductible since we are a not-for-profit organization. It will also go a long way toward helping us reach our goal of raising $20,000 at the event. All of the proceeds will be used to help us stage Fairfield's Arts Week.

If you could email us or call us to let us know of your willingness to donate, we would be very appreciative. We will call you sometime over the next couple of weeks to follow up.

Thank you very much for your continued support.

Sincerely,

Liza Tinsel
Chair, Fairfield Arts Week

Sample Letter 16.48 is also an example of a fund-raising letter, but it is sent as a follow-up to a previous contributor.

Sample Letter 16.48.   Letter attempting to raise funds—sent to previous contributor.

[date]

Mrs. Ann L. Kemper
23 Deerfield Avenue
Rather, MI 48056

Dear Ann:

Three years ago this month, our friend and colleague, *The Chronicle* reporter Ellen Yalter, was killed in a drunk driving accident. This is a somber time for us and for Ellen's family. Even though Ellen is gone, she is not forgotten. Thanks to your overwhelming support and generosity, we've raised $75,000 for the newly established Ellen Yalter Memorial Scholarship at Highlands University. As you know, this will provide a full tuition scholarship to a deserving graduate student in print journalism at the School of Journalism. It is a wonderful tribute to Ellen and her memory.

On June 15, 20X4, we will award the first annual Yalter Scholarship during a special event planned at the Lewis & Carey Inn in Boonton. We will also be doing something else to further honor Ellen's achievements. On that night we will announce the recipient of the first annual Ellen Yalter Memorial Excellence in Reporting Award. This honor will go to a metropolitan area print journalist who has demonstrated outstanding ability during the previous year. A Lifetime Achievement Award will also be made to a nationally known news broadcaster. It should be an exciting night.

Last June, more than 500 of you paid tribute to Ellen at the Morris County Courthouse reception. This summer, we can all get together again on a happier note, with the knowledge that Ellen will continue to be remembered and honored in a variety of ways. Now we can pay tribute to those among us who are striving for the same standard of excellence that Ellen did.

We'll have a buffet style meal, music, and a brief awards ceremony. Mostly, I hope we'll all have fun and share in the kind of camaraderie we all felt the last time around. Tickets will be $75 per person to help raise the additional $75,000 needed to meet our fund-raising goal to continue providing the scholarship. If you make your contribution to the scholarship now, you'll receive your tickets in the mail by early May. Please be as generous as you can.

I look forward to seeing you June 15.

Very truly yours,

Carl B. Combsen
Committee Chairman

cbc/jls

enc.

Sample Letter 16.49 was written by a class agent to her classmates seeking to raise funds for their alma mater. The letter is anecdotal and makes a solid plea for funds.

Sample Letter 16.49.   Letter written to raise funds from fellow alumnus.

[date]

Mr. James Lewis
186-A Savin Hill Avenue
Bethany, NC 27034

Dear Jim:

There's a story told about a conversation between F. Scott Fitzgerald and Ernest Hemingway. Fitzgerald remarks to Hemingway: "The rich are different from you and me." To which Hemingway responds: "Yes, they have more money." The encounter came to mind when I heard a talk given by Jack Temple, one of the beacons of light in the investment world. When he was about to tell the audience what he thought the best investment would be for the future, he had the entire audience on the edge of their seats in anticipation. And then he hit them with it: "The best investment for the future," he said, "is tithing 10% of your annual income." It seems Temple had followed this philosophy for years and felt it had paid off handsomely.

I'm not suggesting you tithe 10% of your income to Clarkson Community College. But there is a lot of merit in what Temple says. If you want to see tangible results from your money, investing in the future of Clarkson Community College is a sure bet. When the stock market languishes, Clarkson Community College continues to flourish doing what it does best—educating students.

The outlook for the future of Clarkson Community College is good. The college is blessed with a growing number of entering students each year. Academically, the college continues to challenge students. Athletically, the teams of Clarkson continue to tough it out on the playing field (or courts or pools). Student publications and productions continue to provide experiential opportunities. All the trappings needed to educate graduates who go out and find success are there.

Please try to give what you can to Clarkson. Be sure to check whether your company has a matching contribution plan.

Think of what you give as an investment, one that you will know is at work every time you visit Clarkson, talk to a Clarksonian, or hear from a recent graduate nervously encountering the world outside of college for the first time—just like we did when we graduated.

Sincerely,

Maxene Right
Class Agent

mr:js

enc.

Sample Letter 16.50 was written requesting that the recipient perform a public service. The letter writer is clear in his request and lays out the details of what he is asking. This letter can easily be adapted to an email. If it is, then enclosures should be referred to as attachments in the text of the email.

Sample Letter 16.50.   Letter requesting public service.

[date]

Mr. Alan T. Pine
45 Trusty Road
Barnstable, GA 30032

Dear Alan:

If you're like me at this time of year, you're searching for the perfect holiday gift and for the bulb that makes the Christmas tree lights stop blinking. And you're not sure when you'll find time to assemble that new bicycle or bake cookies for the neighbors.

With all the joys and hassles of the holiday season, I would like to ask you to add one more item to your Christmas list: to become a Preston Community College Class Agent.

We would like to mail the Class Agent letter in January, which is why we are approaching you during the holiday season. Believe it or not, January is one of the best times of the year for direct mail solicitations, something I learned in my direct mail class at Preston Community College.

As always, you are welcome to write your own letter to your class. As an encouragement, I am enclosing a copy of an excellent article on letter writing that appeared in *Business Communication News*.

I encourage you to write your Class Agent letter just as you would write a letter to a friend. After all, you share two years of special memories with your classmates. Your letter should bring out the bonds that tie your class.

Let people know what's happening at Preston now. Let them know what's changed and what hasn't. If you've visited the campus recently, describe what you saw. Along the same lines, let people know what other classmates are doing. Encourage people to send you news about what's new in their lives—it'll be great material for your spring letter.

If you just can't put pen to paper (and believe me, I know how that feels), I'm also enclosing a "ghost" letter that you can adapt as your own. Write your own, change mine, or use mine without any changes. But please have your letter at the Development Office by January 5, 20X4. Also, complete the enclosed card and send it with the letter so the office will know how it is to be mailed.

This year we have an incentive for our Class Agents: a signed, limited edition watercolor of Old Preston Hall will be given to the Class Agent who has the largest percentage increase in the number of donors from his or her class and to the Class Agent who has the largest percentage increase in the total amount given by his or her class. A copy of the Preston Community College Report describing the limited edition print is enclosed.

I encourage you to be innovative in your appeals to your class. Don't be limited by the two required letters. I'm open to your suggestions, ideas, and spurts of creativity—anything that will help improve the Class Agent program.

Many thanks for your help. Your work as a Class Agent is a year-round gift to Preston.

Sincerely,

Rhett L. Retson
Class Agent Coordinator

rlr:jls

Enclosures

Sample Letters 16.51 and 16.52 are also excellent examples of letters that were written to request a charitable contribution. Sample Letter 16.51's balanced structure opens with a description of the good work that the charitable organization performs and then closes with a polite, firm request for contributions. The writer makes a strong case for giving to this organization and refers to the enclosed postage-paid envelope for the potential donor's convenience.

Sample Letter 16.51.   Charity drive letter to neighbors.

[date]

Emmett and Sarah Rose
186 Ralston Lane
Durston, NY 10607

Dear Neighbors:

I am writing to tell you about an agency that is doing outstanding work in our neighborhood. The Council for Literacy in the Immigrant Community (CLIC) has been hard at work providing educational opportunities for immigrants in Durston for six years. CLIC workers are responsible for teaching reading and writing, offering job training and referrals, and connecting resources for more than 100 newcomers representing many nationalities. CLIC's work has been recognized by several local newspapers and many Durston officials in the past year.

CLIC needs our help. It is time to repay the help that they have given to our city by supporting them now. In order to continue their work they need to hire English teachers, maintain their facility, and build upon their network of resource agencies. Their costs have increased at a higher rate than their state funding, and the founders now need to supplement their revenue with donations from their neighbors. Please consider making a contribution of $50 or more to CLIC. A postage-paid envelope has been provided for your convenience. Several businesses, including mine, are volunteering their time and effort to coordinate this effort to raise funds for CLIC. Please contact me if you have any questions. I can be reached at 706-448-9620.

Sincerely,

Emily Fletcher
Zoom Design
123 Hanes Road
Durston, NY 10607

encl.

Sample Letter 16.52 was written to a business associate to request a charitable donation to an agency that benefits the writer and her reader's community. The author begins by establishing the credentials of the agency and describing the good work it has done, before moving into a succinct statement of what help the agency now needs. Instead of merely asking for help, the writer relates the help she herself has given to this agency, leading by actions, not just words. She offers concrete ways that the recipient can donate and closes by giving her telephone number for further information.

Sample Letter 16.52. Letter to a business associate requesting charitable funds.

[date]

Christine May
Truelove Cosmetics
78 Main Street
Andover, NH 03076

Dear Colleague:

I am writing to let you know of the efforts of an agency in our community that needs our help. CleanUp, a nonprofit agency founded by Susan and Bruce Talia of Andover, has been instrumental in improving our downtown area since 2004. Because of the hard work of the Talias, many dozens of neighbors and businesspeople have volunteered their time and energy over the past several years to make the area more pleasant for visitors to Andover. The lighting and signage have been updated and more trash cans and benches have been added because of the direct work of CleanUp. The visitors to Andover are our customers, and we owe the Talias not only a large "thank you," but also our help.

I have donated my own time and have encouraged some of my employees to do the same. I will be participating in a community meeting at the CleanUp offices on August 2 and would like to invite you to join us. I have also made a donation of $1,000.00 to CleanUp to support its continued efforts on behalf of our town. Please consider doing the same. The money that we donate to CleanUp will allow the Talias to hire support staff and continue their lobbying efforts.

For more information feel free to contact me at 789-987-7890 or contact CleanUp directly at 789-956-4218. I look forward to seeing you on August 2.

Sincerely,

Beth Amy Wedge
Owner, Sundance Books

Letters Declining Requests for Donations

We all know the simplest way to deal with those mass-mailed requests for donation—either write a check, or put the request in the circular file. But sometimes a request comes from a friend, neighbor, or business acquaintance, and although you don't want to donate, you don't want to be rude. Sample Letters 16.53 through 16.55 show how it can be done without losing a friend or destroying a cordial business connection.

Sample Letter 16.53 was written to decline a request to make a donation. Such letters can be challenging to write, but it is good practice to respond to such requests particularly if you want to maintain a relationship with the organization making the request. The letter writer is respectful of the recipient while being clear that a donation will not be forthcoming.

Sample Letter 16.53.   Letter declining a request for donation.

[date]

Ms. Liza Tinsel
Chair, Fairfield Arts Week
52 Motley Way
Fairfield, MN 55088

Dear Ms. Tinsel:

Thank you for your letter requesting donations for your annual auction.

In the past, we have been able to donate pocketknives and other weapons to your annual auction that raises funds for Fairfield Arts.

Unfortunately, we will be unable to make a donation this year. We have already committed to making donations to about a half-dozen charities and have chosen to limit our donations this year. Perhaps next year we will be able to add you back to the list.

We hope you understand that our decision not to donate this year has nothing to do with our perception of the valuable work your organization does.

Please do not hesitate to solicit us in the future.

Sincerely,

Harry Whittlewood, President

hw/lw

Sample Letter 16.54 was written to decline a request for a charitable contribution to a cause. The writer approaches this sensitive issue tactfully, complimenting the reader on her agency's cause before explaining in detail the reasons why the writer's company is financially unable to contribute to that cause. In closing, the writer again commends the recipient's agency and wishes her good luck in her fund-raising drive.

Sample Letter 16.54. Letter declining charitable request because of limited funds.

[date]

Marie Calderone
Tots Love Toys, Inc.
76 Wilkes Street
Burbank, MI 48099

Dear Ms. Calderone:

Thank you for your recent request for a contribution to the Tots Love Toys charity drive. Your organization sounds like it provides a valuable service to the children in the Detroit area.

Unfortunately, though, my company is unable to give funds to you at this time. A substandard performance in the fourth quarter of this past fiscal year has necessitated personnel layoffs and financial restructuring, and I am afraid that we have had to limit our charitable donations across the board this year. I'm sure you can agree that increasing our outside giving at a time when we cannot pay our existing employees would seem inappropriate.

Best of luck in your fund-raising drive. Tots Love Toys plays an important role in making the lives of Michigan's children more enjoyable and rewarding, and I hope your company has much success this year.

Sincerely,

T. E. Mane
Chief Financial Officer

Sample Letter 16.55 was also written to decline a request for charitable giving, but this writer's reason differs in that his company is financially able but philosophically opposed to contributing to this cause. The language is still polite but firm, and the author explains thoroughly the differences in mission statements between his company and that of his reader. Included in this letter is a request to be removed from the recipient's mailing list, effectively terminating any future correspondence in a cordial way. The writer concludes with a wish for success in gathering funds, not just for the reader's company, but for both companies.

Sample Letter 16.55. Letter declining charitable request because of opposition to cause.

[date]

Marie Calderone
Tots Love Toys, Inc.
76 Wilkes Street
Burbank, MI 48099

Dear Ms. Calderone:

Thank you for your recent request for a contribution to the Tots Love Toys charity drive. Your organization sounds like it believes it provides a valuable service to the children in the Detroit area.

Although we understand that your company's philosophy is that children will best benefit from receiving free toys, we at EdCom Enterprises feel that underprivileged children need educational opportunities more than they need a new Barbie doll or PlayStation 3. Perhaps it is due to the nature of our business as a publisher of educational materials for children aged 2–12, but we have chosen to concentrate our charitable giving this year on those companies that are more in concordance with our mission of educating low-income and minority children in the Midwest. Since our goals differ and we do not anticipate future giving to your organization, we would appreciate it if you would remove us from your mailing list.

Best of luck in your fund-raising drive. Tots Love Toys does play a role in making the lives of Michigan's children more enjoyable and rewarding, but unfortunately, it is not a role that we are prepared to invest in. There are many ways to help children, though, and I hope that both our companies will have much success this year.

Sincerely,

T. E. Mane
Chief Financial Officer

Letter Urging Political Representative to Action

Sample Letter 16.56 was written by a concerned individual to a political representative to encourage the politician to support the passage of a bill. The writer displays a knowledge of the bill's content and potential impact. The request for support comes immediately, so that the reader knows what is asked of him; the close reiterates and highlights the importance of the bill.

Sample Letter 16.56. Letter to politician urging support of bill.

[date]

The Honorable Thomas Brockett
250 Kilgo Circle
Washington, D.C. 20003

Dear Mr. Brockett:

I strongly urge you to support the passage of HR 112-290, which is now being considered by the Education Committee. This bill will provide much needed relief for inner-city schools, many of which are struggling under local budget cuts, teacher shortages, and dwindling tax bases.

Over the past six years, urban schools have been forced to choose far too frequently between critical needs programs like free and reduced-cost lunches and after-school tutoring, all because their funding is so sparse that they cannot afford to provide both a meal and extra academic help. Many have adjusted creatively, using unpaid community members as staff for the programs they wish to offer, but community support without federal backing sends the wrong message to these hard-working parents. If HR

112-290 fails to gain passage in the House, the legislators of this nation are telling local parents that their efforts and vision for their schools are not mirrored at the federal level.

This important bill will enable local school districts to renegotiate contracts with key support industries like sanitation, food services, book publishers, and custodial firms, ensuring that school systems can compete with corporations for these much-needed components of the education system. Please give America's urban school districts a fighting chance to do what they want to do best: teach the next generation of young Americans.

Sincerely,

Patricia Tedescho

Congratulations-on-New-Position Letters

Sample Letters 16.57 and 16.58 were written to congratulate people on new positions. Sample Letter 16.57 was written to congratulate the reader on her new position and to take the opportunity to introduce the letter writer's services to the reader. The writer encloses material for the reader to review.

Sample Letter 16.58 is a short letter of congratulations to a business acquaintance on his new position, written in the official-style format. There is no attempt to sell anything here.

Sample Letter 16.57. Letter congratulating someone on new position, using opportunity to promote services.

[date]

Ms. Connie S. Ebergen, President
Smokehouse Restaurants, Inc.
56 Stone Street
Nottingham, MA 02121

Dear Ms. Ebergen:

Congratulations! I read of your recent appointment to president of Smokehouse Restaurants, Inc., in November's issue of *National Dining Out Newsalerts*.

As specialists in the restaurant industry, Naidu Public Relations, Inc., provides a full range of marketing services. For publicity, we have great press contacts, locally and nationally. To serve as an informal introduction to Naidu Public Relations, Inc., I have enclosed our press kit. It contains marketing articles we've written for *Eating Out Often* and *Restaurants of the World*, a client list, my biography, and other relevant materials.

We would truly welcome an opportunity to meet with you and your marketing team at Smokehouse Restaurants, Inc., to discuss how we might contribute to your expansion plans. I'll call your office next week to arrange an appointment at your convenience.

Thank you, in advance, for taking the time to review these materials, Ms. Ebergen. I look forward to speaking with you.

Sincerely,

Leo J. Naidu
President

LJN:JLS

Enc.

Sample Letter 16.58. Letter congratulating a business acquaintance on new position.

[date]

Dear William:

I had the pleasure of learning that you recently became the president of Kismick Department Stores. Congratulations on your new position.

I hope I will have a chance to stop in and see you next time I'm in Guam City. In the meantime, good luck with your new responsibilities.

Best regards,

Pearl Pendleton

Mr. William Martin, President
Kismick Department Stores
One Symphony Place
Guam City, AZ 85012

PP:js

Letters to Sick Employees, Acquaintances

Sample Letter 16.59 was written to express concern for an employee who has been ill. Sample Letter 16.60 was written to an employee who is in the hospital. Sample Letter 16.61 was written to a business acquaintance who is hospitalized. All three letters are brief, but show genuine concern for the letter reader.

Sample Letter 16.59.   Letter expressing concern for ill employee.

[date]

Mr. Edward T. Landsale
45 Beaumont Place
Rose, TX 75076

Dear Ed:

Everyone here at Furomont Building & Engineering joins me in wishing you a speedy recovery from your bout with pneumonia. We hope you take care of yourself so that you can be back on the job soon.

Please accept our best wishes.

Sincerely,

Alan T. Ransdade
Project Supervisor

atr/jls

Sample Letter 16.60.   Letter to employee in the hospital.

[date]

Ms. Patrice R. Chin
Room 756
Medical Hospital
Medino, CA 90067

Dear Patrice:

Please accept my best wishes for a speedy recovery from your surgery. I hope that the doctors and nurses over at Medical Hospital take good care of you so that you are healthy and back on the job as soon as you feel up to it.

We miss you here at Altmont Minerals and hope that you are back on your feet just as soon as possible.

Sincerely,

John U. Uxbridge
Personnel Director

juu/jls

Sample Letter 16.61.   Letter to hospitalized business associate.

[date]

Mr. Jack Wagner
Room 4545
Doctor's Hospital
Newburgh, Connecticut 06056

Dear Jack:

I learned from your office that you have been hospitalized. I wish you the speediest recovery and hope that you will be home and healthy soon.

Regards,

Alice R. Treat
Sales Representative

art/jjj

Condolence Letter

Sample Letter 16.62 is an example of a brief, tactful letter of condolence written to the letter reader on the occasion of his mother's death. Such letters are difficult to write but are appreciated by the person being written to.

Sample Letter 16.62.   Letter expressing condolences.

[date]

Mr. Joshua T. Leopard
Fulton, Carlton & Leopard, P.C.
One Blazen Avenue
Fort Utah, NV 89034

Dear Joshua:

I was sorry to learn of the death of your mother. I hope you will accept the sincere condolences of your friends at Andover Parris Publishing Company.

If I or anyone else here can be of help to you, please let us know. I look forward to meeting with you as soon as you get back into the swing of things.

Sincerely,

Maxwell L. Shorter
Publisher

jls

Letter Congratulating Someone on Opening a Business

The letter writer in Sample Letter 16.63 congratulates a business acquaintance on opening a new business. He also accepts her invitation to a reception she is holding for the opening. This is written in official-style format.

Sample Letter 16.63. Letter congratulating someone on opening a new business.

[date]

Dear Evelyn:

Congratulations on opening your own truck sales business. I know it's been a dream of yours for some time, and I am overjoyed that you finally have gotten your own business up and going.

I must tell you how much I admire you for the determination and fortitude you have had to follow through on your dream. Those of us who have gotten to know you personally and professionally over the past several years are not at all surprised that you've been able to muster up the convictions to act on your passions, and we've little doubt that you will succeed beyond all expectations.

Nancy and I would love to join you at your opening reception next Sunday. We'll be there to cheer you on and share in your joyous occasion.

Regards,

Simon Nelson

Ms. Evelyn Kane
Redwing Trucking Agents
49 Delaware Turnpike
Harvard, MA 02134

Letter Announcing Retirement

The letter writer of Sample Letter 16.64 writes to a business acquaintance that he is retiring. He tells the recipient who his replacement will be and how he can be reached after he's retired. The letter writer uses a personal tone, yet lays out the facts of his retirement in a very professional manner.

Sample Letter 16.64.   Letter announcing retirement.

[date]

Mr. John T. Quackenbush
45 Travelogue Drive
Braintree, NJ 07004

Dear John:

I have decided to take early retirement as of November 1. One of the things I will regret most in leaving Hunker Down, Inc., is that I will no longer have the fun of working with good people like you.

The new director of marketing is Tom North, formerly of Beach & Sand Enterprises. If you have any immediate questions or concerns about the status of your projects, feel free to call him at 222-555-4444. I'm sure you will find him extremely easy to talk with and eager to help in any way that he can.

It goes without saying that if I find myself headed your way, I'll call in advance to see if there's some way we can get together. By the same token, if you are going to be in my area, please call me; my home phone is 201-364-8276 and my cell phone (who is without one these days, even when retired) is 927-368-4995. A reunion one place or another would be great fun.

In any case, let's try to stay in touch. For now, all best wishes.

Sincerely,

Wyatt Z. Samuels

PART III

Appendixes

Rule #1: Remember to never split an infinitive.

Rule #2: Prepositions are something you should never end a sentence with.

Rule #3: Dangling a participle at the end of a sentence is uncouth and requires changing.

Rule #4: Your spelling will improve if you consult your dictionary alot.

· · · · · · · · · · · · · · · · ·

—Larry E. Grimes, from "Rules of the Writing Game"

The two appendixes to *The AMA Handbook of Business Letters* can help make letter writing less arduous.

The first appendix, "Words to Watch," is by no means an all-inclusive list of every word ever used incorrectly. It does, however, include some words and phrases that are either tricky to use or often are used incorrectly. If you have a question about how a word or phrase should be used, look it up here.

The second appendix, "Punctuation," is a discussion of punctuation marks and "how and when to use which." For a more extensive discussion of the proper use of punctuation, there are several good references available. I recommend: *The Chicago Manual of Style*, 16th Edition (Chicago: The University of Chicago Press, 2010) and *Merriam-Webster's Guide to Punctuation and Style,* Second Edition (Merriam-Webster, 2001).

APPENDIX I

Words to watch

The words and phrases listed in this appendix are often used incorrectly in correspondence.

ACKNOWLEDGE WITH THANKS or **ACKNOWLEDGE RECEIPT OF**   Using the words *thank you* is a more direct way of expressing gratitude after receiving something.

AFFECT versus **EFFECT**   When used as verbs, *affect* means "to influence"; *effect* means "to accomplish." Both words can also be used as nouns. The noun *affect* is usually used only in a psychological context, where it means "expression of emotion." When the construction calls for a noun, and you are not using the word in a psychological sense, you will almost always use *effect*. Most of the time you can the mnemonic device RAVEN to remember the appropriate usage: Remember Affect is a Verb and Effect is a Noun.

AFORESAID   Write "named" or "mentioned earlier."

AFTER THE CONCLUSION OF   Write "after."

ALONG THESE LINES   Another trite expression to avoid.

ALLUDE versus **ELUDE**   *Allude* means "to refer to"; *elude* means "to escape from." You allude to a piece of literature. You elude someone who is chasing you.

ALTERNATIVE   Means the choice between two possibilities. In constructions such as "no other alternative," the word *other* is unnecessary.

AMOUNTING TO or **IN THE AMOUNT OF**   Write "for" or "of" or "totaling."

AND/OR   Avoid the use of "and/or" unless it is absolutely necessary as a legal term. It destroys the flow of a sentence and causes confusion or ambiguity.

ANYBODY   An indefinite pronoun meaning "any person." Should be written as one word, as should "somebody," "nobody," and "everybody." Only if you are writing about a body that was looked for but not found, would you write: "The investigators did not find any body." In most business letters such usage would be rare.

ANYONE   Best written as one word unless meaning "any one of them," as in the sentence "He didn't like any one of them."

AS OF EVEN DATE HEREWITH   Legalese (and pretty much unfathomable). Merely give the date.

AS PER COPY   Instead of writing, "We wrote you last Friday as per copy enclosed," it's clearer to write, "We have enclosed a copy of…," or "Enclosed you will find a copy…"

AS REQUESTED/DESCRIBED/MENTIONED   It is a little more personal to write "as you requested," "as you described," or "as you mentioned."

AS SOON AS POSSIBLE   Give a specific date whenever possible, but if you really mean "as soon as you can get around to it," then *as soon as possible* will do; under no circumstances write "ASAP"—unless you are text-messaging a colleague back at the office.

AS TO   Write "about."

AS TO WHETHER   Write "whether."

AS YET   Write "yet."

AT   Do not use after the word *where*. ("I wonder where he's at" is a dire no-no. Erase it from your vocabulary, please.)

ATTACHED HERETO   Forget the *hereto;* write "attached."

AT THE PRESENT TIME or **AT THIS TIME** or **AT THIS WRITING**   Write "now" whenever possible instead of these words.

ATTORNEY versus **LAWYER**   A lawyer who has a client is an attorney.

AT YOUR EARLIEST CONVENIENCE   Encourages delay. Whenever possible, be more specific.

BAD or **BADLY**   The adjective *bad* is used after verbs of the sense—smell, sound, feel, look, taste. For example: "He looks bad." Or: "It tastes bad." *Badly* indicates manner. For example: "He was hurt badly in the accident." If you say "She feels badly," you are saying that her sense of touch is impaired; has she burned her fingers?

BESIDE or **BESIDES**   *Beside* means "at the side of." *Besides* means "in addition to" or "other than."

BETWEEN versus **AMONG**   Where the number exceeds two, use "among" for both persons and things. "Between" is a preposition that takes the objective pronoun (*me, him, her, us, them*). See Chapter 5 for a complete discussion of objective pronouns.

BIMONTHLY   "Every two months" or "twice a month." Since this word can mean either of these, it's better to be explicit and write whichever you mean.

BIWEEKLY "Every two weeks" or "twice a month." As with bimonthly, it's better to be specific and write whichever you mean.

BOTH ALIKE In this phrase, the word *both* is superfluous. Write "alike."

BY MEANS OF Write "by."

COMMUNICATION Avoid using this word to mean "a letter" or "a conversation." Use the specific reference. See section on jargon in Chapter 5.

CONTACT Use more specific words such as "talk to," "write," or "call."

DIRECT versus **DIRECTLY** *Direct* is both an adjective and an adverb. "The man was sent direct (or directly) to Chicago." In the sentence "The professional made a direct trip to Chicago," we are using the adjective *direct*. The word *directly* is always an adverb, as in the sentence "We remit directly to a beneficiary if there is no intermediary."

DISINTERESTED Means "impartial." Do not confuse with the word *uninterested*, which means "expressing no interest in."

DROP IN or **DROP A LINE** Avoid using these colloquialisms in your letters.

DUE TO THE FACT THAT Write "because."

ENCLOSED HEREWITH Forget the "herewith"; write "enclosed."

ENCLOSED PLEASE FIND Write "enclosed is" or "I have enclosed…"

EQUALLY AS WELL Drop the *as*. Write "equally well."

ETC. Don't use unless the omitted context is understood. Because the meaning of *et cetera* is "and so forth," you would never write "and etc." or "etc., etc."

FACTOR This word is overused. Instead of writing "Good salesmanship is an important factor in account management," write "Good salesmanship is important to account management."

FARTHER versus **FURTHER** "Farther" refers to distance. "Further" refers to discourse ("We'll speak further on this matter") or to something additional ("Further meetings on the budget will be necessary"). The distinction between these two words is blurred by many writers who also use "further" to refer to distance. Eventually, this usage may become acceptable.

FOR YOUR INFORMATION Usually superfluous.

GO OVER Write "examine," "look over," or "read."

HE/SHE or **S/HE** Avoid using either of these alternatives. If you cannot rewrite the sentence using a plural pronoun, then write "he or she."

HOPEFULLY An adverb meaning "with hope" or "in a hopeful manner" ("Let me come too, Lavinia said hopefully"). It is used incorrectly by many writers to mean "I hope."

HOWEVER Best used in the middle of a sentence. When *however* is used at the beginning of a sentence, it often means "to whatever extent."

I.E. versus E.G.   The abbreviation "i.e." stands for *id est*, which means "that is" in Latin. The abbreviation "e.g." stands for *exempli gratia*, which means "for example" in Latin. Both of these abbreviations are set off by commas in a sentence.

IN POSITION   Implies "at attention" or "standing around." Write "prepared," "ready," "willing," or "available."

IN RECEIPT OF   Write "We (I) have received" or "We (I) have."

IN REFERENCE TO or **IN REGARD TO** or **IN REPLY TO**   Write "concerning," "proposing," "inquiring about," or "suggesting."

IN THE LAST ANALYSIS   Trite expression. Don't use it.

IN WHICH YOU ENCLOSED   Write "with which you enclosed." Information is given *in* a letter. You receive an enclosure *with* a letter.

IRREGARDLESS versus REGARDLESS   "Irregardless" is not a word. The proper word is *regardless*.

ITS versus IT'S   *Its* shows possession. *It's* is a contraction of "it is."

LIKE versus AS   *Like* is a preposition that introduces a prepositional phrase and is used to compare things: "He looks like his mother." *As* is usually used as a conjunction and introduces a subordinate clause (clauses have a subject and a verb): "He acts as his mother did."

MATTER   Too general a term. Use the specific word: "problem," "request," "subject," "question," or whatever you may be writing about.

MOST   Don't substitute *most* for *almost*. Write "almost everyone" instead of "most everyone."

MYSELF/OURSELVES, HIMSELF/HERSELF/THEIRSELVES, YOURSELF/YOURSELVES (pronouns ending in **-SELF/-SELVES**)   Avoid using any of these as the subject in a sentence. Write "Max and I are approving the purchase," instead of "Max and myself…" Pronouns ending in *-self* (or *-selves*) are used for reference and emphasis in a sentence. In the sentence "I approved the purchase myself," *myself* emphasizes *I* (that is, no one else approved the purchase).

NEITHER, NOR and **EITHER, OR**   These correlatives should be kept together.

PARTY versus PERSON   Use *party* as a legal reference only. *Person* should be used in ordinary reference.

PEOPLE versus PERSONS   Use *people* when referring to large groups; *persons* for small groups.

PER   Use of *per* is acceptable in an economic context, such as "20 shares per dollar." Although writers should usually avoid mixing Latin and English (*per* is Latin), if the construction is made less awkward by using *per*, use it. Avoid writing "per your letter" or "per my last letter," however, because this does nothing to simplify your letter.

PLEASE BE ADVISED THAT Avoid this wordy construction. Just give the information without the long windup.

PREVIOUS EXPERIENCE The word *experience* already tells the reader "we have a prior history with this …" Write "Our experience with this person," instead.

PRINCIPAL versus **PRINCIPLE** *Principle* refers to a basic truth ("The principles of physics do not allow water to run uphill"). *Principal*, as an adjective, means "leading" or "chief." As a noun, *principal* means either a "person in charge" or, in finance, "capital."

SHALL versus **WILL** You may have learned that you should use *shall* as the future indicative of the verb *to be* in the first person—I/we shall—and *will* in the third person—you/he/she/they will—and that to express determination the forms are reversed. You can forget this so-called rule, and just say "will" ("I *will* go to the show, no matter what you say") whenever you want.

TAKING THIS OPPORTUNITY Instead of writing "We are taking this opportunity to thank you," write "We thank you" or "Thank you."

THAN versus **THEN** *Than* is used for comparison. *Then* is used to indicate time.

THAT versus **WHICH** A simple rule is to use the pronoun "which" if the clause it modifies can be separated from the rest of the sentence with commas ("The book, which is on the table, is green"). Otherwise use "that" ("The book that I loaned Tim is terrific").

THEREAFTER Too lofty. Use "after that" when possible.

THIS WILL ACKNOWLEDGE RECEIPT OF YOUR LETTER An answer to a person's letter will let him or her know it was received.

TRY AND versus **TRY TO** Write "try to."

UNDER SEPARATE COVER Write "We are sending separately" or "You will receive."

UNIQUE There are no degrees of uniqueness. "Very unique," "most unique," or "extremely unique" are incorrect. It's just "unique."

UTILIZE/UTILIZATION Inflated language for the verb "to use." And utilization? Equally inflated language for the noun "use." Don't use either of these terms.

VIA Means "by way of" (geographically) and is properly used as a railroad, airline, or steamship term. Write "by express mail" or "by parcel post."

WE ASK YOU TO KINDLY Write "please."

WE WISH TO THANK YOU Write "thank you."

WRITER Write "I" or "me" when you are referring to yourself in a letter.

APPENDIX II

Punctuation

Punctuation is a worrisome thing, not the least because experts differ in their interpretation of its rules. Here we present the system we believe is most useful in business writing. You may encounter other opinions of what is "correct." No matter. Be consistent with your own usage, and remember the cardinal rule: The purpose of punctuation is to help readers follow your meaning.

apostrophe (')

The apostrophe indicates omission, possession, and sometimes the plural of certain letters, nouns, numbers, and abbreviations.

1. The possessive pronouns—its, hers, his, ours, yours, theirs—do not use an apostrophe.
2. The possessive of plural nouns ending in "s" is formed by adding an apostrophe: *10 days' trial.*
3. Joint possession is indicated by adding an apostrophe and an "s" to the last noun only: *Ben and Jerry's Ice Cream.* To indicate separate possession, add the apostrophe and an "s" to each noun: *Ben's and Jerry's ice cream cones.*
4. Add an "s" with no apostrophe to form the plurals of letters, nouns, numbers, and abbreviations, if it is possible to do so without causing confusion: *several YWCAs and YMHAs; in the 1960s; in fours and fives.*
5. Add an apostrophe and an "s" to form the plurals of lowercase letters used as nouns, abbreviations using periods, and capital letters that would otherwise be confusing: *C.P.A.'s; a's and b's; I's, A's, U's.*

colon (:)

The colon warns the reader that what follows will complete what was promised in the preceding words.

The colon is used:

1. After the salutation of a letter.
2. To indicate that pertinent information follows.
3. Preceding a formal or extended quotation.
4. To introduce a list.

The phrases "as follows" and "the following" should be eliminated if possible in your letters. If it is necessary to use either phrase, it should be followed by a colon.

A colon is always placed outside of quotation marks.

The first word following a colon should be capitalized if what follows the colon could be construed as a complete sentence on its own.

comma (,)

Use the comma:

1. To separate distinct, independent statements in a compound sentence: *I turned left, and George kept on marching down the road.*
2. To separate a series of words or phrases having equal value and not connected by conjunctions.
3. To separate a series of adjectives or adverbs that are equal in value and are not connected by conjunctions: *They are predicting a long, cold, storm-filled winter.*
4. To set off a long dependent clause preceding its principal clause: *If you want to come with us tomorrow, you'll have to be ready by nine.*
5. To precede nonrestrictive relative clauses introduced by "who," "which," and similar pronouns: *The boy, who shifted nervously from foot to foot, finally delivered his message.* The pronoun "that" is frequently used in a restrictive sense and does not require a comma preceding it: *The letter that came yesterday contained the check we were waiting for.*
6. To set apart a parenthetical expression: *Thanksgiving, and by the way I really hate turkey, is the most sacrosanct of national holidays.*
7. To separate the year in a complete date from the continuation of the sentence: *June 14, 1981, was his graduation.*
8. To separate the name of the state, following mention of the city located within its borders, from the rest of the sentence: *He lives in a suburb of Omaha, Nebraska, with his wife and two children.*
9. When the thought is broken by a connective, such as "however," "obviously," or "namely."

dash (—)

The dash indicates an abrupt change in thought. Dashes are generally preferable to parentheses. Use dashes to:

1. Set off expressions foreign to the sentence.
2. Set off explanations and repetitions.

ellipsis (...)

When letters or words are omitted in a quotation, use an ellipsis (three periods on the typewriter: "...") to indicate the omission. If the omission ends on a period, use an ellipsis, plus a period (four periods on the typewriter: "....").

exclamation point (!)

An exclamation point should not be overused or it will lose its effectiveness. It should be used:

1. To indicate surprise.
2. To indicate a strong command.
3. To indicate sarcasm.
4. To follow a strong interjection, such as "Ouch!" or "Hurray!"

hyphen (-)

Avoid hyphenation. Excessive use of the hyphen tends to distract from a letter's message and does not add to its appearance. Consult a dictionary on the proper hyphenation of words when you must hyphenate. Here are some general rules:

1. Insert a hyphen in compound adjectives preceding a noun: *absent-minded office manager; fun-loving buddies; twenty-year mortgage.*
2. Insert a hyphen in compound numerals twenty-one through ninety-nine: *thirty-two, forty-six, eighty-seven.*

parentheses (())

Parentheses may be used:

1. To set apart explanatory detail that can be omitted without changing the grammatical structure of a sentence.
2. To enclose a word or clause that is independent of the sentence in which it is inserted.

Punctuation should be placed outside of the closing parenthesis unless it is a part of the parenthetical expression.

period (.)

In addition to the traditional uses of the period, use one after a question of courtesy, which is really a request: *Would you give me a hand with these bundles, please.*

question mark (?)

Use after every direct question: *What is your name?* If your question consists of a polite request you should usually use a period instead of a question mark: *Would you please take out the garbage.*

quotation marks (" ")

Any material quoted within a sentence or a paragraph should be set off with quotation marks.

Use single quotation marks to enclose a quotation within a quotation.

Titles of poems, articles, episodes of television series, or chapters in a book are enclosed in quotation marks. Do *not*, however, use quotation marks for titles of books, magazines, television series, and plays; they should be set in italics.

Lengthy quotations should be set off by indentation—blocking—in which case quotation marks are unnecessary.

If quotation marks are used and the text is continued into two or more paragraphs, use quotation marks at the beginning of each paragraph, but at the end of only the last paragraph of the quotation.

Periods and commas are always placed inside quotation marks, colons always outside. Other punctuation marks go inside quotation marks if they relate to the quoted segment, and otherwise outside.

semicolon (;)

The semicolon is used:

1. To separate the clauses of a compound sentence when the conjunction is omitted.
2. Between the clauses of a compound sentence that are joined by one of the conjunctive adverbs: accordingly, also, besides, consequently, further, hence, furthermore, however, moreover, nevertheless, otherwise, still, then, thus, yet, or therefore.
3. To separate units in a series when they are long and complicated or internally punctuated.
4. Between clauses of a compound sentence that are connected by a conjunction when those clauses are somewhat long, or when a more decided pause is desirable.

Index